Hystories

ELAINE SHOWALTER is Professor of English at Princeton University. Her first book, *A Literature of Their Own* (1975), is a classic study of women writers. She is also a historian of psychiatry, whose books *The Female Malady* (1985) and the co-authored *Hysteria Beyond Freud* (1993), established the background for this study. Showalter writes frequently about movies, theatre and television for newspapers and magazines in the United States and Great Britain.

Also by Elaine Showalter:

A LITERATURE OF THEIR OWN:
   British Women Writers from Brontë to Lessing

THE FEMALE MALADY:
   Women, Madness and English Culture

SEXUAL ANARCHY:
   Gender and Culture in the Fin de Siècle

SISTER'S CHOICE:
   Tradition and Change in American Women's Writing

HYSTERIA BEYOND FREUD *(co-author)*

THE NEW FEMINIST CRITICISM *(editor)*

SPEAKING OF GENDER *(editor)*

DAUGHTERS OF DECADENCE *(editor)*

SCRIBBLING WOMEN *(editor)*

Hystories

Hysterical Epidemics and Modern Culture

Elaine Showalter

PICADOR

For English, Vinca, and Michael

First published 1997 by Columbia University Press, New York

First published in Great Britain 1997 by Picador
This edition published with a new preface 1998 by Picador
an imprint of Macmillan Publishers Ltd
25 Eccleston Place, London, SW1W 9NF
and Basingstoke

Associated companies throughout the world

ISBN 0 330 35477 9

A CIP catalogue record for this book is available
from the British Library

Printed and bound in Great Britain by
Mackays of Chatham PLC, Chatham, Kent

Contents

Acknowledgments

I t was a happy day in 1978 when I first began working at the Wellcome Institute for the History of Medicine in London—an ace caff, a great staff, and a rather nice library attached. Sally Bragg has always made me feel welcome at the Wellcome and helped me make the most of its amazing resources. I'm grateful for the generosity and example of the Wellies, especially Bill Bynum, Roy Porter, Michael J. Clark, and Julia Sheppard. Many friends and colleagues in England aided and encouraged my work, even when they disagreed with my conclusions; my thanks to Juliet Mitchell, Susie Orbach, Lisa Tickner, John Forrester, Lisa Appignanesi, Louise Armstrong, Lisa Jardine, John Clay, Sally Alexander, Linda Grant, Ann Dally, Sarah Dunant, Diane Middlebrook, Anna Furse, Jacqueline Rose, Barbara Taylor, Marina Warner, and Michael Robinson. Erica Davies and Ivan Ward at the Freud Museum organized important symposia on hysteria today. In Paris, Sherrill Mulhern shared her remarkable collection of tapes and books; Jan Goldstein and Rae Beth Gordon offered valuable scholarly advice, and Catherine Saint Louis helped me track down treasures at the Bibliothèque Nationale.

At Princeton University, the Council for Research in the Humanities and Social Sciences has funded my research travel over the past several years. New Hysterian friends, especially Martha Noel Evans, Sander Gilman, Mark Micale, George Rousseau, Dianne Hunter, and Ian Hacking, have been ideal members of a vital, although far-flung, community of scholars. Stuart Burrows found stacks of references at the British Library and on the Internet. I have been blessed with a wonderful family, to whom I have dedicated this book, and with friends never too busy to listen, talk, or e-mail: Michael Cadden, Wendy Martin, Joyce Carol Oates, Larry Danson, Richard Kaye, and Carol Smith. My literary agents, Elaine Markson and Mary Clemmey, deserve thanks for years of good advice and advocacy. Finally, my brilliant and meticulous editor, M. Mark, made me account for every sentence, and Jennifer Crewe and Anne McCoy at Columbia University Press and Tanya Stobbs at Picador saw this project through its many stages with exemplary patience, professionalism, and panache.

Preface to the Paperback Edition

When I finished writing *Hystories* in fall 1996, I noted that although some hysterical epidemics seemed to be waning, others were springing up to take their places. A year later, I am nonetheless surprised at the hystories that have emerged since the book's publication. Who would have guessed that members of the Heaven's Gate cult would commit mass suicide in hope of joining an alien spaceship they believed lay behind the tail of the Halle-Bopp comet? That the fiftieth anniversary of Roswell would become a media circus, and that the town would turn into an alien theme park? That a Wisconsin doctor would be sued for diagnosing a patient with 120 personalities, including a duck, and for billing her insurance company for group therapy? That rumors about the fate of TWA Flight 800 would still be circulating on the Internet? That a doctor in Los Angeles would claim he caught Gulf War syndrome from his patients and it made his teeth fall out, and an ex-army nurse who never went to the Gulf would be sure she had given GWS to her dog? Or, uncannily and tragically, that Princess Diana, who had courageously overcome her own hysterical eating disorder, would die at the Salpetrière Hospital in Paris, where modern hysteria began; that journalists would be asking about the hysterical reaction to her death; and that conspiracy theories about it would be raging?

I anticipated that *Hystories* would upset some special-interest groups, and it did. Angry responses come with the territory of this applied research, and have to be expected by anyone who challenges the belief systems of sufferers. Dr. Paul McHugh, Director of the Department of Psychiatry and Behavioral Science at the Johns Hopkins School of Medicine, has written that challenges to such systems are "not for the faint-hearted or inexperienced. They seldom quickly succeed because they are often misrepresented as ignorant or, in the cant word of our day, uncaring." In a 1997 study of online support groups used by chronic fatigue syndrome patients, Kathyryn P. Davison and James W. Pennebaker reported that on the Internet, "discussions of chronic fatigue authors who include in their writing suspected psychological factors or psychosocial treatment strategies are viewed as anathema, practically subhuman in their callous and ignorant statements."

But I didn't predict that I would become the subject of conspiracy theories myself, that I would be accused of writing the book with secret "major corporate funding" and attacked as a "fascist" trying to "bolster a flagging career in academia." I didn't foresee that my editors at Columbia University Press would be called "cunt-sucking maggots to let this one slither through." I didn't anticipate that people would bombard me with hate mail, offer me blood transfusions, advise me to get a bodyguard, threaten to rip me apart, or warn me of assassination unless I recanted. In fact, although another year's accumulated scientific evidence has supported my arguments, the inflammatory reaction to the book from some quarters has only confirmed my analysis of hysterical epidemics of denial, projection, accusation, and blame.

On the other hand, I've had the opportunity to meet and correspond with many doctors, scientists, journalists, scholars, and government officials who have extended and enriched my understanding of these syndromes. These personal exchanges with other investigators have strengthened my resolve to make connections between my academic research and controversial public issues of our time. The expansion of the Internet and the World Wide Web have have made medical information more accessible than ever before, and e-mail has made it possible for me to be in dialogue with colleagues all over the world.

With regard to chronic fatigue syndrome, little has changed. Much-touted medical studies suggesting that neurally mediated hypotension, or brain lesions, or an enzyme, could be definitively connected to the syndrome have not been replicated or proven, and the community remains resistant to psychological treatments and interpretations. Meanwhile, patients tell stories of prolonged illness, worsening disability, and deepening distress. The CFS diagnosis is increasingly being applied to adolescents.

As for Gulf War syndrome, the real gulf is still the one between alleged causes and proven effects. Despite the conclusions of five U.S. independent commissions that there is no single illness and that stress is the major factor, conspiracy theories about Gulf War syndrome continue to flourish. Suspicions were undoubtedly reinforced on July 24, 1997, when CIA and Department of Defense officials announced that the vaporized sarin plume from the explosion at Kamisayah may have reached 99,000 service members. But whether 100 or 100,000 troops may have been exposed to vaporized sarin, the likelihood that it could have caused any long-term symptoms remains remote. Nerve gases cause symptoms immediately upon exposure, and there was not a single complaint of nerve gas poisoning during the conflict, though such poisoning causes unmissable symptoms: pinpoint pupils, runny nose, eye pain, sweating, nausea, diarrhea, convulsions, and wheezing. In addition, three decades of research on nerve gases have produced no evidence of long-term damage from low-level exposure. In the U.K., where the troops were not exposed to any nerve gas, Gulf War syndrome has been blamed on everything from flea collars to sheep dip; but although British and American conspiracy theories of government cover-ups continue to diverge in their hypotheses, the overall belief in government cover-up remains unshakable.

With regard to recovered memories, ritual abuse charges, and multiple personalities, however, the tide seems to have turned. Courts are continuing to reverse decisions, and in a few highly publicized cases, day-care center workers convicted of abusing children, such as the "Edenton Seven" in North Carolina, have been released from prison and charges against them have been dropped. Yet many of these people's lives have been wrecked by false allegations. In the U.K., local health-care officials have still not released a highly critical report about a satanic ritual abuse scare of 1989. Television documentaries, tabloid newspapers, and sensational movies continue to spread the imagery of recovered memory, Satanism and alien abduction around the world. If, as some polls claim, millions of Americans still believe in alien abduction, we have a long way still to go before credulity, superstition, and hysterical epidemics are on the wane. Confronting these syndromes may indeed generate heat, but without heat, there can be no light.

ELAINE SHOWALTER
October 1997

PART ONE

Histories

I

The Hysterical Hot Zone

In the Midwest, a nurse with chronic fatigue syndrome commits suicide with the help of Dr. Jack Kevorkian. In Yorkshire, a young Gulf War veteran struggles with a mysterious illness that has destroyed his marriage and his career. In California, an executive is disgraced after his daughter, who has been treated by her therapist with the hypnotic drug sodium amytal, says he abused her when she was a child; the court later awards him half a million dollars' damages. In Massachusetts, a Pulitzer Prize—winning Harvard professor claims that little gray aliens are visiting the United States and performing sexual experiments on thousands of Americans. In Oklahoma, accused bomber Timothy McVeigh tells his lawyers that the government planted a surveillance microchip in his buttocks during the Gulf War. In Montana, right-wing militias announce that the federal government, armed with bombs and black helicopters, is chemically altering the blood of U.S. citizens as part of its conspiracy to create a New World Order.

These sensational cases exemplify individual hysterias connecting with modern social movements to produce psychological epidemics. In books like Laurie Garrett's *The Coming Plague* (1994) and Richard Preston's *The Hot Zone* (1994), we've learned a lot about large-scale viral epidemics caused by killer microbes from the rain forest and the jungle. Fifty years ago scientists believed that antibiotics had conquered infectious disease and that the age of epidemics had passed into history. According to Garrett, these "boosters of the 1950s and early 1960s had some basis, born of ignorance, for their optimism; they knew comparatively little about genetics, microbial evolution, the human immune system, or disease ecology."[1] But infectious diseases had not been vanquished; they have proved remarkably resistant to medical triumphs and medical complacency. From Toxic Shock Syndrome to AIDS and the Ebola virus, emergent and resurgent diseases threaten societies that have believed themselves immune from pandemics.

Just as scientists prematurely proclaimed infectious diseases to be dead, so too psychiatrists prematurely announced the death of hysteria. In her 1965 study, Ilza Veith marveled at the "nearly total disappearance" of the disorder.[2] "Where has all the hysteria gone?" psychologist Roberta Satow asked a decade later.[3] Some doctors explained that the diagnostic tools of modern medicine had conquered hysteria by identifying it as unrecognized organic illness. A number of historians and sociologists argued that hysteria was really a Victorian disorder, a female reaction to sexual repression and limited opportunities, which diminished with the advent of modern feminism. Many psychiatrists believed that widespread awareness of Freudian psychoanalysis had made somatic conversion hysterias like limps and paralyses unfeasible as expressions of anxiety. According to the British analyst Harold Mersky in *The Analysis of Hysteria* (1978), conversion hysterias occur only in psychoanalytically unsophisticated areas such as East Africa, South Korea, Sri Lanka, or Nigeria. Whatever the cause, "hysteria is dead, that is certain," wrote the French medical historian Étienne Trillat, "and it has taken its secrets with it to the grave."[4]

But hysteria has not died. It has simply been relabeled for a new era. While Ebola virus and Lassa fever remain potential, psychological plagues at the end of the twentieth century are all too real. In the 1990s, the United States has become the hot zone of psychogenic diseases, new and mutating forms of hysteria amplified by modern communications and fin de siècle anxiety. Contemporary hysterical patients blame external sources—a virus, sexual molestation, chemical warfare, satanic conspiracy, alien infiltration—for psychic problems. A century after Freud, many people still reject psychological explanations for symptoms; they believe psychosomatic disorders are illegitimate and search for physical evidence that firmly places cause and cure outside the self.

When well-meaning crusaders see hysterical syndromes in the context of social crises and then publicize their views through modern communications networks, these misconceptions can give rise to epidemics and witch-hunts. In *The Pursuit of the Millennium*, the historian Norman Cohn describes the paranoias that accompany apocalyptic moments. "Those who are first attracted," he writes, "will mostly be people who seek a sanction for the emotional needs generated by their own unconscious conflicts. It is as though units of paranoia hitherto diffused through the population suddenly coalesce to form a new entity: a collective paranoiac fanaticism. But these first followers, precisely because they are true believers, can endow their new movement with such confidence, energy and ruthlessness that it will attract into its wake vast multitudes of people who are themselves not at all paranoid but simply harassed, hungry or frightened." When "a paranoiac mass movement captures political power," Cohn warns, disaster follows.[5]

Cohn writes about the year 1000 but he could be describing the mood right now. In the interaction between 1990s millennial panic, new psychotherapies, religious fundamentalism, and American political paranoia, we can see the crucible of virulent hysterias in our own time. The heroes and heroines of 1990s hysteria call themselves traumatists and ufologists, experiencers and abductees, survivors and survivalists. As their syndromes evolve, they grow from microtales of individual affliction to panics fueled by rumors about medical, familial, community, or governmental conspiracy. As the panic reaches epidemic proportions, hysteria seeks out scapegoats and enemies—from unsympathetic doctors, abusive fathers, and working mothers to devil-worshiping sadists, curious extraterrestrials, and evil governments.

Hystories

Hysteria not only survives in the 1990s, it is more contagious than in the past. Infectious diseases spread by ecological change, modern technology, urbanization, jet travel, and human interaction. Infectious epidemics of hysteria spread by stories circulated through self-help books, articles in newspapers and magazines, TV talk shows and series, films, the Internet, and even literary criticism. The cultural narratives of hysteria, which I call *hystories*, multiply rapidly and uncontrollably in the era of mass media, telecommunications, and e-mail.

As we approach our own millennium, the epidemics of hysterical disorders, imaginary illnesses, and hypnotically induced pseudomemories that have flooded the media seem to be reaching a high-water mark. These hystories are merging with the more generalized paranoias, religious revivals, and conspiracy theories that have always characterized American life, and the apocalyptic anxieties that always accompany the end of a century. Now they are dispersing globally to infect other countries and cultures.

I am a literary critic and a historian of medicine, rather than a psychiatrist. Above all, hysteria tells a story, and specialists in understanding and interpreting stories know ways to read it. As hysteria has moved from the clinic to the library, from the case study to the novel, from bodies to books, from page to stage and screen, it has developed its own prototypes, archetypes, and plots. Many of these motifs are adapted from myth, popular culture, folklore, media reports, and literature. Drawing on literary and medical history, I try to unravel some of the threads that make up the narratives of epidemic hysteria in the 1990s.

Hystories have internal similarities or evolve in similar directions as they're retold—which has convinced many doctors and researchers that these stories must be true. A century ago, Freud insisted that the stories his patients told him under hypnosis must be fact because of the "uniformity which they exhibit in certain details."[6] Dealing with chronic fatigue syndrome patients at the Centers for Disease Control in Atlanta, researcher Walter Gunn "asked himself the fundamental question: how could so many people—all of whom told a story that was, with only minor variations, the same—be making this up?"[7] Advocates of alien abduction also have faith in narrative similarity. "All the major accounts of abduction in the book share common characteristics and thus provide a confirmation of one another," writes David Jacobs in *Alien Encounters*. "Even the smallest details of the events were confirmed many times over. There was a chronology, structure, logic—the events made sense . . . and they displayed an extraordinary internal consistency."[8]

Literary critics, however, realize that similarities between two stories do not mean that they mirror a common reality or even that the writers have read each other's texts. Like all narratives, hystories have their own conventions, stereotypes, and structures. Writers inherit common themes, structures, characters, and images; critics call these common elements *intertextuality*. We need not assume that patients are either describing an organic disorder or else lying when they present similar narratives of symptoms. Instead, patients learn about diseases from the media, unconsciously develop the symptoms, and then attract media attention in an endless cycle. The human imagination is not infinite, and we are all bombarded by these plot lines every day. Inevitably, we all live out the social stories of our time.

The New Hysterians

While physicians and psychiatrists have long been writing obituaries for hysteria, scholars in the humanities and social sciences have given it new life. Social historians, philosophers, anthropologists, literary critics, and art historians have taken up the subject of hysteria because it cuts across historical periods and national boundaries, poses fundamental questions about gender and culture, and offers insights into language, narrative, and representation. This informal international network of scholars does not yet have an organization, a journal, or an official name, but we meet at conferences, correspond through e-mail and snail mail, and exchange manuscripts, articles, and books. I call the group the New Hysterians.

New Hysterians ask questions about the self, sexual and gender identity, cultural meaning, and political behavior. According to Roy Porter, a dauntingly prolific and energetic historian of medicine and science who teaches at the Wellcome Institute in London, the story of hysteria is "a history in which the very notions of mind and body, and the boundaries and bridges between them, are constantly being challenged and reconstituted."[9] In *Approaching Hysteria*, Mark Micale, who teaches at Yale and the University of Manchester, writes that hysteria is "not a disease; rather, it is an alternative physical, verbal, and gestural language, an iconic social communication."[10]

Throughout history, hysteria has served as a form of expression, a body language for people who otherwise might not be able to speak or even to admit what they feel. In the words of Robert M. Woolsey, hysteria is a "protolanguage," and its symptoms are "a code used by a patient to communicate a message which, for various reasons, cannot be verbalized."[11] It appears in the young as well as the old, in men as well as women, in blacks as well as whites. It happens to the powerful as well as the obscure. In October 1993, the Empress of Japan lost her voice after she had been criticized in the press and did not speak for three months: "It is possible," the official Japanese Household Agency declared, "for a person who suffers some strong feelings of distress to develop a symptom in which the person temporarily cannot utter words."[12] A seasoned soldier may experience stress as disabling as that of a helpless child. Circumstances silence people, not their rank or position.

Micale suggests that the new hysteria studies express the age as much as the disorders they analyze. He sees New Hysterians as products of the "gender revolution" inspired by the "great metacritique of

gender that in retrospect is certain to be regarded as one of the defining features of the thought, culture, and society of the late twentieth
century." He also speculates that this generation of scholars has come
of age in the context of the AIDS epidemic, reflecting "the rapid and
traumatizing reintroduction of the reality of epidemic disease" into
their mental life. Since mass psychogenic disorders are metasymbols
of the deep structures of our culture, Micale concludes that for the
New Hysterians, "rewriting the history of hysteria becomes a way of
achieving an understanding of, and perspective on, ourselves and our
social world."[13]

Beyond Scapegoats

I expect that defining recovered memory, chronic fatigue, and Gulf War
syndrome as contemporary hysterias, and analyzing them on a continuum with alien abduction stories and conspiracy theories will infuriate
thousands of people who believe they are suffering from unidentified
organic disorders or the aftereffects of trauma. I don't wish to offend
these sufferers, but I know that many assume the term *hysteria* has
insulting connotations. Being hysterical means being overemotional,
irresponsible, and feminine. During an argument, "hysterical" is what
you contemptuously call your opponent when you're keeping your
cool and he's losing his. It's a term that particularly enrages some feminists because for centuries it has been used to ridicule and trivialize
women's medical and political complaints.

Americans also tend to feel defensive about hysterical disorders
after the recent spate of accusations that this country is becoming a
hysterical victim society. It's a standing joke that Americans no longer
view themselves as sinners struggling with the guilt of lust, avarice, or
greed but rather as sick people addicted to sex, shopping, or sweets.
Books like Charles Sykes's *A Nation of Victims* (1992), Robert Hughes's
The Culture of Complaint (1993), Wendy Kaminer's *I'm Dysfunctional,
You're Dysfunctional* (1993), and Alan Dershowitz's *The Abuse Excuse*
(1995) mock and denounce what they see as the twelve-step, self-help
culture of contemporary America. Because many of these books have
an ideological ax to grind, they seek political scapegoats and simple
answers for a complex phenomenon. Pundits blame the recovery
movement on Freud and psychoanalysis, changes in sexuality, or a collapse of American family values. These attacks are so sweeping and so
vitriolic, so one-sided and so unfair, it's no wonder patients, psychia-

trists, and therapists feel threatened and panicky. In the *Journal of Psychohistory*, Nielltje Gedney, for example, charges that critics are after "the total annihilation of therapy and therapists."[14]

I don't regard hysteria as weakness, badness, feminine deceitfulness, or irresponsibility, but rather as a cultural symptom of anxiety and stress. The conflicts that produce hysterical symptoms are genuine and universal; hysterics are not liars and therapists are not villains. Instead, hystories are constructed by suffering patients, caring psychologists, dedicated clergy, devoted parents, hardworking police, concerned feminists, and anxious communities. While I criticize some forms of therapy, some uses of drugs in recovering memories, and some self-help literature, I also see a vital place for psychotherapy, psychopharmacology, and psychological guidebooks in everyday life. We should no more attempt to struggle alone with crippling depressions than to run the marathon with broken legs.

Unfortunately, though some critics claim that psychoanalysis is passé, Freud's message never got through to millions of people, who still distrust and fear the unconscious and its power over us. As a result, they suffer needlessly. Class, race, gender, and cultural attitudes play an underestimated role in the legitimation of psychotherapy. A 1995 *New York* magazine poll showed that 44 percent of New Yorkers living in Manhattan had sought psychological counseling—more than twice the percentage of those New Yorkers in Brooklyn, Staten Island, or Queens.[15] Black Americans distrust psychoanalysis more than white Americans do. Women have more leeway than men to seek psychological help.

Hysteria is inevitably a feminist issue, because for centuries doctors regarded it as a female reproductive disease. Charcot and Freud collaborated with female patients who have become known as the classical or canonical hysterics. Some modern psychoanalysts suggest that the golden age of hysteria vanished with the great hysterical divas of the nineteenth century. Jacques Lacan regarded these women as bygone stars, like Mistinguette or Judy Garland: "Where have they gone, the hysterics of yesteryear ... these marvelous women, the Anna Os, the Emmy von Ns?"[16] he asked in 1977. But even in the 1990s, women patients outnumber men in virtually every category of unexplained illness and recovered memory. According to a study at Harvard Medical School, 80 percent of those with chronic fatigue syndrome are women. More than 90 percent of those who say they've recovered memories of childhood sexual abuse are women. Ian Hacking concludes that nine out of ten patients diagnosed with multiple personality disorder are women. Researcher Debby Nathan observes that accusations of satanic ritual abuse come primarily from women. Even among those who claim to have been abducted by aliens, a field where science fiction and technology mix, women outnumber men about three to one and, according to ufologist David Jacobs, "seem to have a larger number of more complex experiences."[17]

Hysteria concerns feminists because the label has always been used to discredit women's political protest. Conservatives have pressed ancient stereotypes into popular service to interpret all women's frustrations as sexual and irrational, and to stigmatize the sharing of women's experiences as hysterical confession. Lynne V. Cheney's *Telling the Truth* (1995), for instance, blames women's studies classrooms in universities for the recovered memory movement. Cheney draws a sinister analogy between women's studies discussions and therapeutic coercion: "Indeed, there are many parallels between the recovered memory movement and feminism as it has come to be practiced on campuses. The encouragement—even the requirement—in feminist classrooms to confess personal views and traumas establishes an environment very much like the one that exists in victim recovery groups."[18] Feminist activists are understandably angry about these attacks and about related attacks on the concepts of child abuse, date rape, and wife-battering. They argue that these crimes are underreported and underbelieved, that women and men have fought for years to create an atmosphere in which women's testimony is taken seriously.

Nonetheless, in a surprising reversal, hysteria has been adopted since 1970 by a number of feminist intellectuals, psychoanalysts, writers, and literary critics as a rallying cry for feminism itself. Some of these women have claimed hysteria as the first step on the road to feminism, the sign of women's protest against patriarchy. Hysteria, writes Diane Price Herndl, "has come to figure as a sort of rudimentary feminism, and feminism as a kind of articulate hysteria."[19] In my book *The Female Malady* (1985), I speculated that although epidemic hysteria exists on one extreme of a continuum with feminism, as a body language of women's rebellion against patriarchal oppression, it is a desperate, and ultimately self-destructive, form of protest. But for many feminist writers, the nineteenth-century hysterical supermodels—the canonical or articulate hysterics—epitomize universal female oppression. Some contemporary feminist theorists and therapists have inadvertently helped to spread new hysterical disorders.

The feminist interpretation of hysteria as a product of women's social circumstances has been an important contribution to our understanding of female psychology. But I deplore the credulous endorsements of recovered memory and satanic abuse that have become part of one wing of feminist thought. I try to ask feminist questions about the sources behind these syndromes, accusations, and conspiracy theories. What needs are women attempting to meet through these therapeutic investments, sickness lifestyles, and emotional hystories? Can we find more constructive ways to meet these needs than succumbing to the epidemic of suspicion and blame that threatens us all at the end of our century? Can we redefine hysteria in a way that allows more space for the mysteries of human emotions?

The Anatomy of Epidemics

In this book, I look at the forces that shape hysterical epidemics. Part I, "Histories," reviews the rise of modern hysteria and the cultural and religious matrix where it takes shape. Hysteria needs a doctor or theorist, an authority figure who can give it a compelling name and narrative. As Roy Porter points out, "The nineteenth century was hysteria's golden age because it was then that the moral presence of the doctor became normative as never before in regulating intimate lives."[20] The greatest of these physician-advocates were Jean-Martin Charcot, Sigmund Freud, and Jacques Lacan. But hysteria is dialogic: it depends on the needs of patients as well as the decisions of doctors. Until World War I, most of the famous hysterical patients were women. Many historians and analysts have maintained that hysteria is the product of a dialogue or collaboration between the hysterical woman and the medical man. Male doctors have been reluctant to confront the reality of male hysteria, but hysterical men play an underestimated role in the evolution of the disorder. I trace the theories and prototypes of male hysteria from the nineteenth century to the present and question the assumption that hysterical men must be homosexual.

In part II, "Cultures," I look at hysteria's intersections with literature, theater, and film. Models and metaphors of hysterical illness have always been circulated through fiction and drama, and Freud even defined hysteria as narrative incoherence. Today many syndromes are bracketed with a particular genre of popular fiction—multiple personality disorder with the confession, satanic ritual abuse with horror stories, alien abduction with science fiction. Movies and television also popularize the narratives of these syndromes, and even literary criticism can contribute to the blurring of fiction and reality.

Part III, "Epidemics," analyzes six psychogenic syndromes of the 1990s: chronic fatigue, Gulf War syndrome, multiple personality disorder, recovered memory of sexual abuse, satanic ritual abuse, and alien abduction. The hystories of these syndromes are linked and overlapping. Some doctors attribute Gulf War syndrome to chronic fatigue syndrome. Some therapists regard anorexia and bulimia as symptoms of childhood sexual abuse that must be remembered in therapy. Recovered memories of childhood sexual abuse can lead to cases of multiple personality disorder and satanic ritual abuse. Traumatologists believe that stories of alien abduction are screen memories for child sexual abuse, while ufologists maintain that narratives of child sexual abuse often shield experiences of alien abduction. All these syndromes move toward suspicion, conspiracy theories, witch-hunts, and mass panics.

Can we interrupt or halt these epidemics? I believe that we already have the power to control epidemic hysteria, though it will take dedication and persistence to counter sensational news reports, rumors, and fear. We must accept the interdependence between mind and body, and recognize hysterical syndromes as a universal psychopathology of everyday life before we can dismantle their stigmatizing mythologies. When anti-Freudian zealots make sweeping attacks on psychoanalysis and psychiatry, we can defend Freud's insights and try to restore confidence in serious psychotherapy. We need professional regulation that can establish licensing requirements for psychotherapists. We also need encouragement and financial support for people trying to cope with the painful dilemmas and tragedies of life in the 1990s. Psychiatry and pharmapsychology offer new and effective treatments for debilitating depression, compulsive behaviors, and anxiety disorders. TV talk shows and self-help literature are easy targets for scornful intellectuals, but they reach and teach a wide audience, largely female, that cannot always afford or manage other forms of counseling.

New Hysterians and other scholars can place hysteria in its fullest sexual, historical, and cultural contexts. We can use the media to fight rumors as well as to spread them, through op-ed pieces, magazine stories, TV documentaries, and books. Modern forms of individual and mass hysteria have much to tell us about the anxieties and fantasies of western culture, especially in the United States and Europe. We can use our knowledge of the past to interpret what is happening today. We can educate the public about the long history of war neurosis and transform the prevailing atmosphere of skepticism and contempt for psychogenic symptoms in men.

Feminists have an ethical as well as an intellectual responsibility to ask tough questions about the current narratives of illness, trauma, accusation, and conspiracy. We also have a responsibility to address the problems behind the epidemics—including the need to protect children from sexual and physical abuse. And we can lead the way in making distinctions between metaphors and realities, between therapeutic narratives and destructive hystories. If hysteria is a protolanguage rather than a disease, we must pay attention to what it is telling us.

Finally, as a critic of hysteria's stories, I want to emphasize my belief that hysteria is part of everyday life. Whenever I lecture about hysteria, I cough. French psychoanalyst André Green, an internationally honored member of the Freudian community, has joked that "we are all hysterics . . . except when we are writing papers." Any honest scholar knows that we are all hysterics, *especially* when we are writing papers. I do not have a quarrel with hysteria's symptoms, but with its social appropriations. In this book, I hope to show the difference.

2 | *Defining Hysteria*

H ow do individual hysterias become social epidemics? How do these epidemics differ from mass hysteria? And how do hysterical epidemics or mass hysterias lead to witch-hunts?

What Is Hysteria?

Hysteria is not a single, consistent, unified affliction like malaria or tuberculosis. At first, as Dr. Philip Slavney of Johns Hopkins explains, hysteria "was regarded as a disease—an affliction of the body that troubles the mind." Later, the terms were reversed, and hysteria "was believed by many physicians to be an affliction of the mind that was expressed through a disturbance of the body," which converted unconscious desires into pathological changes and physical symptoms through an obscure neural process. Now hysteria "has come to imply behavior that produces the *appearance* of disease," although the patient is unconscious of the motives for feeling sick.[1]

Hysteria has been the designation for such a vast, shifting set of behaviors and symptoms—limps, paralyses, seizures, coughs, headaches, speech disturbances, depression, insomnia, exhaustion, eating disorders—that doctors have despaired of finding a single diagnosis. In 1878, a French physician, Charles Lasègue, proclaimed that "the definition of hysteria has never been given and never will be. The symptoms are not constant enough, nor sufficiently similar in form or equal in duration and intensity that one type, even descriptive, could comprise them all."[2] A century later, Edward Shorter lamented: "Writing a history of something so amorphous, whose meaning and content keep changing, is like trying to write a history of dirt."[3]

But another way into the history of hysteria is to see it as plural rather than singular, cyclical rather than linear—not, according to Roy Porter, "a single, unbroken narrative but scatters of occurrences: histories of hysterias."[4] Hysteria is a mimetic disorder; it mimics culturally permissible expressions of distress. An Englishman can legitimately complain of headache or fatigue but not that his penis is retracting into his body—a perfectly acceptable symptom in Malaysia and South China. Edward Shorter calls the legitimate symptoms in a given culture at a given time "the symptom pool." "By defining certain symptoms as illegitimate," he writes, "a culture strongly encourages patients not to develop them or to risk being thought 'undeserving' individuals with no real medical problems. Accordingly there is great pressure on the unconscious mind to produce only legitimate symptoms."[5]

A constant cultural negotiation goes on, of course, over both the symptom pool as a whole and the legitimacy of its contents. In the nineteenth century, Porter writes, the "visibility of real biomedical neurological disorders," like limps, paralyses and palsies, the result of birth defects, industrial accidents, alcoholism, venereal disease, and so on, provided "a sickness stylistics for expressing inner pains."[6] But many of these symptoms have declined or disappeared in the twentieth century and been replaced by new ones; the quantity of hysterical energy does not decrease but flows into new channels and takes new names.

Throughout most of its medical history, hysteria has been associated with women. Its name comes from *hystera*, the Greek word for uterus. Classical healers described a female disorder characterized by convulsive attacks, random pains, and sensations of choking. They believed the uterus traveled hungrily around the body, unfettered—Monday in the foot, Tuesday in the throat, Wednesday in the breast, and so on—producing a myriad of symptoms in its wake: a choking sensation, as if a ball were in the throat, called the *globus hystericus*; coughs and loss of voice; pains in various parts of the body; tics and twitches; paralyses, deafness, blindness; fits of crying; fainting; convulsive seizures; and sexual longings.

When anatomists proved that the uterus did not migrate, doctors relocated the centers of hysteria to the nervous system. Women were then described as a nervous sex, suffering from vapors, spleen, and fainting fits, or eroticized as hysterical nymphomaniacs. In fact, hysteria was often a wastebasket diagnosis. In his *Essay on the Pathology of the Brain* in 1684, Thomas Willis candidly acknowledged that hysteria was the term doctors used when they didn't know what they were seeing but wanted to say something: when "at any time a sickness happens in a Woman's Body, of an unusual manner, or more occult original, so that its causes lie hid, and a Curatory indication is altogether uncertain, . . . we declare it to be something hysterical . . . which oftentimes is only the subterfuge of ignorance."

By the eighteenth century blaming the nerves or the brain for hysterical symptoms also made it possible to recognize that men too might be sufferers, even though women still predominated as patients since they had fewer outlets for nervous energy (98 percent of the hysteria cases at Edinburgh Infirmary, for example, were female). As the English physician Henry Maudsley wrote in 1879, "The range of activity of women is so limited, and their available paths of work in life so few, compared with those which men have in the present social arrangements, that they have not, like men, vicarious outlets for feelings in a variety of healthy aims and pursuits."[7]

During the late eighteenth and early nineteenth centuries, some advanced physicians treated hysterical symptoms with mesmerism and animal magnetism, early experiments in hypnosis. Franz Anton Mesmer became a celebrity, demonstrating his techniques on French and Viennese ladies during the 1780s, when superstition contended with enlightenment rationalism. Mesmerism fell into disrepute by the middle of the nineteenth century, and hysteria remained a messy mystery. Although the number of hospital patients diagnosed as hysterical was small, the symptoms continued to fascinate doctors, who wrote about hysteria more than any other medical disorder. It also fascinated journalists, who quickly picked it up as a way of describing society. By 1900 hysteria had become widespread in the United States and Western Europe. Doctors explained the epidemic as a product of hereditary weakness and cultural degeneration.

Since Freud, psychology has sought an explanation for hysteria in theories of the volatile, histrionic personality; psychoanalysis has attributed it to Oedipal conflicts. Despite denials that hysteria is a female malady, questions of femininity are still central to psychoanalytic theory. The British psychoanalyst Gregorio Kohon has argued that all women go through a hysterical stage in their psychosexual development, during which they transfer their desires from the mother to the father. According to Kohon, "*A woman always at heart remains a hys-*

teric."[8] The French psychoanalyst Janine Chasseguet-Smirgel has hypothesized a female "aptitude for somatization." Women, she contends, turn emotions into physical manifestations because their sexuality is more diffuse than men's. Rather than being centered on a single visible organ, a woman's sexuality makes her entire body available for sexual symbolism.[9]

In recent years, hysteria has disappeared from consulting rooms, hospital wards, and psychiatric textbooks, as many of its traditional symptoms were reclassified as anxiety neuroses, obsessional disorders, manic depression, or borderline personality disorders. "In reality," wrote Georges Guillain, a French medical historian of hysteria, "the patients have not changed . . . but the terminology applied to them has."[10] What used to be called hysteria is now diagnosed as somatization disorder, conversion disorder, or dissociative identity disorder.

Despite this adoption of new terminology, many doctors and researchers feel that the concept of hysteria is still misleading, moralistic, and judgmental, either exaggerating the wisdom of the physician or trivializing the patient's pain. Richard Webster suggests that we might instead describe patients as suffering from "imaginary illness" and "imaginary symptoms," or postpone judgment altogether by calling them "unexplained physical symptoms." Perhaps, he adds, we should call the symptoms "spectral" rather than "imaginary," to give them more credence and weight.[11] While I recognize the difficulties of terminology, it makes sense to use the words *hysteria* and *hysterical*, both to draw on extensive records and to emphasize the continuities between past and present. Redefining hysteria as a universal human response to emotional conflict is a better course than evading, denying, or projecting its realities.

Modern Epidemics

Hysterical epidemics require at least three ingredients: physician-enthusiasts and theorists; unhappy, vulnerable patients; and supportive cultural environments. A doctor or other authority figure must first define, name, and publicize the disorder and then attract patients into its community. "Like invisible ink when heat is applied," writes Roy Porter, hysteria was "rendered visible by the medical presence."[12] The most influential doctors of hysteria are also theorists who offer a unified field theory of a vague syndrome, providing a clear and coherent explanation for its many confusing symptoms. Beginning with a small sample of patients, these doctors diagnose a puzzling disorder and give it a name. As Robert Aronowitz observes, the process works two ways; diagnosis is "an anticipated and necessary part of the healing ritual, bestowing a certain legitimacy on the patients' malaise, and at the same time undergirding the diagnostician's claim to social authority."[13] Doctors advocate a systematic method of treatment and hold out hope for a cure.

Influential diagnosticians have connections to institutions—clinics, hospitals, medical schools—which teach and promote their theories. The most famous and effective doctors have charismatic personalities and establish schools of devoted disciples. Interacting with modern media and culture, they become legends, caricatured in cartoons, satirized in drama, but also lionized in novels, plays, and movies.

Having diagnosed a new syndrome, physicians advertise prototypes of patients. For example, Gary Peterson, a psychiatrist who specializes in multiples, advises his followers to begin presentations with "a life course story." He provides them with a script about the life of a twenty-eight-year-old woman and urges them to "read the story slowly and emotionally, stopping at appropriate places to let the audience absorb the impact of what has just been said."[14] Self-help books also use real and composite prototypes to personalize a disorder. Like horoscopes, these prototypes are often broad enough to seem uncannily relevant. The media disseminate information about the prototype and encourage patients to come forward. Overall, clinical centers, professional newsletters and journals, and doctor-advocates increase a culture's investment in the syndrome as a real disease.

Yet no matter how persuasive the medical catalysts, hysterical epidemics would not erupt without the collaboration of patients. Edward Shorter writes that "hysteria offers a classic example of patients who present symptoms as the culture expects them or, better put, as the doctors expect them."[15] By the beginning of this century, some physicians had learned that hysteria could be *iatrogenic*—created by the interaction between doctor and patient. "It is not merely that his hypothesis is apt to color a physician's way of looking at a case," wrote the English doctor S. A. K. Wilson in 1901, "but also that in some obscure and little understood manner the patients come in a sense to respond to his hypothesis."[16] Cornell University historian Joan Jacobs Brumberg says the "interactive and evolving process" of a disease begins with social and cultural recruitment, as troubled individuals respond to prototypes.[17]

Initially, patients are people with a bewildering set of troubling symptoms and a wide range of explanations for them. Once they see their problems reflected in a prototype, come to believe that the laws of a disorder describe their lives, and seek the aid of a therapist, some patients rewrite their personal narratives. They may become addicted to their symptoms, and embark on the career of being a particular kind of patient, one with chronic fatigue syndrome, Gulf War syndrome, or multiple personality disorder. For some, the patient career may be a permanent way of life, with a self-supporting network of friends, activities, doctors, and treatments.

Many historians of psychiatry think the symbiotic relationship between male doctors and female patients explains the prevalence of women hysterics. In *The History of Sexuality*, Michel Foucault wrote that women have been made the passive, inert objects of a medical will to power. At the end of the nineteenth century, he wrote, women's bodies were "hystericized"—that is, turned into a collection of physical and psychological symptoms—by the medical profession. Henri Ellenberger, however, saw the relationships between young psychiatrists and hysterical female patients as more equal. These women tended to enter their physicians' lives at intellectually formative times in the doctors' careers, and they often served as clinical models—founding cases—of the doctors' theoretical work. The doctors needed hysterical women as muses; hysterical women needed doctors to speak for them.[18]

The third side of the hysterical triangle is environmental and cultural. Epidemics of hysteria seem to peak at the ends of centuries, when people are already alarmed about social change. The Salem witch trials took place in the 1690s; the mesmerism craze after the French Revolution, in the 1790s. In the 1890s, rebellions against imperialism and the class structure, controversies over prostitution and homosexuality, the rise of feminism, and the sexual plague of syphilis all joined with apocalyptic fantasies to produce the perception of a hysterical epidemic. In a supportive cultural environment, after entering the mainstream of popular culture, hysterical syndromes multiply as they interact with social forces such as religious beliefs, political agendas, and rumor panics. Traditional enemies or social scapegoats become part of the scenario, further fueling fears. The longer the epidemic continues, the greater the participants' need to believe it is genuine. In a sense, they feel their honor and integrity are at stake. The chain is hard to break, because each wave of publicity recruits new patients, who feel more and more invested in the search for an external cause and a "magic bullet" cure.

Anorexia and Bulimia

Anorexia and bulimia are examples of modern hysterical epidemics. Although anorexia nervosa was identified in 1874 and fasting behaviors had been observed for centuries before that, the rate of anorexia doubled between 1960 and 1976, and bulimia started its rise in the 1980s. By the late 1980s, these two disorders were thought to affect up to a million young women, and a U.S. House Subcommittee issued a report entitled "Eating Disorders: The Impact on Children and Families."

How did these epidemics occur? First, the cultural environment was supportive. American society from the 1960s on became increasingly obsessed with thinness, dieting, and exercise; anorexics seen in hospitals showed more severe weight loss than in earlier generations. Second, adolescent girls constituted a susceptible patient pool. And third, anorexia nervosa attracted a gifted physician-advocate who offered a coherent theory of the disease. Hilde Bruch, sometimes called "Lady Anorexia," was a professor of psychiatry at Baylor University Medical School in Houston, Texas. In two books, *Eating Disorders: Obesity, Anorexia Nervosa, and the Person Within* (1973) and *The Golden Cage: The Enigma of Anorexia* (1978), Bruch supplied a theoretical and sociological context for understanding food refusal. In her view, anorexia was about an adolescent's "struggle for control, for a sense of identity, competence and effectiveness," in a society that demanded slenderness, beauty, and obedience from its daughters. Bruch wrote compassionately about the anorexic's "paralyzing sense of ineffectiveness" and defined the prototype of the patient:

> The patients were described as having been outstandingly good and quiet children, obedient, clean, eager to please, helpful at home, precociously dependable, and excelling in school work. They were the pride and joy of their parents and great things were expected of them. The need for self-reliant independence, which confronts every adolescent, seemed to cause an insoluble conflict, after a childhood of robot-like obedience. They lack awareness of their own resources and do not rely on their feelings, thoughts, and bodily sensations.[19]

Often these adolescents had domineering mothers and equated eating with undesirable female sexual maturity.

Bruch's books humanized anorexia and, as Joan Jacobs Brumberg has explained, "provided an intimate account of the inner life of the anorectic." They connected anorexia to the "developmental crisis of adolescence," and "presented a nearly complete script" of the family tensions that provided the context for the disorder.[20] But even though *The Golden Cage* sold 150,000 copies and had a huge impact on young readers, medical books alone could not have created the epidemic. Beginning in the 1970s, the mass media circulated information about anorexia through news, articles in magazines like *Mademoiselle* and *Seventeen*, TV specials, movies, and best-selling novels.

Between 1980 and 1985, several anorexia autobiographies and celebrity revelations also came into the market. In 1983, when Jane Fonda revealed her problems with bulimia, girls who may not have known about vomiting as a form of weight control were exposed to the information. A decade later they could learn about bulimia through the tribulations of Princess Diana.

In young adult fiction, a set of narrative conventions described the inner world of an anorexic girl, and her eventual recovery. According to Brumberg, the plots were remarkably similar, even "formulaic," emphasizing "family tensions and the adolescent's desire for autonomy and control." The typical heroine is an attractive, ambitious high school girl, precisely five feet five inches tall, from a two-career family. "Like virtually all American girls, she embraces the current social ideal of slimness. . . . For various reasons all having to do with the difficulties of adolescence, ordinary dieting becomes transformed into a dominating pattern of ritualistic food and eating behavior."[21]

As these stories circulated, they put the blame for anorexia on the mother. Young adult novels about anorexia nervosa targeted the demanding, fashionable, often professional mother as the source of the heroine's conflicts about eating. "Because the main characters are depicted as still in high school and living at home," Brumberg explains, "mothers are central to the story. The fictive anorectic both dislikes and loves her mother and feels perpetually guilty about hurting and deceiving her." In fiction as well as reality, mothers rather than fathers seek out professional help for anorexic daughters. Despite their concern, mothers seem to be the daughters' antagonists across the dinner table.

By the late 1970s, through peer support groups, dormitory bull sessions, and college counseling, anorexia acquired a social life. Many of the eating disorder groups took a feminist position on the causes and contexts of the disorder, seeking to reduce the burden of individual or maternal responsibility by looking at social forces that demand thinness and passivity in women. At the same time, feminist writers and literary critics interpreted anorexia as a form of social protest, comparing it to the hunger strikes of imprisoned suffragettes and IRA terrorists. In *The Madwoman in the Attic* (1979), Sandra M. Gilbert and Susan Gubar described anorexia as a parodic or renunciatory gesture against patriarchal socialization. Other feminist critics speculated that Emily Brontë, Emily Dickinson, and Virginia Woolf may themselves have suffered from anorexia. Brumberg argued that anorexia nervosa has a spiritual dimension, that it substitutes for a code of meaning in the lives of young women: "Sadly, the cult of diet and exercise is the closest thing our secular society offers women in terms of a coherent philosophy of the self."[22]

As a result of all this attention, anorexia became epidemic. By the 1990s, some researchers recognized that publicity accorded to anorexia and bulimia was creating a secondary wave of patients, and that men too were developing eating disorders. The eating disorders unit at New York Hospital–Cornell Medical Center's Westchester Division admitted its first male patients in 1988. By 1995, men made up 13 percent of the cases.[23]

Mass Hysteria

A psychogenic epidemic like anorexia nervosa which develops and grows over a number of years is not the same as mass hysteria. When, because of panic and fear, people simultaneously contract physical or mental symptoms without any organic cause, that's mass hysteria. It's contagious; it spreads from one afflicted person to another but is usually abrupt and brief.

Mass hysteria has been recognized for centuries. In *Extraordinary Popular Delusions and the Madness of Crowds* (1841), Charles Mackay, a London journalist, described what he called "moral epidemics," including tulipomania and witchcraft. One hundred fifty years later, Mackay's book still has relevance. As Simon Wessely, a senior lecturer in psychological medicine at King's College School of Medicine in London, explains, "All that has changed is the precise nature of false explanation. In previous times mass hysteria would be blamed on demons, spiritism and diabolic possession. Nowadays we are oppressed by equally invisible gases, viruses and toxins." He points to such recent headline-grabbing phenomena as panics among Japanese commuters and shoppers following a poison gas attack on a Tokyo subway and nausea among children in Rhode Island, London, Osaka, the Palestinian West Bank, Albania, and Portsmouth.

Mass hysteria takes place within a community. According to Wessely, "The trigger is often trivial—one person has a heat-induced faint or a panic attack. Normally bystanders take little notice, but if the community is already in a state of tension a rumor can develop, usually 'we are being poisoned.' If the rumor is plausible to a wider group, it spreads rapidly." Witnessing someone else faint or collapse spreads the panic faster, and social networks sustain it. "If you do not know, or do not like, the person you see collapse in front of you, you are less likely to collapse. Hence outbreaks in tight-knit communities such as isolated villages or islands last the longest." Episodes are most severe when there is an obvious enemy; witness the Iraqi Scud missile attacks on Israel during the Gulf War, when some citizens believed they had been gassed and became nauseated or faint.

The reaction of authorities to these incidents and rumors is crucial. If ambulances arrive on the scene with sirens, if scare headlines ensue, and if a search for poisons takes precedence over calming fears, the situation rapidly gets out of control. "Things only go wrong," writes Wessely, "when the nature of an outbreak is not recognized, and a fruitless and expensive search for toxins, fumes, and gases begins. Anxiety, far from being reduced, increases. It is only then that long-term psychological problems may develop."[24]

Such episodes can affect men as well as women and children, health professionals as well as laymen. In February 1994 several emergency room workers in Riverside, California, fainted after treating a patient who vomited, went into cardiac arrest, and died. Although complications from cervical cancer caused the patient's death, hospital workers were convinced that they had been poisoned by a substance she emitted. The lawyer for one hospital worker objected to a report by the Department of Health that called the episode "an outbreak of mass sociogenic illness." "Clearly people were poisoned by something that night," he insisted. "These are all professional emergency room workers. They don't become hysterical because of a heart attack."[25] In January 1996 dozens of people in Canovanas, Puerto Rico, claimed to have seen a huge, vampirelike beast killing goats, sheep, rabbits, chickens, cats, and dogs. "It was about four or five feet tall and had huge elongated red eyes," said one witness. Although health authorities insisted that autopsies on the animals showed various causes of death, including parasites and feral dogs, panic about the monsters increased. Skeptics, according to the *New York Times*, recalled that "Puerto Ricans seem to have suffered almost cyclically from collective bouts of fear set off by sensationalist press accounts."[26] Soon after, the beast was spotted in Miami.

Witch-Hunts

When hysterical epidemics or mass hysterias target enemies, when they develop links with religious fundamentalism, political paranoia, or apocalyptic panic, they can turn into witch-hunts or pogroms. In his classic essay "The Paranoid Style in American Politics," historian Richard Hofstadter outlined millenarian paranoia, mass hysteria with a political form. Hofstadter wrote that while some paranoia may always be present in American politics, "movements employing the paranoid style are not constant but come in successive episodic waves," suggesting that "the paranoid disposition is mobilized into action chiefly by social conflicts that involve ultimate schemes of values and that bring fundamental fears and hatreds, rather than negotiable interests, into political action."[27]

Other scholars have argued that anxieties about social and economic change were relieved by attacks on witches. "Witchhunting," wrote Brian Levack, "became one of the ways that people could maintain their equilibrium at a time of great stress."[28] It guaranteed one's own sanctity and salvation despite theological and spiritual uncertainty. Norman Cohn described popular psychopathologies that attended the last millennium: many people "lived in a state of chronic and inescapable insecurity, harassed not only by their economic helplessness and vulnerability, but by the lack of the traditional social relationships on which, even at the worst of times, peasants had normally been able to depend. These were the people whose anxieties drove them to seek messianic leaders and they were also the people who were most prone to create demonic scapegoats." Mixed with old prophecies, wrote Cohn, paranoia "became a coherent social myth which was capable of taking entire possession of those who believed in it. It explained the suffering, it promised them recompense, it held their anxieties at bay, it gave them an illusion of security—even while it drove them, held together by a common enthusiasm, on a quest which was vain and often suicidal."[29]

Preconditions of a witch-hunt were consistent, whether the events took place in Scotland or Salem. The community had to know something about the practices of witches and to be convinced of their habits. Lawyers and judges also had to believe in witchcraft, since they controlled the judicial process and could halt the hunts. For successful prosecutions, specific antiwitchcraft legislation and the establishment of jurisdiction were necessary. Witch-hunts were smaller where inquisitional procedures and torture were prohibited, as in seventeenth-century England.

In addition, witch-hunts required an emotional atmosphere stirred up by sermons, discussions, and rumors. They often began with individual denunciations stemming from personal grudges. Sometimes malice played a role. Sometimes disturbed individuals confessed. In England, witch-hunts were usually limited to those originally accused. In Switzerland, Germany, and Scotland, medium-size witch-hunts, what Brian Levack calls "small panics," prevailed: the accused were tortured and implicated a group of accomplices. These panics burned themselves out when the local group of suspicious persons had been exhausted. As Levack remarks, "In communities where medium-sized hunts occurred, there may not have been a sufficient amount of popular hysteria for the less rigorous standards to be invoked."[30]

Large witch-hunts, "characterized by a high degree of panic or hysteria," took place in France, Sweden, and of course in Salem. These were driven by both the clinical conversion hysteria of the demoniacs and the collective hysteria of the community. Levack cautions that

> we must be careful to distinguish between the mass hysteria of some witch-hunts and the individual psychological problems of some of the participants in these hunts. The occasional sadistic judge or hangman, the compulsive witch-finder, the insane or 'melancholic' witch all manifested abnormal forms of behaviour, but these should not be confused with the general, collective mood or group psychosis with which we are concerned. We must also be careful not to apply a simple label such as the 'witch-craze' or the 'witch-mania' or 'mass delusion' to the entire European witch-hunt. But within the context of specific witch-hunts we can legitimately—although at the same time hypothetically—talk about mass hysteria."[31]

In the notes to his prophetic play *The Crucible*, Arthur Miller explored the psychology and politics that created the Salem witch-hunt and, by extension, McCarthyism. Salem, Miller writes, "was a perverse manifestation of the panic which set in among all classes when the balance began to turn toward greater individual freedom." For some individuals it was a catalyst for repressed emotion, "a long-overdue opportunity for everyone so inclined to express publicly his guilt and sins, under the cover of accusations against the victims." It provided an opportunity to express "long-held hatreds of neighbors" and to take vengeance, "despite the Bible's charitable injunctions." The Salem witch-hunt began for political, social, and economic reasons; but it grew because "these people had no ritual for the washing-away of sins. It is another trait we inherited from them, and it has helped to discipline us as well as to breed hypocrisy among us."[32]

Cultures and Conspiracies

American culture has been particularly hospitable to hysterical movements. In the past, such movements have centered on the Masons, Catholicism, communism, the Kennedy assassination, and the fluoridation of water. In the 1990s, hysteria merges with a seething mix of paranoia, anxiety, and anger that comes out of the American crucible. Many observers see millennial America in the grip of what journalists Katherine Dunn and Jim Redden call "a mind-numbingly vast conspiracy theory."[33] *New Yorker* writer Michael Kelly terms this mix of conspiracy theories "fusion paranoia": "In its extreme form, paranoia is still the province of minority movements, but the ethos of minority movements—anti-establishmentarian protest, the politics of rage—has become so deeply ingrained in the larger political culture that the paranoid style has become the cohering idea of a broad coalition plurality that draws adherents from every point on the political spectrum."[34] These fantasies protect the real villains. Even a mother whose two little sons were killed in the bombing of the Federal building in Oklahoma City insists that the attack was part of a mysterious conspiracy: "Now I feel like I'm in some bad movie," she told a journalist. "Before this all happened, I never voted, never watched the news. Now I'm in the middle of a government conspiracy and cover-up. It just blows my mind."[35]

Some scholars warn that fusion paranoia has carried over to medicine and psychiatry, with conspiracy theories to explain every unidentified symptom and syndrome. Sherrill Mulhern, an outspoken American anthropologist who works in Paris at the wonderfully named Laboratoire des Rumeurs, des Mythes du Futur et des Sectes, sees a deeper problem behind the ostensible debate over memory: "the emergence of conspiracy theory as the nucleus of a consistent pattern of clinical interpretation. In the United States during the past decade, the clinical milieu has become the vortex of a growing, socially operant conspiratorial mentality, which is undermining crucial sectors of the mental health, criminal justice, and judicial systems."[36]

Americans may lead the world in these behaviors and attitudes, but other countries also provide breeding ground for hysterical epidemics. When Miller wrote *The Crucible* in the 1950s, he believed that "only England has held back before the temptations of contemporary diabolism," not only in religious tolerance, but in the absence of political persecution.[37] Even in the nineteenth century, British doctors believed that hysteria was rarer in the British Isles than elsewhere in Europe because of the sturdy and sensible quality of English culture and heredity. "The Gallic nature," wrote T. S. Dowse in 1889, "seems to be of less enduring stability than that of the Saxon, and is more liable to exhibit exalted hysterical manifestations."[38] "Certain races are more liable to the disease than others," wrote Edward Bramwell and John Tuke in 1910. "Thus the Latin races are much more prone to hysteria than are those who come of a Teutonic stock, and in more aggravated and complex forms."[39] In England doctors felt that hysteria was not only "un-English" but also un-Christian. As J. Mitchell Clark declared in *Hysteria and Neurasthenia*, "No race is exempt from hysteria, but it is more common in some than in others; thus the Jewish race is especially prone to suffer from it, and it appears to be more frequent, at any rate in a severe form, in France than in Germany or England."[40] While one hundred thirty-three book-length studies of hysteria were published in France between 1880 and 1900, England and Scotland together produced only four.

Today the English invariably reach for the metaphor of hysteria when they're confronted by political intensity or national drama. Hysteria is the opposite of the cherished national trait of irony. It is overstatement rather than understatement, wearing one's ambitions on one's sleeve, getting excessive, running it out. In English journalism, the term hysteria signifies disapproval of intensity, a put-down of both the antismoking lobby and the tobacco industry, of AIDS activists and homophobics, of feminists and misogynists.

In the 1990s, even the most cursory survey of the English press makes clear that too open a display of passion or ambition is regarded as hysterical. When John Major's sudden resignation as Tory Party leader in July 1995 led to a brief, ferocious public tussle among potential successors, the British press reacted with horror. A paradigmatic cartoon in *The Times* showed a staid John Major labeled "Englishman" and a rabid, foaming-at-the-mouth John Redwood (his Tory challenger) as "mad dog." In one essay, Simon Jenkins deplored the "hysterical talk" of "shell-shocked politicians": "The entire Tory party is engaged in a collective *crime passionnel*. If these are frigid Englishmen, Britain would be better run by a gang of mafiosi gigolos. We are at one of those alarming moments in our island story when someone (a Prime Minister, no less) peels back the skin of office to reveal, not a devotion to public duty or good government, but raw insecurity and ambition seething beneath."[41] The furor over Mad Cow Disease in 1996 owed some of its intensity to British fear and denial of anything mad.

On the other hand, at the Freud Museum's 1995 conference on "Hysteria Today," David Bell, a Kleinian analyst, observed that florid symptomatology of hysteria could still be seen in English psychiatric hospitals and that the full range of hysterical symptoms was far more common than many believed.[42] England has had its own outbreaks of hysterical panics over satanic ritual abuse, and Dr. Charles Shepherd estimated in 1992 that the country had one hundred thousand patients with chronic fatigue. English fiction and theater have taken the lead in exploring the meanings of hysteria for men and women today.

The French intellectual tradition of Cartesian hyper-rationality, skepticism, and anticlericalism has kept France relatively untouched by the more virulent recent panics. Sherrill Mulhern, a forceful critic of recent extremes, regards Paris as the perfect outpost from which to investigate flammable societies of hysteria. When it gets too hot in the brushfire conference circuit where recovered memory is debated, Mulhern can retreat to the relative academic safety of Neuilly and the cool intellectual detachment of her Parisian colleagues.

Nonetheless, France has a long hystory of its own. Throughout the twentieth century, while most psychiatrists have relegated hysteria to the dusty back shelves of the library, French doctors have showcased it under racy new titles, declared their affection for it, and pioneered its historiography. "When a foreign professor is asked to express his ideas in another country, he is expected to expose one of the most characteristic studies of his native land, just as, when we have landed in a new country, we seek to taste the dishes that characterize its cookery," said Dr. Pierre Janet in 1920 on the eve of his inaugural lectures at the Harvard Medical School. "It seems to me," he went on, "that what has been most characteristic in France for a number of years . . . is the development of pathological psychology," an interest that "has as its object a special disease: Hysteria."[43] Many French psychoanalysts still feel nostalgia for the heyday of hysteria and value national variants like *spasmophilie* that keep it alive.

Finally, even if contemporary hysterical epidemics begin in the United States, it was a nineteenth-century Parisian physician-enthusiast who pioneered the modern marketing of hysteria, who took it out of the medical books and made it a star. To understand modern hysterical epidemics, we must first look at Jean-Martin Charcot, and how he pioneered the synthesis of medical authority, institutional prestige, and cultural spectacle that initiated hysteria's golden age.

3

The History of Hysteria: The Great Doctors

Jean-Martin Charcot:
The Invention of Modern Hysteria

The modern medical history of hysterical epidemics begins with Jean-Martin Charcot (1825–1893) and his clinic in the Paris hospital La Salpêtrière just over a century ago. Here doctor, patients, and culture came together for the first time. From the late 1870s until his death in 1893, Charcot, according to his student Axel Munthe, "was the most celebrated doctor of his time. Patients from all over the world flocked to his consulting-room in Faubourg St. Germain, often waiting for weeks before being admitted to the inner sanctum where he sat by the window at his huge library. . . . A word of recommendation from Charcot was enough to decide the result of any examination. . . . He ruled supreme over the whole faculty of medicine."[1] Magazines, newspapers, and fiction popularized Charcot's theories, and doctors from Europe and the United States sat at his feet. His French colleagues thought him the daring Caesar of hysteria. At the banquet for Charcot's election to the Institut de France, Professor Charles Bouchard said, "The study of hysteria could have brought you triumphant to Rome or dragged you into the mud. You were courageous and Fortune has rewarded your audacity."[2]

Charcot defined hysteria as a physical illness caused by a hereditary defect or traumatic wound in the central nervous system that gives rise to epileptiform attacks. His definitions and prototypes attracted thousands of clients; at the height of his power, approximately ten hysterical women arrived at his clinic every day for diagnosis and treatment. Under Charcot's direction at the Salpêtrière, the percentage of women diagnosed with the disorder and hospitalized for it rose dramatically, from 1 percent in 1841 to 17 percent by 1883. In Paris, among the *charcoterie* of disciples and patients at the hospital, a particular kind of *grande hystérie* became epidemic; elsewhere, the syndrome was rare, leading some doctors to suspect that Charcot was creating iatrogenic illness or, indeed, inventing hysteria.

Charcot had extraordinary personal as well as intellectual gifts. He brought an artist's eye—the observational gift Freud would later term *visuel*—to the study of hysterical bodies. Many of his contemporaries described his mesmerizing gaze, and Dr. Alexandre Souques never forgot his "scrutinizing eyes . . . deeply set in the shadow of their orbits."[3] Charcot had planned to become an artist and always maintained a studio in his home where he could paint. He and his interns sketched hysterical patients during their attacks, and he even installed a full photographic studio, with a professional photographer, Albert Londe, to record the women's movements and expressions. These photographic images appeared in three volumes called *iconographies*; sketches, drawings, and paintings of the women were also reproduced and sold. The best known, André Brouillet's engraving of Charcot and his most famous hysterical patient, Blanche Wittman, hung in the lecture hall at the Salpêtrière, and Freud always had a copy in his office.

In the late 1870s Charcot, a showman with great theatrical flair, instituted two weekly public performances at the Salpêtrière. Every Friday morning, he gave a prepared lecture-demonstration, often involving hysterical patients. On Tuesdays, in the celebrated *leçons du mardi*, he publicly diagnosed patients he had never seen before—like a magician, or an acrobat working without a net. This bravado and virtuosity drew huge, spellbound audiences of as many as five hundred. Pierre Janet recalled, "Everything in his lectures was designed to attract attention and to captivate the audience by means of visual and auditory impressions."[4] According to Henri Ellenberger, "The podium was always decorated with pictures and anatomical schemata pertaining to the day's presentation. Charcot . . . entered promptly at ten o'clock, often accompanied by a distinguished foreign visitor and a group of assistants who sat down in the first row."[5] He illustrated his lectures with chalk drawings on the blackboard and imitated the behavior of patients he was about to present. Charcot certainly had a sense of the dramatic; on one occasion, when he planned to discuss tremors, he brought in three women wearing hats with long feathers, each of which trembled in a way characteristic of its disease.

Charcot undertook his studies at a propitious time. Because government ministers appointed medical directors at public hospitals, medicine and politics were intertwined. Political liberals and scientists shared anticlerical sentiments; Charcot explicitly set out to refute religion through his practice of medicine and, literary critic Martha Noel Evans asserts, to "reclaim hysteria from former religious interpretations of the disorder as diabolic possession, or, alternatively, saintly ecstasy."[6] He and his assistants wrote essays debunking miracles of the church, describing even Saint Joan of Arc as a case of hysteria. Paradoxically, however, Charcot himself used techniques that suggested the diabolism of the witch-hunt, such as searching for hysterical "stigmata" and pricking or writing on the sensitive skin of patients. In addition, Charcot's descriptions of hysterical seizures seemed influenced by religious imagery, and the epidemic hysterias at the Salpêtrière coincided with the reemergence of belief in miracles at the end of the century. In the late 1880s and early 1890s Charcot himself sent patients on a pilgrimage to Lourdes, and as Mark Micale points out, "Lourdes functioned as a kind of popular nonmedical counterculture of hysteria in late nineteenth-century Europe."[7]

Charcot had the advantage of working in a major medical institution, which he had redesigned in order to pursue his own interests. The Salpêtrière was a huge, old, rambling women's hospital in the 13th *arrondissement*, more poorhouse and medical warehouse than clinic. But even as an intern, Charcot saw in its thousands of long-term cases a living medical laboratory, a "reservoir of material," where he could test out theories through the "anatomical-clinical" method, performing autopsies for signs of organic disease and then tracing these signs back to their physical symptoms through close observation of patients. This old hospital was an ideal environment for the manufacture and marketing of hysterias, and Charcot made it an up-to-date "temple of science."[8] By the end of the nineteenth century, the Salpêtrière had become one of the sights of the city, a three-star attraction on any serious visitor's tour.

As chief physician at the Salpêtrière after 1862, Charcot made several important discoveries using the anatomical-clinical method. He differentiated multiple sclerosis from Parkinson's disease; defined the symptoms of poliomyelitis; mapped out the spinal forms of neurosyphilis; and described the pathology of amyotrophic lateral sclerosis, now called Lou Gehrig's disease.[9] In the 1870s, Charcot decided to use some of the same techniques to define the organic laws of hysteria. He theorized that hysteria was an inherited disease of the nervous system that could be triggered by an emotional or physical trauma in vulnerable men or women. Its symptoms ranged from stigmata, ovarian sensitivity, pain, visual disturbances, local numbness or anesthesias, particularly on the left side of the body, and convulsive fits. Charcot imposed a persuasive set of laws on the anarchic shapelessness and multiple symptoms—paralyses, muscle contractures, convulsions, and somnambulism—of hysteria. Furthermore, he set out to demonstrate that the dramatic seizures of *grande hystérie* could be induced or stopped by hypnosis, allowing doctors to examine its stages and determine its "laws." Jan Goldstein writes that he "took the old, amorphous 'wastepaper basket' of symptoms and replaced it with a coherent and conceptually elegant array."[10]

Though Charcot treated at least ninety male hysterics, about ten times that number of women were diagnosed as hysterics in the hospital. In his autopsies of hysterical women, Charcot concentrated on the ovaries—which, according to the reflex theories of medicine then popular, could send signals along the spinal cord to other organs. In examining patients, he found ovarian sensitivity, particularly on the left side, and began to use pressure on the ovaries to initiate and stop attacks. Soon he invented a physical apparatus, the ovarian compressor, a heavy leather and metal belt strapped onto the patient and often left for as long as three days. Later he would try to find parallel "hysterogenic" regions on men's bodies, compressing the testicles in an effort to affect the course of a seizure. (Unsurprisingly, the procedure did not always work, and some doctors discovered that squeezing the patient's testicles actually made the convulsions stronger.)

Charcot viewed seizures as the central sign of hysterical disorders. He outlined four stages: a premonitory period in which there might be visual disturbances or the classic *globus hystericus*; involuntary movements, building to backbending athletic acrobatics; stagy poses, which Charcot called *attitudes passionnelles* and suggestively titled "summons," "amorous supplication," "mockery," "menace," "eroticism," and "ecstasy"; and resolution. Predictably, he announced his unified theory of hysteria with dramatic panache and argued it with incontrovertible authority.

In 1878, Charcot reintroduced hypnosis, which had been discredited since the vogue for mesmerism and animal magnetism. He argued in

fact that the capacity to be hypnotized was itself a sign of hysteria. At
the Tuesday demonstrations in the hospital's semi-circular amphitheater,
women diagnosed as hysterics were put on display and hypnotized by
Charcot's interns. The Swedish doctor Axel Munthe recalled that one
woman "would crawl on all fours on the floor, barking furiously when
told she was a dog. . . . Another would walk with a top hat in her arms,
rocking it to and fro and kissing it tenderly when she was told it was her
baby."[11] Hypnotic suggestion was also used to stop hysterical attacks.
Charcot's theatrical demonstrations aroused controversies. Other doctors agreed that hypnotic suggestion was a powerful therapeutic tool but
disputed its special relationship to hysteria. Munthe complained, "If the
statement of the Salpêtrière school that only hysterical subjects were
hypnotizable was correct it would mean that at least eighty-five percent
of mankind was suffering from hysteria."[12]

Despite Charcot's insistence that hysteria was neither a sexual disorder nor one limited to women, both he and his staff repeatedly fell
back on stereotypes that equated it with the female personality.
Hysterics were seen as vain and preoccupied with their appearance,
deceitful and self-dramatizing. Charcot's assistant Charles Richet saw
these traits as "varieties of female character. . . . One might even say that
hysterics are more womanly than other women."[13]

At the Salpêtrière, two-thirds of the hysterical patients were working-class women. The nascent French feminist movement demanded
political, social, and educational reform but also provoked a backlash
of virulent misogyny. In addition, working women were neglected by
feminist thinkers and ignored—even betrayed—by the labor movement. Many working-class women migrated to the cities, where by
1866 they made up a third of the labor force. As Martha Noel Evans
comments, "Poor women were thrust into a new and often disorient-
ing freedom in urban centers. Alone, unsupported by the family
groups they were accustomed to, often paid below subsistence wages,
they faced a stressful lot. The astronomic increase in the number of
prostitutes in Paris at this time is a sad witness to the fate of many of
these displaced, young working women."[14]

Some of Charcot's working-class women patients became stars of his
public lectures and supermodels in his photography albums. Blanche
Wittman, known as the Queen of the Hysterics, and Augustine, later
the Surrealists' pinup girl, were among the most famous. Blanche
Wittman entered the Salpêtrière in 1877 at the age of fifteen. The
daughter of a carpenter who had himself been institutionalized, she had

worked as a laundress, a furrier's apprentice, and a nurse. Her symptoms of convulsions and "nervous crises" began when the furrier attempted to rape her. In the Salpêtrière, Wittman proved to be an excellent hypnotic subject; George Frederick Drinka writes in *The Birth of Neurosis* that her "astonishing cataleptic, lethargic, and somnambulistic feats were reported in detail throughout the Western medical world."[15] Painted, displayed, and photographed, she stayed in the hospital for her entire life. After Charcot's death she became a laboratory technician and eventually a radiologist. Even on her death bed she insisted that her fits had been genuine.

Augustine spent only five years in the Salpêtrière, from October 1875, when she was a fifteen-year-old domestic servant, to September 1880; but she became the most photographed of all the hysterical patients. At age thirteen, she had been raped by her mother's lover, who had threatened her with a knife; soon after, she began to have seizures in which she imagined that she was being bitten by wild dogs or rats and chased by a knife-wielding man. In the hospital, she was treated with drugs, straitjackets, and solitary confinement as well as hypnosis, and posed frequently for Londe. After many attempts to run away, she finally succeeded by disguising herself as a man.

Charcot's images of the hypnotized hysterical woman inspired novels and plays, which in their turn influenced popular understanding of the hysterical trance. In the 1880s, art students who had been to performances at the Salpêtrière amused themselves by hypnotizing their models. "The chief culprit," wrote one contemporary, "was a young fellow who for some considerable time had attended the lectures of the late Dr. Charcot, and, rather than waste the knowledge he had acquired, he applied it indiscriminately to no matter whom—models and fellow-workers alike. . . . Our amateur Charcot continued to experimentalize, and finally selected for his "subject" a girl of great plastic beauty; . . . the well-known Elise Duval, the favorite model of MM. Gérôme and Benjamin Constant. . . . One day at the beginning of a seance, she was thrown into a trance which lasted for four hours, at the end of which time she was awakened more dead than alive." The atelier of Gérôme was closed for a month over the scandal.[16]

The idea of the vulnerable artist's model entering a trance in order to pose for hours resurfaced in George Du Maurier's best-selling novel *Trilby* (1894), which became a great hit play of the fin-de-siècle stage. The young artist's model Trilby suffers from crippling migraine headaches; she is cured by the mesmerism of the Jewish musician

Svengali, under whose hypnotic gaze and instruction she becomes a great singer. *Trilby* sold over two hundred thousand copies in its first year and generated a craze—"Trilby-mania"—for sequels and spin-offs. The stage and film versions played up Svengali's Jewishness and further demonized the mesmerist; Trilby became a popular icon of hysterical suggestibility and feminine attractiveness.

Even in Charcot's day, these theatrical poses and fictional heroines taught women how hysterics looked. The performances took place in a hall of mirrors, for the hysterics were coached and surrounded by pictures of *grande hystérie*. Some of the women in the Salpêtrière acquired symptoms related to the photography itself; a sixteen-year-old seamstress, Hortense, came down with "photophobia," a spasm and paralysis in one eye induced by the flash—a squint that made her face mimic that of the cameraman.[17] Charcot's favorite model, Augustine, had episodes of color blindness when she saw everything in black and white. Indeed, as Jan Goldstein has concluded, "The 'iconography' of hysteria as defined by Charcot—with all its vividly theatrical contortions and grimaces—seems to have been so widely publicized ... in both pictorial and verbal form, as to constitute for that historical moment a reigning 'cultural preconception' of how to act when insane."[18]

Despite his brilliance, Charcot made a number of mistakes. According to Henri Ellenberger, he wrongly emphasized the most complex forms of hysteria and oversimplified the disease descriptions to make them fit into his scheme. He was not interested in his patients as people; he cared about them only as cases. "Charcot hardly ever made clinical rounds himself; rather, he saw his patients in the hospital examining room while his students, who had examined them in the wards, reported to him. Charcot never suspected that his patients were often visited and magnetized repeatedly on the wards by incompetent people."[19] The Goncourt brothers reported in their diary that Charcot gossiped about patients' personal secrets.

Having started with the intention of making objective scientific discoveries about hysteria, Charcot ended with a rigid model, a theoretical cage into which he squeezed all his patients. In the highly contagious environment of the hospital, hysteria took on the immense power of suggestion. People came in with problems—with psychosomatic conversion symptoms, post-traumatic stress disorders, and other emotional responses to their unhappy lives. Charcot gave them a diagnosis; he gave them a certain degree of legitimacy; he even gave some of them a warped celebrity. But he took away their dignity and their hope. They were pressed into mass conformity, put into solitary confinement, turned into chronic, even lifelong patients. Through hypnotic suggestion, Evans notes, "hysterical patients were already becoming iatrogenic monsters."[20]

Toward the end of his life, Charcot suspected that his theories were flawed and that he needed to pay more attention to the psychological and social elements in his patients' lives. Moreover, the liberal political atmosphere in France that had supported his work was shifting to the right in the early 1890s. After his death in 1893, Charcot's fame rapidly declined. As Mark Micale writes, the empire of hysteria that had made France "for a single, glorious generation . . . the international epicenter of the hysteria industry" began to "break apart" and "scatter."[21] Charcot's medical rivals, such as Hippolyte Bernheim in Nancy, challenged his theories, and some of his own interns suggested that he had coached his patients in their performances. In his savage novel *Les Morticoles* (1894), Léon Daudet portrayed Charcot as the sinister Doctor Foutange, who manipulates his patients like a puppeteer. Swiss neurologist Paul Dubois noted that in the Salpêtrière, "All cases of hysteria resemble each other. At the command of the chief of the staff, or of the interns, they begin to act like marionettes, or like circus horses accustomed to repeat the same evolutions."[22]

By 1900, writes Micale, "the age of Charcot, and with it the *belle époque* of French hysteria, had effectively come to a close," and a backlash against his theories had set in.[23] A German doctor predicted that "within a few years the concept of hysteria will belong to history." What Charcot had called hysteria, he claimed, was "a tissue woven of a thousand threads, a cohort of the most varied diseases, with nothing in common but the so-called stigmata, which in fact may accompany any disease."[24] A year later, Charcot's former pupil Joseph Babinski presided over a meeting of the Paris Neurological Society that systematically dismantled all the assumptions of the Charcotian model of hysteria. In an article for a medical journal, Babinski announced the "dismemberment of traditional hysteria."[25] By the 1930s, only one dissertation on hysterical disorders was written at French medical schools.[26]

Sigmund Freud: The Talking Cure

Charcot had publicized the idea of hysteria as a unified organic disease; Sigmund Freud, who had studied at the Salpêtrière in 1885 and 1886, defined it as a neurosis caused by repression, conflicted sexuality, and fantasy. Freud felt that the course of his intellectual and professional life had been changed by his encounter with Charcot, who was brilliant, cultivated, and bold in his thinking, with an extraordinary ability to encapsulate and theorize. Among Charcot's many admirers and disciples, only Freud had the charisma and determination to build a theoretical empire. Indeed, Richard Webster contends, "Freud himself consciously identified with Moses, and the prophetic and messianic dimensions of his character."[27]

Like Charcot, Freud was a showman who publicized psychoanalysis through his writings and lectures. Although Charcot worked with, and perhaps created, the florid behaviors of *grande hystérie*, Freud worked with the much more subtle, everyday symptoms of *petite hystérie*: coughs, limps, headaches, loss of voice—conversion hysterias with less dramatic potential. In the 1890s, when Charcot's career had reached its apex and Freud's was on the rise, hysteria coincided with the unconscious anxieties and fantasies of the fin de siècle to produce a powerful mix unequaled until the end of our own century. Freud's ideas on hysteria are scattered throughout his writing, but they peak in the 1890s, when, as John Forrester and Lisa Appignanesi point out, they became "grand theories, colossal structures, breathtaking speculative leaps."[28] These ideas are fundamental to our century's way of thinking about hysteria.

Along with his colleague Joseph Breuer, Freud took the crucial step of actually listening to hysterical women and paying serious attention to their stories. In the lengthy *Studies on Hysteria* (1895), Freud and Breuer proposed a new explanation for the origin of hysteria and a new therapy for its treatment, arguing that all hysteria, male and female, had traumatic origins, but that the traumas did not have to be injuries or hereditary lesions. Instead, they could be disturbing sexual experiences patients had repressed, thus creating symptoms through a process of symbolization. The original traumatic injuries, they speculated, had occurred when the patient was in a "hypnoid state," moments of daydreaming or resistance to pain. The memories were then banned from consciousness and converted into bodily symptoms that were "mnemonic symbols" or physical metaphors of the suppressed trauma. If the patient could retrieve these memories through hypnosis, along with their original force or affect, her symptoms would vanish.

In 1880, Breuer thought he had relieved the symptoms of his first patient, Bertha Pappenheim (1859–1936), whom he named "Anna O.," through the process of hypnosis and analysis she called "the talking cure." Breuer described Anna O. as "markedly intelligent, with an astonishingly quick grasp of things and penetrating intuition. She possessed a powerful intellect which would have been capable of digesting solid mental pabulum, and which stood in need of it." Although she was "bubbling over with intellectual vitality," Anna O. "led an extremely monotonous existence in her puritanically-minded family." Her hysterical conversion symptoms—including a severe cough, headaches, contractures of her right arm and leg, sleepwalking, and loss of voice—seemed in part an expression of intellectual frustration. In lengthy sessions Breuer invited her to speak, often under hypnosis, about her memories, dreams, and hopes. This attention seemed to help, but the therapy ended abruptly when Anna O. hallucinated that she was giving birth to Breuer's baby. She had also become addicted to pain-relieving drugs and spent several months in sanatoriums between 1883 and 1887. In the 1890s, Pappenheim worked with Jewish immigrants from Eastern Europe and found a satisfying outlet for her talents in feminist journalism, politics, and philanthropy.[29]

In his early work with hysterics, Freud used techniques he had learned from his teachers, especially Charcot. He attempted to provoke hysteria by pressing the "hysterogenic" ovarian zones of his women patients' bodies. And like Breuer, he used hypnosis to help patients recall early childhood memories he believed had been forgotten or repressed. This technique, the "cathartic method," he later explained, differed from hypnotic suggestion and involved "questioning the patient upon the origin of his symptoms, which in his waking state he could only describe very imperfectly or not at all."[30] Like theorists of neurasthenia, Freud blamed masturbation for such symptoms as fatigue, constipation, and bed-wetting. For a decade, influenced by the theories of an eccentric friend, the Berlin doctor Wilhelm Fliess, he even believed that sexual problems had their source in the nose.

Freud hypothesized that the doctor must insist on taking memories back to their sources in order to bring about a cure. Treating twenty-seven-year-old Emma Eckstein for vague complaints, including stomach aches and menstrual irregularities, in 1895, Freud initially concluded that her hysteria was caused by masturbation and the cure was to operate on her nose. Fliess performed the operation but bungled it, leaving a piece of gauze in the nasal cavity that caused a severe postoperative infection. Meanwhile, Freud had convinced himself that Emma's postoperative symptoms and hemorrhages were merely hysterical manifestations. When discussions of her childhood masturbation did not help,

Freud urged Emma to come up with other "memories"—an account of sexual abuse when she was eight, and even a story about satanic ritual female circumcision.

By 1896, Freud was convinced that repressed childhood or even infantile sexual abuse caused hysteria; he called this early model of hysteria the seduction theory. In a paper read to the Viennese Society for Psychiatry and Neurology in April 1896, based on his experiences with eighteen hysterical patients, Freud announced his views on the etiology of hysteria. "At the bottom of every case of hysteria," he said, "there are *one or more occurrences of premature sexual experience*, occurrences which belong to the earliest years of childhood but which can be reproduced through the work of psycho-analysis in spite of the intervening decades." Hysterical symptoms were the "derivatives of memories which are operating unconsciously." As he wrote to Fliess in December 1896, he had come to believe that in most cases the fathers were the seducers and abusers. "It seems to me more and more that the essential point of hysteria is that it results from *perversion* on the part of the seducer, and *more and more* that heredity is seduction by the father."[31]

But unlike Charcot, who died before he could revise his own too sweeping and too simple theory of hysteria, Freud moved through several stages. By late 1897, he had abandoned the seduction theory for a concept that depended much more on the patient's unconscious and on sexual and Oedipal fantasy. Freud announced his new theory in another letter to Fliess, listing the reasons he had been forced to abandon his seduction hypothesis. First, the theory did not lead to therapeutic success. Second, the incidence of fathers abusing children would be improbably vast, because it would have to exceed the incidence of hysteria. Third, no one could distinguish between truth and fantasy in narratives elicited from the unconscious. And finally memories of abuse never surfaced except when his patients were under hypnosis, "even in the most confused delirium." Therefore, Freud concluded, instead of remembering real incidents of incestuous abuse, hysterical patients were expressing fantasies based on their unconscious Oedipal desires.

Freud's abandonment of the seduction theory has long been the center of heated debate about hysteria, psychoanalysis, and the character of Freud as a man. In 1980, as he recalls in *The Assault on Truth: Freud's Suppression of the Seduction Theory* (1984), psychoanalyst Jeffrey M. Masson, then projects director of the Freud Archives, "was given the freedom of Maresfield Gardens, where Freud spent the last year of his life. Freud's magnificent personal library was there, and many of the volumes, especially from the early years, were annotated by Freud."[32] Masson made several discoveries, including letters about the sexual seduction of children, and a pattern of omitting such discussions in Anna Freud's abridged edition of the Freud/Fliess letters. Masson pursued the issue of a cover-up, and in August 1981 the *New York Times* reported his discoveries, leading to a furor in which he was dismissed from the Freud Archives.

The furor over Freud, however, has never really subsided. Freud was a fraud, some angry feminists charged. For Freud "to incriminate daughters rather than fathers," wrote Judith Lewis Herman in *Father-Daughter Incest* (1981), "was an immense relief to him, even if it entailed a public admission that he had been mistaken." Freud, she protested, all but forgot the incestuous wishes of parents in his new zeal, which did not "matter very much in the case of boys, for, as it turns out, boys are rarely molested by their parents. It matters a great deal in the case of girls, who are the chief victims."[33]

Masson declared that in publicly renouncing his seduction theory, Freud backed away from the true complaints of his women patients and that he did so out of self-exculpation and professional cowardice. "By shifting the emphasis from an actual world of sadness, misery, and cruelty," Masson wrote, "to an internal stage on which actors performed invented dramas for an invisible audience, Freud began a trend away from the real world that, it seems to me, is at the root of the present-day sterility of psychoanalysis and psychiatry throughout the world."[34]

But many other recent critics of Freud, including Allen Esterson, Morton Schatzman, Frederick Crews, and Richard Webster, argue persuasively that Freud pressured his patients to produce narratives congruent with his theories. In other words, Freud's patients were not molested by their fathers and did not fantasize about them. Instead, they fabricated stories along the lines of Freud's own hysterical hypotheses. "Before they come for analysis," Freud himself admitted in "The Aetiology of Hysteria," "the patients know nothing about these scenes." Their "memories" of abuse were responses to Freud's hints, suggestions, and persuasion. Indeed, Freud wrote that he preferred a method of diagnosing the causes of hysteria "in which we should feel less dependent on the assertions of the patients themselves." When the patient's memories did not satisfy the therapist's expectations of traumatic causation, Freud explained, "We tell our patient that this experience explains nothing, but that behind it there must be hidden a more significant, earlier experience; and we direct his attention by the same technique to the associative thread which connects the two memories—the one that has been discovered and the one that has still to be discovered."

Clearly, Freud was a stubborn, bullying interrogator of hysterical women. In *Studies on Hysteria*, he explained how the therapist must fight to overcome the patients' defenses: "We force our way into the internal strata, overcoming resistances all the time." By March 1896, Freud argued that the stories must be true *because* the patients were not conscious of remembering them and stammered or cried while describing them under hypnosis. A month later, he defended himself against the idea that "the doctor forces reminiscences of this sort on the patient" by pointing to the "uniformity" of the narratives.[35]

Looking closely at Freud's letters and essays from this time, I am convinced that he did force such reminiscences on his patients, eliciting confabulations rather than actual memories. As Berkeley professor Frederick Crews puts it, "Freud himself laid down the outlines of the seduction plots, which were then fleshed out from 'clues' supplied by his bewildered and frightened patients, whose signs of distress he took to be proof that his constructions were correct."[36] Richard Webster endorses this view and adds that renouncing the seduction theory moved Freud further away from hypotheses based on evidence: "What happened when Freud repudiated his seduction theory, then, was not that he abandoned the real world of human emotions for an invisible world of internal biological processes. . . . What happened was that this invisible world was at last almost completely freed from the constraints of empirical reality."[37]

We see effects of this shift to internal, invisible dramas in Freud's case study of Ida Bauer, or "Dora," whom he treated in 1900. Brought to Freud's Vienna consulting room by her father when she was eighteen, Dora was an intelligent young Jewish woman stifled by the limitations of her role as the marriageable daughter of a bourgeois family. She was a Viennese version of the New Woman of the 1890s, the feminist who seeks higher education and wishes to avoid marriage, but she was also dealing with the rising anti-Semitism of Austrian society. Freud never met Dora's mother, whom he regarded as an obsessive housewife. Although Dora felt contempt for her mother's monotonous domestic life, it was the life for which she too was destined. Her mother was "bent upon drawing her into taking a share in the work of the house." Dora could find no support for her intellectual aspirations from either parent. Although she had a governess who was "well-read and of advanced views," Dora believed that the governess was neglecting her and was really in love with her father. She arranged to have the woman dismissed. Afterward, she struggled alone with the effort to keep up her serious reading, and she attended lectures specially given for women. Her older brother, Otto, went off to the university and later became a prominent Austrian politician.

Dora was treated like a pawn or a possession by her father and denied the rights to privacy or personal freedom. For six years her father had been having an affair with Frau K., whose husband had attempted to seduce Dora when she was fourteen. Dora felt that "her father had handed her over to Herr K." in exchange for his complicity in the adultery. Professing to be anxious about her depressive state of mind but really, Dora believed, afraid that she would betray his sexual secrets, her father then "handed her over" to Freud for psychotherapeutic treatment. He wanted Freud to persuade Dora that her keen perceptions were simply adolescent imaginings. He hired Freud hoping for an advocate to "bring her to reason."[38]

As Jeffrey Masson observes, Dora had good reason to be upset: "She felt conspired against. She was conspired against. She felt lied to. She was lied to. She felt used. She was used."[39] Freud's determination to label her as a hysteric did not depend upon the severity of her symptoms, which were few and slight; she had a chronic cough, headaches, depressions. Although he acknowledged that Dora's case was no more than *petite hystérie*, Freud believed that the ordinariness of her symptoms made her an ideal psychoanalytic subject. Committed from the start to the hysteria diagnosis, he interpreted all Dora's behavior and statements in accordance with his theories. He told her that she was really attracted to Herr K., in love with her father, and with Freud himself. He ignored the appalling circumstances of Dora's family situation, and after only eleven weeks she broke off the therapy.

Unlike the impoverished working-class women at the Salpêtrière, who had to give Charcot what he wanted, Dora had the financial and social resources to resist her therapist. Yet Dora failed as well. She was not a willing participant and did not collude with Freud, but she couldn't manage to tell her own story. Instead, Freud used her to publicize psychoanalysis at the moment of its inception and rising fortunes. Freud's account, called "Fragment of an Analysis of a Case of Hysteria," was published in 1905 and has become the most famous study of any hysteric.

Analysts today believe that psychoanalysis could only have evolved out of work with hysterics because hysterics formed strong, explicit transferences to their doctors and thus provided examples of projection and sexual conflict. Kurt Eissler has hypothesized that "the discovery of psychoanalysis would have been greatly impeded, delayed, or even made impossible if in the second half of the nineteenth century the prevailing neurosis had not been hysteria."[40] "I think . . . that psychoanalysis had to start from the understanding of hysteria," Juliet Mitchell writes. "It could not have developed from one of the other neuroses or psychoses. Hysteria led Freud to what is universal in psychic construction and it led him there in a particular way—by route of a prolonged and central preoccupation with the difference between the sexes. . . . The question of sexual difference—femininity and masculinity—was built into the very structure of the illness."[41] However, Freud relied on cultural myths of masculine and feminine identity in shaping his interpretation of hysteria. Had he written a case study of "Dorian" rather than "Dora," the history of psychoanalysis might look very different.

On the whole, Freudians make strict distinctions between hysterical symptoms and psychosomatic symptoms. Hysteria, Martha Noel Evans sums up, is "primarily a pathological personality structure resulting from inner psychic conflict."[42] The conversion symptom of hysteria is a particular form of symbolic somatization; it represents a transfer of libido to a bodily organ that expresses a forbidden wish and its feared consequences. Freudians view paralysis in a leg, without organic cause, as a hysterical symptom, both an erection and a castration, while hysterical blindness is both a wish to look at something forbidden and the punishment for such transgression. Migraine headache or stomach pain, however, might be merely somatic and have no symbolic content. How psychiatrists tell the difference between hysterical and psychosomatic symptoms is hard for a layman to figure out, but as a result of this distinction hysteria has been severed from ordinary experience. Everyone admits to having the occasional psychosomatic episode. But rather than explaining hysteria as a point further along a spectrum of universal human behavior, psychoanalysis has made it seem aberrant and enigmatic.

As we approach the second century of Freudian studies, the Freudian empire seems to be collapsing, just as Charcot's empire did a century ago. While Freud was long the subject of hagiography, he is now the subject or object of pathography, as biographers vie with one another to produce the most demonic and maniacal life history. In a 1993 essay called "The Unknown Freud," which appeared in the *New York Review of Books*, Frederick Crews, who began his career as a psychoanalytic literary critic, denounces Freud as "willful and opportunistic," and calls psychoanalysis so scientifically feeble that it could be sustained only "in popular lore, the arts, and the academic humanities, three arenas in which flawed but once modish ideas, secure from the menace of rigorous testing, can be kept indefinitely in play."[43] British literature professor Richard Webster goes even further: in *Why Freud Was Wrong* (1995), Webster denounces Freud as a man with a Jewish Messiah complex who ruthlessly twisted the facts and sacrificed his patients.

Both Crews and Webster hold Freud responsible for the recovered memory movement, which they deplore. In the fall of 1995, Freud's critics protested so vociferously against the Library of Congress's planned Freud exhibition that it was indefinitely postponed. The exhibit, Crews charged, was "conceived as a means of mobilizing support for the besieged practice of psychoanalysis."[44] Even as psychoanalysts celebrated the centenary of Freud and Breuer's *Studies on Hysteria* in 1995, Freud bashing reached a peak of frenzy. Some predicted that like Marxism, psychoanalysis was an ideology that could not survive the millennium.

Of course, some intellectuals have always scoffed at Freud. But Crews, Webster, Masson & co. offer little to replace his insights or vision. Webster argues that virtually all psychological symptoms are organic, and that every case of hysteria has been misdiagnosed. Crews enjoys the traditional position of the critic, who does not have to do more than attack. Whatever the assaults of academics and renegades, artists and writers will continue to cherish Freudian insights. The British novelist Sebastian Faulks comments, "Most people have a Freud-shaped cavity in their minds which no other writer can satisfactorily fill. The climate of opinion he created will take an age to alter. He offers intellectual excitement, literary pleasure, magical solutions, and all in the cause of healing humankind. One would as soon discard God or Santa Claus."[45] Despite his mistakes, Freud in my view was a truth seeker, willing to revise his ideas and to criticize himself. The therapy he pioneered has changed drastically since the days when he treated hysterics in Vienna, and Freud would probably not recognize or even endorse some of its current forms. Yet at its heart and at its best, psychotherapy offers a safe space within which we can examine the most frightening, damning, and forbidden parts of ourselves, and come to take responsibility for our future.

Jacques Lacan

Since Freud's death in 1939, the strongest contender for the position of hysterical impresario has been Jacques Lacan (1901–1981), who founded the École Freudienne de Paris in 1964. In his rereadings of Freud with a structuralist/poststructuralist twist, Lacan became a French Freud who interpreted hysteria as a linguistic and cultural phenomenon and a metaphor for Woman and femininity. Like the 1880s in Paris and the 1890s in Vienna, Paris in the 1970s and 1980s was a hospitable milieu for psychoanalytic gurus and theories of hysteria. In her important book *Psychoanalytic Politics*, MIT professor Sherry Turkle examines the ways psychoanalysis displaced and assimilated Marxism and other radical political movements after the collapse of the 1968 student revolution. Disappointed intellectuals turned from political action to philosophical inquiry.

"Since 1968," Turkle writes, "a Frenchman often finds a psychoanalyst in places where he might once have expected to find a priest, a teacher, or a physician. Analysts lived through the May–June events to find that by the time the dust had settled, they were no longer marginal men and women but were very much at the center of things. For many people, psychoanalysis, which was once seen as subversive and alien, was now a welcome source of expertise for solving the problems of everyday life."[46] According to his biographer Elisabeth Roudinesco, Lacan was leader and savior for a generation: "like Charcot at the Salpêtrière and like Freud in Viennese society, Lacan, as of 1969, became the iconoclastic doctor of a society sick with its symptoms, its mores, and its modernity."[47]

Many of Lacan's critics and disciples have remarked on his similarity to Charcot; Martha Noel Evans writes, "Not since the clinical lessons of Charcot a century earlier had a master of French medicine exercised the same kind of influence and charisma as Jacques Lacan."[48] Like Charcot, Lacan was a dazzling theoretician, a charismatic and iconoclastic clinician, an aesthete with links to the Surrealists, and a connoisseur of the arts. In the 1920s, the French Surrealists adopted hysteria as the model for their avant-garde art, a language of the unconscious and dreams opposed to science and the academies. In their 1928 manifesto, "Le cinquantenaire de l'hystérie," the poets Louis

Aragon and André Breton acclaimed hysteria as the "greatest poetic discovery of the nineteenth century."[49]

Beginning in 1964, Lacan presented a public seminar every Wednesday at the École normale supérieure. The feminist writer Catherine Clément attended regularly. As she recalls, "You had to get there quite early: an hour in advance was barely sufficient to get a seat. . . . The hall quickly filled to overflowing. Besides the psychoanalysts and the *normaliens*, curious at first and quickly conquered, there were actors and writers. With each new term new faces were added to the crowd." At these lectures, Lacan put forth his theories and case studies. "Having an audience," Clément notes, "gives a theatrical atmosphere to the event. Something of the spirit of Charcot is in the air: hysteria passes in review, offering bits and pieces of narrative as it struts upon the stage."[50]

At the École Freudienne, Lacan presided over a corps of devoted disciples and continued to see patients as well. He promoted his own arcane theories of hysteria, which had a tremendous influence on French intellectual life and especially on women analysts. He attempted to "hystericize" psychoanalysis, by which he meant restoring to it the playfulness, wildness, and mystery that had made it so exciting at the beginning of the century. On the theoretical level, Lacan gave hysteria pride of place in the psychoanalytic system. He believed hysteria, women, femininity, and gender were knotted together; the hysteric was most likely a woman struggling with her sexual identity.

But Lacan never created the alliance with hysterics that Charcot and Freud had achieved. He was the star of his lectures, unwilling to share the spotlight with hysterical performers. And although his ideas and his style certainly had a huge effect on French culture, and had their heyday in academe, Lacan's relentless difficulty and personal arrogance cut him off from the popular following others had won, and he might have gained.

Hysteria Today

Like it or not, we live in a psychoanalytic century. As Mark Micale and Roy Porter observe, "We turn to the psychosciences to run our private relationships, to raise our children, to try our criminals, to interpret our works of art, to improve our sex lives, to tell us why we are unhappy, depressed, anxious, or fatigued."[51] In the United States, the number of therapists has grown enormously during the past two decades. Although psychiatry, which demands a medical degree and special training, had a relatively modest increase between 1975 and 1990, the number of clinical psychologists almost tripled, and the number of clinical social workers and marriage and family counselors multiplied even more.[52]

But the expansion in mental health specialists has not produced consensus about hysteria. A century after Charcot and Freud, psychotherapists are still divided about what hysteria means and baffled by how it works. The twists and turns of psychoanalytic thought as it has attempted to come to terms with hysteria are interesting mainly to psychoanalysts, and probably even they find some of it tedious. Yet throughout the century, psychoanalysis has struggled to define hysterical syndromes, and despite attacks on Freud, the disorders he treated have continued to mutate. Though modified, the image of the doctor-guru is still strong in psychotherapy; every current hysterical syndrome has its own therapeutic advocates and promoters. As we shall see, the presence of these authority figures has been crucial to the growth of modern epidemic hysterias.

4 | *Politics, Patients, and Feminism*

"Without the context of a political movement," writes Judith Lewis Herman, "it has never been possible to advance the study of psychological trauma."[1] For over a century, the political context for hysteria has been feminism. Hysteria became a hot topic in medical circles during the 1880s and 1890s, when feminism, the New Woman, and a crisis in gender were also hot topics in the United States and Europe. Fin-de-siècle feminism coincided with the pseudoscientific discourses of race degeneration: degenerationists believed that women's activism—particularly the fight to be admitted to universities and to enter the professions—led to a decline in marriage and a falling birth rate. Women, they argued, were cultivating their brains but neglecting their biology. Conservatives saw feminism as the woman's form of degeneration; doctors viewed hysterical women as closet feminists who had to be reprogrammed into traditional roles, and politicians attacked feminist activists as closet hysterics who needed treatment rather than rights. The New Woman, one English journalist wrote, "ought to be aware that her condition is morbid, or at least hysterical."[2]

In England at the turn of the century, hysteria, feminism, and political speech merged in the popular mind. Women who spoke out in public for women's rights were caricatured as "the shrieking sisterhood," a term coined by the English antifeminist novelist Eliza Lynn Linton. In 1910 Arnold Ward warned that giving women the vote would "incorporate that hysterical activity permanently into the life of the nation."[3] In Austria, too, hysteria was blamed for women's pioneering efforts to become doctors. Fritz Wittels, a Viennese contemporary of Freud's, declared, "Hysteria is the basis for a woman's desire to study medicine, just as it is the basis of women's struggle for equal rights."[4]

New Women, intellectuals, and feminists like Olive Schreiner, Eleanor Marx, and Bertha Pappenheim were the most conspicuous of the women diagnosed as hysterics in England and Austria. American feminist intellectuals also consulted doctors: Morton Prince in Boston and Silas Weir Mitchell in Philadelphia specialized in treating women with artistic and literary aspirations who had mysterious symptoms of anxiety and depression. Although male physicians often suffered from hysteria, they blamed higher education and professional ambition for the epidemic of female nervous illness: "For me," Mitchell wrote in 1888, "the grave significance of sexual difference controls the whole question. . . . The woman's desire to be on a level of competition with man and to assume his duties is, I am sure, making mischief, for it is my belief that no length of generations of change in her education and modes of activity will ever really alter her characteristics. She is physiologically other than man."[5]

Doctors diagnosed the nervous complaints of female intellectuals and feminists as neurasthenia, a chronic fatigue syndrome first identified in the United States as "American nervousness" or N.E. (Nervous Exhaustion). Its origins can be traced at least to the 1870s, when the American neurologist George M. Beard argued that life in the fast lane for educated and professional men and women had precipitated mental and physical fatigue with organic causes beyond the diagnostic capacities of nineteenth-century medical science. Neurasthenia soon appeared in Europe, where it became the hysteria of the elite at the turn of the century.

Middle-class women might be called neurasthenics rather than hysterics, but however flattering the euphemism, female neurasthenia differed substantially from the male variety. Doctors defined its most significant causes as disturbances of reproduction and childbirth, emotional trauma, exhaustion, and intellectual strain. The Weir Mitchell rest cure, often prescribed for women intellectuals and artists in the United States and England, required the patient to spend six weeks or more in bed without any work, reading, or social life, and to gain large amounts of weight on a high-fat diet. Many women found the treatment itself maddening, and indeed Mitchell wanted the treatment to be more unpleasant than the symptoms so that patients would be eager to get out of bed.

Why were feminism and hysteria "two sides of the same coin or two ends of a continuum"? John Forrester and Lisa Appignanesi conclude that one reason was "the sexual conservatism of so much feminist activity."[6] They explain in *Freud's Women* that many late-nineteenth-century feminists also belonged to the temperance, hygiene, social purity, or eugenics movements, so that they attempted to embody ideals of asceticism and sexual morality. Living up to these ideals created unconscious conflicts that hysterical symptoms like paralysis or loss of voice might express.

American Hysterics

Changing sexual mores and attitudes toward appropriate roles for women affected both symptoms and treatment. In *The Psychiatric Persuasion: Knowledge, Gender and Power in Modern America* (1994), Princeton University historian Elizabeth Lunbeck studied Boston Psychopathic Hospital records from the early decades of this century. Although hysterical women made up less than 1 percent of the hospital's clientele, they were 25 percent of the case load of the hospital's only Freudian doctor, L. E. Emerson. His case studies reflect Freud's techniques of bullying women patients and pressuring them to come up with stories of sexual trauma. Emerson "urged women to sift through their memories . . . for the unpleasant sexual experiences that might help explain their ailments, and he expected women would find, then divulge, these memories quickly." When they did not, he blamed repression or ignored what they had to say. "Chews the rag," he complained about one patient. Although he theoretically understood the danger of influencing his patients, Emerson's records show "the mix of subtle suggestion and emotional incentives that in nearly every case yielded the information he sought." Because many of his patients were woefully ignorant about sexuality, and even about menstruation, Emerson felt that it was his duty to enlighten them; "to woman after woman he explained the facts of sex."

The women Emerson treated for hysteria were generally young, single, and white. About a third of them reported that they had been victims of sexual assault or incest. Another third reported sexual incidents with employers or boyfriends that they experienced as aggression, though these encounters fell within the bounds of "what men, and their culture, considered 'normal' heterosexuality." The last third were so terrified by adult female sexuality that they had withdrawn from courtship or heterosexual activity, despite longing for love and marriage. Lunbeck writes, "In a culture that nurtured male sexual aggressiveness and in which even heterosexual couplings that had been openly entered into were suffused with this aggression, it was sometimes difficult for women to draw a firm line between abuse on the one hand, and consensual sexual activity on the other." Psychiatrists responded unsympathetically to this dilemma of culture and gender because they themselves had inherited both a tradition of disdain for the hysterical woman and distrust of the sexual woman. Thus, Lunbeck concludes, "In psychiatrists' evolving discourse, the hypersexual and the hysteric served as emblematic representations of modern womanhood and its possibilities gone awry."[7]

Feminists Fight Back

How did women doctors and psychiatrists contend with epidemic hysteria? The feminist critique of the treatment of hysteria is at least a century old. Feminist activists in the antivivisection movement challenged Charcot's exploitation of hysterical women patients in the 1880s and 1890s. In 1888, a distinguished Russian woman scientist, Madame S.V. Kovalevskaia, gave a scathing account of her visit to the Salpêtrière: "Charcot is the master of this kingdom of neurosis," she noted. "To him all here relate with awe bordering on servility." She was embarrassed by his treatment of the women, especially charity cases, who had to put up with any humiliation: "He relates to them extremely unceremoniously; it never enters his head whether they feel things or not. He examines them, sounds their chests, exposes their ailments to the gaze of the students just as indifferently as if he were doing it to a mannequin, and right there in front of them gives his diagnosis and voices what are frequently very sad prognoses, not in the least worrying about what it means to them to hear their own sentences."[8]

Some women doctors came to study hysteria under Charcot and offered socially aware interpretations of its sources in women's restricted lives. Mademoiselle Georgette Déga argued that women's susceptibility to hysterical disorders was the result of their milieu and upbringing. Whatever women's social class, she explained in her doctor's thesis, all were "novices of hysteria," discouraged from making full use of their intellectual capacities, rewarded for developing their emotional side: "This female mode of reaction is called sensitivity and is encouraged and praised in women although it entails a disequilibrium of their psychic being."[9]

However, as a member of a minuscule group of women physicians, none of whom had an institutional base, Déga was unable to translate these insights into an effective and persuasive program. She certainly did not have the power and visibility of a Charcot. Thus instead of recommending a wider field of activity to women, she argued that girls should study mathematics and stop reading novels. In Martha Noel Evans's view, Déga revealed her own helplessness and ambivalence in this remedy. "Rather than turning the enormous strength she perceives in herself and in her patients outward in transforming action, she returns, in a self-punishing reversal, to a horrifying stiffening of women which tragically resembles the cataleptic state of the hysterics she set out to cure."[10]

What's much more surprising is that in the twentieth century, Freud's first female disciples—pioneering and influential women psychoanalysts such as Karen Horney, Melanie Klein, and Helene Deutsch—largely ignored hysteria. In a recent study, Nancy Chodorow suggests some explanations. Chodorow conducted interviews with forty-four women psychoanalysts trained in the 1920s through the mid-1940s, in the United States, Great Britain, and the Netherlands.[11] She found an absence of feminist awareness in these women analysts' lives that initially struck her as dismaying and incredible. They did not find it notable that many women became analysts in the early decades of the movement; they did not think the presence of women and/or mothers among the leading analysts had any significance for the field; they did not think of femininity as an aspect of their own professional histories; they had noticed very few gender differences in the way they were treated; they did not relate psychoanalytic theories of femininity and castration anxiety to their own careers or career motivations.

Eventually, Chodorow concluded that the women analysts' blindness to issues of gender represented concerns faced by their generation. During training, the profession gave no "theoretical prominence to gender or to gender-specific sexuality." Men and women clashed over the theory of femininity, but Chodorow insists that "most analysts of both sexes felt themselves actively engaged in other struggles that were more salient—in cultural and medical struggle, controversy and debate about Freud's theories of the unconscious and infantile sexuality. In these debates, they were certainly on Freud's side." On the whole, despite some prejudicial male attitudes, women analysts "clearly received substantial recognition." And their marital patterns allowed them to avoid some conflicts between maternity and professionalism. "Modally, they married in their early to mid-thirties, and had children in their mid-to-late thirties; even those who seem the most domestic members of psychoanalytic couples didn't marry until at least their late twenties. Thus their careers were already established by the time they were confronting the demands of motherhood."[12] In addition, having children was a functional solution to the Freudian dilemma; Lisa Appignanesi and John Forrester write, "For Freud there was no problem in a woman having a masculine identification once this was combined with motherhood."[13]

Becoming analysts represented for these women a radical break with their mothers' domestic lives, and moving into the public sphere satisfied their feminist impulses. "Participation in an exciting professional movement as equals and notions of socialist comradeship characterized their experience of work relations, women's natural roles as mothers and (equal but different) wives their experience of home roles. They assumed a division of labor in the home, assumed women's natural maternitality, assumed innate, and desirable, gender personality differences." Chodorow concluded that her own generation had been sensitized to feminist concerns in a way that had not existed before: "The pervasiveness of gender as a category to me simply did not resonate with their own life experiences, and I began to realize how much my perceptual and analytic categories had been shaped by my coming of age in the women's movement and my immersion in the recent literature of gender theory."[14]

The Herstory of Hysteria

Feminist academic interest in hysteria first emerged through the writing of women's history. Early in the women's liberation movement, reclaiming the hostile labels attached to rebellious or deviant women became a popular feminist strategy. Although "hysteria," like "witchcraft," had always been pejorative, it became a positive term for those trying to write the "her-story" of hysteria, a story that emphasized the cultural construction of women's hysterical symptoms, diagnosis, and treatment. Nineteenth-century hysterical women suffered from the lack of a public voice to articulate their economic and sexual oppression, and their symptoms—mutism, paralysis, self-starvation, spasmodic seizures—

seemed like bodily metaphors for the silence, immobility, denial of appetite, and hyperfemininity imposed on them by their societies.

Feminist historians focused especially on nineteenth-century America and England. What the cultural historian Ann Douglas called the "fashionable diseases" of nineteenth-century women were Victorian versions of hysterical complaint. In 1973, Douglas kicked off a lively debate about male doctors' complicity in creating and maintaining the disorders. Did these doctors despise their patients? Did they invent punitive treatments to express their own hostilities toward female discontent?

From a more sociological perspective, feminists have seen hysteria as the product of nineteenth-century conflicts over sex roles and female sexuality. According to historian Carroll Smith-Rosenberg, many American women escaped the realities of adult life by regressing to hysterical illness. In her view the clash between women's sheltered upbringing and their real domestic responsibilities "may have made the petulant infantilism and narcissistic self-assertion of the hysteric a necessary social alternative to women who felt unfairly deprived of their promised social role and who had few strengths with which to adapt to a more trying one."[15] Medical sociologists today argue that women are more likely to seek medical and therapeutic help, and thus to predominate in statistical studies. On the other hand, Mark Pendergrast suggests that women may actually be conduits for the hysteria of a culture; women, he writes, have long been socially encouraged to "act out the 'symptom pool' of the era and accept an inappropriate diagnosis."[16]

Reviewing feminist scholarship of the 1970s, medical historian Nancy Tomes finds an impasse over a fundamental contradiction:

> In these early works, feminist historians wrestled long and hard with the implications of interpreting women's nervous conditions as modes of protest against their limited gender roles. The notion of mental illness as a form of "protofeminism" had an obvious appeal. The well-known cases of talented women . . . who had nervous breakdowns and recovered only by forging unconventional lives for themselves seemed to suggest that feminism and madness were two sides of the same coin.

But the escape to madness was a costly one:

> The difficulties of reconciling these two interpretations of female madness remained a fundamental ambiguity in feminist portrayals of nineteenth-century psychiatry and its treatment of women.[17]

I'm Hysterical, You're Hysterical

In France after 1968, feminist intellectuals moved beyond historical analyses and celebrated nineteenth-century hysterical women as heroines, sisters, and political martyrs. What Martha Noel Evans calls "the hysterical phase of French feminism" focused attention on "the hysteric as the representative of femininity."[18] Women in the French feminist movement, many of whom were psychoanalysts themselves, saw hysteria as symbolic of women's silencing within the institutions of language, culture, and psychoanalysis. Lacan had proclaimed that women spoke the discourse of the hysteric rather than the discourse of the master; Lacanian women "proposed to speak directly from the place of the hysteric as it was formulated in Lacan's theory . . . to question psychoanalytical theory from within psychoanalysis itself."[19]

In the 1970s, Hélène Cixous, Catherine Clément, and other French women in the analytic community seized hysteria as a political cause. From the Lacanian "hystericization" of psychoanalysis, French feminists moved to the hystericization of feminism. Overall, writes Evans, "the French feminist critique of the place of women in psychoanalytic theory thus had the effect of uncovering a stifled symbolic system in the symptoms of hysterics. The feminist aim became to recover this lost language which would reconnect their bodies and minds, and women to each other. Indeed, the feminist effort to establish a female descendancy took the precise shape of claiming their inheritance as speakers of a hysterical mother tongue."[20] Hysteria, they maintained, was a semiotic female language with "a privileged relation to the maternal body."

Such French feminist theorists as Hélène Cixous, Luce Irigaray, and Michèle Montrelay connected the hysteric's silences, symptoms, and distorted speech to female symbolism, semiotic, or infantile wordless verbalization. In "The Laugh of the Medusa" (1975), Hélène Cixous called for a revolutionary body of language by women writers that would verbalize the silent discourse of the "admirable hysterics." In "Sorties," she identified with hysterical women: "The hysterics are my sisters. . . . I am what Dora would have been if woman's history had begun."[21]

The French feminists' view of hysteria had tremendous intellectual and emotional appeal. They located the origin of "hysterical" discourse in the pre-Oedipal phase of feminine development, when the baby daughter takes the mother as her primary object of desire. In the writing of Julia Kristeva particularly, the pre-Oedipal phase has its own linguistic character, including orality, rhythms, intonations, and babble. For French feminists, the hysteric occupies the place of female absence in linguistic and cultural systems. According to Martha Noel Evans, for the psychoanalyst Luce Irigaray, it is "precisely the silence of the female produced by the absence of femininity in representational systems of language and logic which has defined women as hysterics."[22] Thus the silent or nonverbal "body language" of hysteria can be seen as a Mother Tongue that contests patriarchal culture.

The "hysterical phase of French feminism" peaked in a 1972 meeting in Paris at which feminists chanted, "Nous sommes toutes des hystériques!"—"We are all hysterical women!" Ironically, they came dangerously close to acting like hysterical divas, reasserting traditional views of women as emotional and irrational at the same time they were trying to undermine tradition. Women analysts also paid dearly for their protest; the Freudian and Lacanian establishments dismissed or punished many of them. Claiming hysteria is not the wisest strategy for professional success.

Dora Returns

In *The Newly-Born Woman*, Hélène Cixous posed a dramatic rhetorical question: "What woman is not Dora?" A century after Freud treated or mistreated her, Dora returned as Everywoman, a cult heroine of literary criticism, especially feminist criticism. Psychiatrists and literary critics have written more on Dora than on any other hysterical case. She has been the heroine of plays and has appeared in movies about Freud. She has become a saint in the pantheon of feminist martyrs. As the most famous of Freud's women, she almost seems to take the place of his wife in the popular imagination. For many feminists who write about hysteria, Dora is all they know.

In 1985, two professors of comparative literature, Claire Kahane and Charles Bernheimer, edited *In Dora's Case*, an anthology of feminist literary essays about Freud's famous study; it was so successful that in 1990 it went into an expanded second edition. In her introduction to the original collection, Kahane wrote that feminist scholars read "Dora" as "an urtext in the history of woman, a fragment of an increas-

ingly heightened critical debate about the meaning of sexual difference and its effects on the representation of feminine desire." Feminist
poststructuralist critics Jacqueline Rose, Toril Moi, and Jane Gallop
contributed to the volume; they agreed, as Kahane wrote in the introduction, that "Freud's interpretive strategies were critically determined
by his inability to deal with the feminine and its relation to the
mother."[23] They emphasized Freud's hostility to Dora and Dora's sexual attraction to both men and women.

What is it about this case that so fascinated and attracted feminist
critics in the 1980s? Describing "the critical cult of *Dora*," Mandy
Merck suggests that feminist critics were retroactively *healing* Dora,
performing the acts of remembering they believed Freud had
neglected.[24] In retrospect, it seems to me that these feminists were
redefining and even denying hysteria. They made Freud the fall guy,
pinning the blame for Dora's symptoms onto him, onto Viennese society, onto Herr K. and Dora's selfish father. New Hysterian Mark
Micale sees *In Dora's Case* as a form of intellectual revenge, with critics doing "to Freud today what Freud did to Dora ninety years ago."[25]
Janet Malcolm writes sardonically that interest in Dora is a form of
unconscious revenge on Freud for being a disturbing genius: "We
cherish the Dora case because it proves that Freud, who told us such
unpleasant truths about ourselves, was himself just another pitiful,
deluded, dirty-minded neurotic."[26]

But feminist criticism of the great hysterical women patients also
filled in historical and cultural lacunae around the case studies and
suggested important relationships between hysteria, psychoanalysis,
and feminism. In her work on Anna O., Dianne Hunter concludes
that Anna's linguistic hysterical symptoms expressed her cultural
silencing, and that when she became an activist, she transcended her
hysteria. Hunter suggests that hysteria is "a self-repudiating form of
feminist discourse in which the body signifies what social conditions
make it impossible to state linguistically."[27] Comparing Anna O. and
Charlotte Perkins Gilman, Diane Price Herndl proposes a "writing
cure" as well as a "talking cure": "Hysteria can be understood as a
woman's response to a system in which she is expected to remain
silent, a system in which her subjectivity is denied, kept invisible. In
becoming a writer, a woman becomes not just a subject, but a subject
who produces that which is visible."[28] Feminist literary critics defended hysterical women patients as responsible beings who had the
power to tell their own stories.

Feminist Therapy, Therapeutic Feminism

In 1985, when *In Dora's Case* and my book *The Female Malady* appeared, the feminist therapy movement was a new force within the North American and English psychotherapeutic communities. I ended *The Female Malady* with a utopian endorsement of feminist therapy: "The best hope for the future is the feminist therapy movement. In the 1970s, for the first time, women came together to challenge both the psychoanalytic and the medical categories of traditional psychiatry, to propose alternatives like feminist psychotherapy, women's self-help groups, and political activism. . . . Its work is essential to the future understanding of women, madness, and culture, and to the development of a psychiatric theory and practice that, by empowering women, offers a real possibility of change."

But since 1985, the field of feminist therapy has changed in ways I had not foreseen. First, from being a vocal minority of mental health workers, women have come to dominate the field. "What do women want?" Freud famously asked. "If Freud were alive today," one therapist replies, "he most likely would be surprised to learn that what increasing numbers of women want is to become psychologists, psychiatrists, and psychoanalysts." By 1986, women constituted 34.9 percent of all psychiatrists in the United States under 35. By 1988, 47 percent of medical students who chose psychiatry were women. Psychological counseling too is rapidly becoming a female profession.[29]

Sociologists argue that when a profession becomes feminized, or perceived as a woman's field, men move out. Indeed, therapists acknowledge that the profession has suffered both from overcrowding and a loss of status which may be associated with feminization. The old-style authoritarian shrink, modeled on a stern Charcot or a bullying Freud, has been replaced by a softer, more approachable figure. Rather than shaman or guru, the image of the therapist is changing into that of a comforting friend. The therapist's role is more and more to affirm, support, and endorse the patient's narrative, to provide a "safe space" for disclosure, and not to challenge the truth or historical reality of the patients' assertions. Clinical psychologist Ilene Philipson warns, "While the relational model's technique might better fit today's client, and may simply be a better means of treating people than classical practice, it may also be true that it tacitly incorporates into its tenets the historical decline of therapeutic authority. Moreover, women will increasingly turn to other women for therapies that are almost extensions of the

maternal role," but "the increasing likelihood of being matched with a
female practitioner may make the therapeutic encounter appear even
more menacing to the prospective male client."[30]

One of the most far-reaching achievements of feminist therapy and
the women's movement has been a campaign to confront incest and
child sexual abuse. In *The Courage to Heal* Ellen Bass and Laura Davis
attribute the recovered memory movement to this feminist effort:
"The advances of the past twenty years are a direct outgrowth of the
women's liberation movement that gained force in the 1970s. Women
courageously spoke out about rape and battering, wrote books analyzing the ways in which our society condoned such violence, and
worked to establish battered women's shelters and rape crisis centers.
Simultaneously, a few pioneering clinicians and researchers, both men
and women, were beginning to study child sexual abuse and set up
models for treatment."[31] In May 1977, *MS* magazine's cover story was
"Incest: Child Abuse Begins at Home." Nearly two decades later, Ian
Hacking writes, "Child abuse was molded to take in a range of acts that
had never before been put together as one single kind of behavior. On
the one hand, incest came to mean any type of sexually oriented activity involving an adult and a child in the same family. Or even, by an
implicit slide of meanings, in the American extended family, which
includes baby-sitters and day-care centers. On the other hand, the
concept of child abuse picked up a whole range of behavior, all of
which became colored by the horror of incest."[32]

Initially, incest and child abuse were kept secret because of shame,
guilt, and fear of skeptical reception, but they did not have to become
lifelong traumas. In her first book, *Father-Daughter Incest* (1981), Judith
Lewis Herman wrote, "It would be an exaggeration to state that victims of sexual abuse inevitably sustain permanent damage."[33] But during the 1980s, feminist therapists fought to expand the definition and
diagnosis of posttraumatic stress syndrome to include routine or
repeated experience, as well as exceptional episodes that were, according to the DSM-III-R, "outside the range of human experience."
Thus, they argued, women's traumatic experiences might also be
chronic, and secret. "For girls and women," writes Laura S. Brown,
"most traumas *do* occur in secret. They happen in bed, where our
fathers and stepfathers and uncles and older brothers molest us in the
dead of night; behind the closed doors of marital relationships where
men beat and sometimes rape their wives and lovers; in the back seats
of cars, where women are forced into sex by their boyfriends, not

knowing until years later that they can call this rape; in the offices of physicians and therapists who sexually exploit patients, knowing that their status is likely to protect them."

Brown is among the feminist therapists who believe the concept of trauma should include all these events, plus sexual harassment and conflicts with men on the job. "The private, secret, insidious traumas to which a feminist analysis draws attention," she writes, "are more often than not those events in which the dominant culture and its forms and institutions are expressed and perpetuated. Feminist analysis also asks us to understand how the constant presence and threat of trauma in the lives of girls and women of all colors, men of color in the United States, lesbian and gay people, people in poverty, and people with disabilities has shaped our society, a continuing background noise rather than an unusual event."[34] Other feminist therapists take the definition of trauma even further. Maria Root believes that the category should be broadened to include "insidious trauma," the psychic effects of living in a culture that fosters fear of sexual assault and rape.[35] In *The Mismeasure of Woman* (1992), Carol Tavris writes, "The sexual-abuse-victim story crystallized many of society's anxieties, in these insecure times, about the vulnerability of children, the changing roles of women, and the norms of sexuality. It draws like a magnet those who feel vulnerable and victimized."[36]

There is no question that the feminist effort to rethink hysteria has had a major positive effect on literary criticism. It has also had real impact for psychiatry and psychoanalysis. But the feminist embrace of all abuse narratives and the treatment of all women as survivors have troubling implications. Claiming hysteria and admiring its victims may have had inspirational functions in the 1970s: feminism, like other insurgent movements, needed martyrs. But Saint Dora's days are over. Today's feminists need models rather than martyrs; we need the courage to think as well as the courage to heal.

5 | Hysterical Men

"A Case of Uncomplicated Hysteria in the Male"

In the winter of 1876, Robert Conolly, a married, childless, white man in his thirties, came to S. Weir Mitchell's Philadelphia clinic with a serious problem: he had begun to tremble; his left hand and arm were stiffly contracted; and he could not practice his trade. In his notes on the case, Mitchell described Conolly as "a rather thin, pallid man, with a nervous, uneasy, anxious look. He was a person of unusual refinement, very gentle and timid, but clearly intelligent and well pleased to be considered as an uncommon case." Conolly's case history was unremarkable. "Gentle" and "reserved," he had no organic diseases, no anaesthesis, speech trouble, or loss of consciousness, and no dramatic memories of trauma. The worst he could remember was becoming excited and emotional after witnessing Decoration Day ceremonies in 1874.

During the next several months, however, despite Mitchell's attention, medical tests, and efforts to discover the cause, Conolly's symptoms did not improve. In fact, his left arm took on a peculiar swinging motion, which, according to Mitchell, "so much resembled the steady, rapid movement of a pendulum that I spoke of it once to my assistants as a case of what might be called descriptively 'pendulum spasms.' In fact its rhythmic regularity was astonishing." Mitchell and his assistants could virtually set their watches by it. In October 1876, the pendulum spasms stopped, and Conolly began involuntary rotary movements with his right arm. Edward Muybridge photographed him, and he consulted many doctors, all of whom failed to alleviate his symptoms. For most of his adult life, he was an invalid. In 1897, hypnosis gave him temporary relief, but after a few weeks of work, Conolly relapsed. Upon his death in 1904, he left his body in gratitude to Mitchell, who performed an autopsy and found no organic problems. It was, he concluded, "a case of uncomplicated hysteria in the male."[1]

In his notes, without any special emphasis, Mitchell mentions Robert Conolly's trade: watch-case maker. Post-Freudian readers might immediately note that Conolly had turned himself into a watch case, mimicking with his body the precise measuring out of time in which he spent his days. Could it have been that Conolly's distaste for his finicky and monotonous labor was so great, his inability to articulate it so deep, that his body simply created compelling symptoms/ symbols of his dilemma? Nineteenth-century male breadwinners could not admit that they hated their work and found debilitating symptoms useful. Like Melville's Bartleby, Conolly developed a body language that expressed his preference not to fulfill his role.

If Mitchell understood Conolly's motivations—and his symptoms resembled those of "battle fatigue" he'd seen in traumatized Civil War soldiers—he did not mention them in his notes. Yet even to diagnose Conolly as a hysteric was bold. Mitchell knew that calling a respectable American working man "hysterical" seemed like a gross insult to his masculinity. But Conolly himself was never given this diagnosis, and Mitchell never published the case in a medical journal or presented it at a professional meeting. It remains in his papers at the Medical College Library of Philadelphia. Mitchell's women patients—including Charlotte Perkins Gilman, Edith Wharton, and Jane Addams—are well known, but Robert Conolly has until now disappeared from psychiatric history.

Where Have All the Male Hysterics Gone?

Robert Conolly is not exceptional; Charcot's male patients also remain mysterious and anonymous, although he had begun to gather materials on male hysteria as early as 1878. Charcot eventually published sixty-one case histories of male hysteria, and left notes on over thirty more. These case studies are as crucial to understanding the construction of masculinity as his studies of women are to the construction of femininity. They reveal, as Mark Micale puts it, "normative gender representations, encoded ideals of normal and abnormal masculinity that repay investigation by the social, cultural, and medical historian."[2] Indeed, in the words of Charcot's successor Pierre Marie, "What dominates the work of Charcot on hysteria, that which will never perish and will continue to serve as a guide to future medical generations, was his demonstration of the existence of hysteria in the male."[3] Yet only during the 1990s have Charcot's accounts of male hysteria been translated into English.[4]

We know that Freud treated many male hysterics, but they have not been turned into mythic figures like Dora. In England, the handful of essays on hysterical boys and men that appeared in medical journals in the 1880s and 1890s have never been collected or reprinted. In the United States, one must turn to unpublished archives to find reports on hysterical men in civilian life. The cultural denial of male hysteria is no accident: it's the result of avoidance, suppression, and disguise. Although male hysteria has been clinically identified at least since the seventeenth century, physicians have hidden it under such euphemistic diagnoses as neurasthenia, hypochondria, phthiatism, neurospasia, eleorexia, koutorexie, Briquet's syndrome, shell shock, or post-traumatic stress disorder.

For centuries, doctors denied that hysteria was also a male malady. As late as 1819 French physician Jean-Baptiste Louyer-Villermay unequivocally declared, "A man cannot be hysterical; he has no uterus." Those who believed hysteria had a uterine cause found it obvious that men could not be hysterical. The male genitalia did not wander about inside the body; they were firmly attached and plainly in sight. When Vesalius and other Renaissance anatomists argued that the uterus too was anchored in the body, medical theories of hysteria shifted to the mobile, capricious, unstable, and emotional female personality, to the fragile female nervous system, and the cyclical and spasmodic manifestations of female sexuality. Real men, many doctors believed, were immune to emotion. In the male, wrote the Victorian specialist Robert Brudenell Carter, "strong emotion is a matter of comparatively rare occurrence, scarcely called forth except to demand immediate and energetic action of some kind."[5]

Predictably, nineteenth-century doctors forced to acknowledge strong emotion and other hysterical traits in men often concluded that their patients were unmanly, effeminate, or homosexual. The English physician Thomas Laycock had noted cases of hysteria among his male patients in the 1840s but attributed the phenomenon to a lack of virility. Laycock described "fat, pale-faced, effeminate looking men," with "flabby wasted testicles."[6] "When men are attacked by genuine hysterical fits ... which certainly does occur," wrote Ernst von Feuchtersleben in 1847, "they are for the most part effeminate men."[7] "One can imagine a perfumed and pomaded *femmelette* suffering from this bizarre malady," wrote Charcot's intern Émile Batault in 1885, "but that a robust working-man should have nerves and vapours like a society woman, that's too much!"[8] The innuendoes of homosexuality further stigmatized male hysteria; male physicians found it even harder to diagnose, and male patients found it almost impossible to accept the diagnosis.

Executive Hysteria

Doctors have worked particularly hard to come up with an inoffensive terminology for the nervous disorders of middle-class men. In the 1880s, neurasthenia became the diagnosis of choice for depression and anxiety among urban male intellectuals, ambitious professionals, and overworked executives. Indeed, about 10 percent of George Beard's neurasthenic patients were doctors. Beard blamed urban industrialization, professional competition, and refined intellect for the epidemic. In his view, men in simpler or primitive cultures—Bushmen or Sioux Indians—did not become neurasthenic, like Boston bankers or New York lawyers. Because neurasthenics came from the same social class as doctors, included a high proportion of men, and appeared eager to cooperate, they also had higher status than hysterical women, whose "belle indifférence" was a cliché of medical literature. Charcot noted that "the young men who graduate from the École Polytechnique, who intend to become heads of factories and rack their brains over mathematical calculations, often become victims of these afflictions. When one has responsibilities, plays the stock market, risks his fortune, and spends sleepless nights worrying, one will often come to this state."[9] In London, as the English doctor Brian Donkin confessed, the diagnosis was "often applied to cases where hysteria might seem a term of reproach."[10] Donkin even suspected it might be caused by multiple chemical sensitivities, especially to mercury poison.

The most significant causes of male neurasthenia were thought to be overwork, sexual excess, overambition, sedentary habits, and abuse of alcohol or drugs. According to the historian F. S. Gosling, "Because men normally led more varied lives than most women, involving themselves in career, family, and social activities both within and outside the domestic circle, physicians made greater distinctions in the causes to which they attributed male nervousness. Physicians also questioned men in more detail about their habits and personal affairs, partially because they were more likely to suspect men of hidden vice and partially because of the delicacy of raising intimate issues with members of the opposite sex."[11] Doctors frequently prescribed the rest cure for neurasthenic women, but not for men. The medical establishment has always made a clear gender division in treating neurasthenia, with women encouraged to rest and withdraw. The feminine personality, doctors argued, is innately changeable, volatile, mobile; but women themselves are healthier if they remain still. On the other hand, as Chicago neurologist Archibald Church observed, men could not be immobilized: "We cannot put men to bed with any expectation that they will stay there. . . . Men do not take to the recumbent position for any considerable time with equanimity."[12]

With middle-class men the preferred treatment for neurasthenia was travel, adventure, vigorous physical exercise. In the United States not only Teddy Roosevelt but also the painters Thomas Eakins and Frederic Remington and the Western novelist Owen Wister were packed off to the Dakotas for a course of rough-riding to cure neurasthenic crises. Unfortunately doctors didn't transfer their discoveries about the treatment of neurasthenic male disorders to women, who might have benefited from a little rough-riding as well.

The mythology of neurasthenia drives the plot of the popular Billy Crystal film *City Slickers* (1992). Three suburban middle-aged men, experiencing vague symptoms of depression, fear of aging, and fatigue, have been taking adventure vacations (baseball camp, running the bulls at Pamplona) to revive their self-esteem and *joie de vivre*. "I just feel lost," Crystal's character tells his long-suffering wife, who urges him to take one last trip—a Western cattle drive—so he can "find his smile." The friends go west, and their confrontations with physical hardship, death, and the birth of a calf, as well as a memorable encounter with a real cowboy, Jack Palance, renew their hope and manliness. The men's movement, with its tribalism and drum-beating, seems like another version of the male adventure cure.

From Railway Spine to Male Hysteria

During the 1880s, English physicians began to describe numerous cases of "traumatic hysteria": men suffering from physical symptoms and emotional distress after railway accidents. John Eric Erichsen at

University College Hospital in London argued for a physical disorder called "railway spine," but Herbert Page, surgeon to the London and Northwest Railway, insisted that the symptoms were caused
by post-traumatic neurosis. In *Injuries of the Spine and Spinal-Cord
Without Apparent Mechanical Lesion*, Page cited over 200 cases of hysterical aftereffects of railway accidents, when passengers in a crash
narrowly escaped injury and saw others wounded and dying.[13] Most
of Page's cases were women, but Charcot read his work and applied
it to cases of male traumatic hysteria caused by industrial accidents
or physical injuries. Fright alone, he theorized, could cause hysterical symptoms.

Charcot had treated upper-class male neurasthenics in his private
practice, but at the Salpêtrière, where he opened a small men's ward in
1882, his patients were working-class men: fifty-six urban or agricul-
tural workers; three beggars. His experience led him to dispute Beard's
assumption that neurasthenia was an upper-class syndrome. "When we
speak today of neurasthenia or male hysteria," Charcot wrote, "it still
seems that we almost exclusively have in mind the man of the privileged classes, sated by culture, exhausted by pleasures' abuses, by business preoccupations, or an excess of intellectual exertion." But, he continued, "We must not forget that the psychological constitution [of
working-class people] is fundamentally the same as ours, and that, perhaps even more than other people, they are subjected to the destructive effects of painful moral emotions, of anxieties related to the material difficulties of life, to the depressing influence of the exaggerated
effect of physical forces." In fact, poor and marginal males suffered
from hysteria much more often than successful ones did. "Where does
hysteria hide?" he asked rhetorically. "In the last few years, I have often
shown [that it hides] in the working class and among manual artisans.
We must also search for it in the gutter, among the beggars, the
vagabonds, and the dispossessed, in the poor houses and perhaps the
jails and penitentiaries."[14]

Charcot set out to prove that masculine hysteria was identical to the
female form, whatever its origins. He insisted that men as well as
women exhibited the four stages of *grande hystérie*. Indeed, men had an
even *grander* hysterical seizure, more athletic, acrobatic, and violent.
Charcot believed that the athletic contortions of the fit came more naturally to boys and men than to women, and named one phase of the
four-stage hysterical attack "clownisme," reflecting his own lifelong fascination with the circus. Male convulsive attacks at the Salpêtrière were

elaborate and spectacular; one admiring doctor called them "a sort of storm in the hysterical atmosphere."[15]

Male hysterics, Charcot maintained, were influenced by hereditary factors: "alcoholism, hysteria, epilepsy, insanity, suicide of the father or grandfather; hysteria, nervousness, eccentricity, madness in the mother; hysteria, insanity, and chorea in the more distant relations." He stressed that "in men hysteria is more often hereditary . . . hysteria in the mother often engenders hysteria in the son."[16] And first Charcot, then Freud, maintained that male hysteria was more severe, intractable, and worrisome than its feminine form. "Singular thing, this male hysteria," Charcot wrote in 1887, "very different in this regard from that of the women. Seems to be much more serious and to bring with it an infinitely more serious prognosis."[17]

The physical patterns of hysteria were the same for both sexes, but not the emotional patterns. In the *leçons du mardi*, Charcot noted that "the hysterical men of the working class who . . . fill the hospital wards of Paris today are almost always somber, melancholic, depressed and discouraged people. . . . We should not expect to find in the male that morbid *con brio* frequent in reality in the female."[18] His male hysterics displayed few extreme emotions, except for depression, and his case histories report only two instances of men crying.[19] Indeed, overall, working-class male hysterics did not behave the way physicians expected. With women hysterics, Charcot wrote, "symptoms are mobile and fleeting, and the capricious progression of the malady is frequently interrupted by dramatic outbursts."[20] Ruth Harris reports that "fear, shock, and terror" appeared frequently as possible causes of male hysteria, but "rarely disappointment, abandonment, or betrayal."[21]

Opening the Male Case

Case studies of male hysterics in the Salpêtrière vividly describe *grande hystérie* and present interesting and even bizarre characters, but Charcot did not do for his male hysterics what Freud did for Dora. We have to piece together a composite picture of the men from various sources, including reports by Charcot's interns. Gui—, for example, was a twenty-seven-year-old locksmith who came to the hospital in February 1884, suffering from nightmares, extreme anxiety, and convulsive attacks. Charcot discovered a "hysterogenic zone" in Gui—'s right testicle. When it was pinched or pressed, his attacks could be started or stopped. As Charcot described them:

These attacks . . . are always preceded by the sensation of a well-defined painful *aura* starting from the right testicle, mounting upwards into the epigastric and cardiac region, thence into the throat, where it produces a feeling of constriction, finally reaching the head, where it produces buzzings, chiefly in the right ear, and beatings, principally in the temple on the same side. Then the patient loses consciousness and the epileptoid stage commences. The tremors of the right hand become much increased, and the eyes become convulsed upwards. The limbs stretch out, and the wrists flex and become twisted in a position of exaggerated pronation. Next the arms cross one another in front of the abdomen owing to a convulsive contraction of the pectoral muscles. After this the period of contortions comes on, characterised by extremely violent movements of salutation accompanied by disorderly gestures. The patient breaks or tears everything on which he can lay his hands, and he assumes the strangest and most outrageous attitudes in a manner that fully justifies the denomination of *clownism*. . . . From time to time the contortions above described stop for a moment and give place to the characteristic attitude of an "arc of a circle."[22]

Batault called Gui—'s fit "an acrobatic performance as beautiful as it was varied,"[23] and Albert Londe photographed it. Yet these rare photos of a male hysteric were not like those of Augustine or Blanche. Everyone at the Salpêtrière agreed that Gui— was "a well-built, vigorous young man";[24] in these photographs, he is seen at a distance, and his body is impressive in its muscularity and flexibility. It is also quite anonymous: the camera avoids his face, and he might be in a gym rather than a hospital.

Charcot's case studies of male hysterics recall other late nineteenth-century and early modernist stories, like Conrad's *Heart of Darkness*, in which one man talks about another and expresses his identification, doubling, and denial. Charcot's narrative structures resemble French naturalist fiction of the period, especially the Rougon–Macquart novels of Émile Zola. Like Zola, Charcot begins with genealogical histories complicated by alcoholism, suicide, criminality, and insanity. Charcot gave little space to the emotional and affective components of male hysteria but used a wide range of literary allusions and linguistic codes to communicate rhetorical, metaphorical, and symbolic messages about his male hysterical patients.

At his Tuesday clinics Charcot identified his female patients by their names and last initials, and often by feminine pseudonyms such as "Louise" or "Augustine." For male patients he used gutted versions of their surnames. In 1888 Charcot introduced a case of "hysteria and degeneration":"La ... sonne," forty-eight, who worked as the wild man in a carnival.[25] Charcot saw him as a victim of a hereditary doom no less implacable than the fatality of Greek tragedy. Indeed, he could cry out to the gods, "What have we done, O Zeus, to deserve this destiny?"

Like Freud's Dora, La ... sonne is a classic hysterical narrator: "He does not have a memory, and he confuses and combines the more distant events according to the time they occurred." At age twelve, he had contracted typhoid fever, which had possibly left him with some retardation. "He had always been something of a vagabond; he liked to roam about and avoided going to school as much as possible." At eighteen, after some years of wandering, he joined the navy, and served successfully for six years. But on the eve of his discharge, he got into a fight with an officer and was condemned to death. The sentence was commuted to ten years of hard labor, eight of which he served on a chain gang in Algeria, and two in New Caledonia.

During this time La ... sonne acquired a number of tattoos. "You can see," Charcot told his interns, "he wears on the left side of his chest a phony croix d'honneur; on his left forearm you can read the inscription 'death to policemen.' Right in the middle of his torso, just below his sternum, is the face of a woman, decently covered, which he says is 'the night.' Why 'the night' he has never been able to explain. I would also like to point out, on his right arm, the drawing of a man 'in a musketeer's outfit,' intended to represent, it seems, the supervisor of a prison colony, and a bit lower, this one of another man in a Scottish costume. There are many more tattoos in various bizarre locations that I should show you, but most of them are too offensive to describe!"

Charcot was more prudish about the body of another man than about the bodies of his female patients. In a clinic where every gesture of the women patients was obsessively sketched or photographed, no one took pictures of La ... sonne. Nor did Charcot speculate on the connection between La ... sonne's paralyzed right arm and the image of the prison colony superintendent tattooed upon it. La ... sonne had created a body language of protest during his incarceration. Like Robert DeNiro in *Cape Fear*, or the Soviet prisoners in labor camps, he had inscribed his anger on his skin.[26] Charcot knew that the tattoos had significance ("the scrutiny of these inscriptions, of these symbolic images, is not to be taken lightly"), but the rigidity of his model did not permit him to study the images with the care they deserved.

In the decade following his release, La . . . sonne scraped a precarious existence on the streets of Paris, sinking ever lower. He began to have nightmares in which he was threatened by ferocious beasts, especially lions; on one occasion he cut himself with a knife as he tried to defend himself during the delirium. Unable to work as a laborer because of increasing paralysis in his right arm, he became first a zookeeper and then, "aiming to advance in his profession," attended the classes of a man who taught street acrobatics. "Under this instructor he learned to swallow swords and fire and to eat broken glass." But his chief source of income came from playing "wild man" in Parisian fairs. Locked in an iron cage, with chains around his feet, blackened from head to toe, wearing a feathered headpiece, he performed his act, as Charcot explained: "To the great wonder of the spectators, we see him, snarling, devouring raw meat, and even, according to him—although perhaps he's bragging here—live rabbits." Then, as he stumbled through this miserable existence, he began to have convulsive attacks.

Charcot believed La . . . sonne's problems had much to do with his "errant and shiftless life" and his holding "what could barely be called professions," along with alcoholism and a general lack of self-discipline. He recommended institutionalization: "I have laid before your eyes an unfortunate creature lacking intelligence, memory, and judgment; weak morally, of course, and emotionally clearly stamped by the seal of mental degeneration. . . . I think the best would be to try and secure the admission of the poor 'wild man' in an institution where he will be protected against his own outbursts at the same time as he is prevented from hurting others." That La . . . sonne's symptoms might be a reaction against brutal injustice, against a whole life of poverty and frustration, did not fit into Charcot's analytic framework.

Vagabonds and Wanderers

Although he had few street and carnival performers among his male patients, Charcot's case studies of them are remarkably powerful. These runaways and migrants can be seen as social equivalents of the unruly migratory uterus traditionally associated with female hysteria. Michèle Ouerd argues that the working class is itself the wandering womb of Paris, moving "often convulsively as in the Commune—and it is thus necessary to suppress it, to channel it into its faubourgs, care for it if possible by all means available—hygienic, prophylactic, and mental medicine."[27]

Jan Goldstein persuasively argues that Charcot's concept of male hysteria did not transform late nineteenth-century understanding of gender because the social backgrounds of his male patients distanced them from male physicians. "While female hysterics could be found in all social strata," she explains, "male hysterics—at least those identified by Charcot—were, if French and Christian, almost invariably members of the working class or of the unemployed underworld. They might also be Jews or Arabs, in which case they could be either middle class or working class. In other words, from the vantage point of the male, bourgeois, Christian doctor who made the diagnosis, the male hysteric remained the 'other,' as radically foreign and as extruded from the self as the female hysteric."[28]

Soldiers and Shell Shock

With the collapse of Charcot's reputation in the 1890s, the study of male hysteria went into decline. But World War I brought with it a great epidemic. In every European country, soldiers and officers were returning from the trenches with limps, loss of voice, paralyzed limbs, headaches, amnesia, incapacitating insomnia, and emotional distress. When an English military doctor, Charles S. Myers, first encountered these symptoms in 1914 among British soldiers in France, he immediately saw their relation to hysteria. But Myers did not want to describe British soldiers as hysterical, and so he suggested that the symptoms might be caused by the physical or chemical effects of proximity to an exploding shell. He christened the disorder "shell shock," a name that stuck, although doctors soon realized that many victims had never been under fire. By the end of the war, 80,000 men with shell shock and war neurosis had sought medical help.

In dealing with shell shock, doctors seemed to forget Charcot's work on male hysterics, but their prototypes showed the same class differentiation. Among officers, symptoms tended toward the emotional: anxiety attacks, depression, insomnia, nightmares. Their prototype was the aristocrat with the stiff upper lip, trained in public-school and university codes of manly understatement and bravery. Siegfried Sassoon, known as "Mad Jack" for his reckless daring on the battlefield, or Lord Peter Wimsey in fiction, embody the debonair hero of shell shock, the officer who stoically disguised his emotions for the sake of his men, but broke down afterwards.

Among the ranks, doctors saw conversion hysterias: limps, paralyses, contractures. The most common symptom was mutism. English tabloid newspapers like the *Evening Standard* called these soldiers "degenerates." Class prejudice influenced military views that soldiers who broke down came from the "dregs of society." Some military authorities saw shell shock as cowardice or malingering, and argued that patients should be court-martialed and shot. Dr. Lewis Yealland, who treated shell-shock victims at the Queen Square Hospital in London, thought they were sulky and negative. Even sympathetic doctors theorized that ordinary soldiers were more childlike and less prepared by their education and background to withstand the pressures of combat. Some Freudians insisted that war neurosis had a sexual origin, and that the latent homosexuality of fighting men was brought to the surface by the male environment.

But psychiatrists who worked with shell-shock patients in World War I recognized that the most courageous, intelligent, and virile soldier could break down under the pressures of combat. The British psychologist Cyril Burt noted in 1935, "It was perhaps the First World War that most effectively brought home the artificiality of the distinction between the normal mind on the one hand and its abnormal conditions on the other. In the military hospitals the study of so-called shell-shock revealed that symptoms quite as serious as the well-defined psychoses might arise through simple stress and strain and yet prove quickly curable by psychotherapeutic means. And thus it gradually became apparent that much of what had been considered abnormal might be discovered in the mind of the average man."[29]

Remarkably, war neurosis became more common after the armistice. One American commentator wrote: "To our astonishment the majority of the neuroses that are hospitalized today in the convalescent hospitals are people who have developed either the first signs of their neurosis on return to this country or have become worse after landing on these shores." Another writer described the distress of the men who returned from the front to civilian life: "They had not come back the same men. Something had altered in them. They were subject to queer moods and queer tempers, fits of profound depression alternating with a restless desire for pleasure. Many were easily moved to passion where they lost control of themselves, many were bitter in their speech, violent in opinion, frightening."[30] By 1929, about 114,600 ex-servicemen had applied for pensions for "shell–shock–related" disorders. In 1932, 36 percent of the British veterans receiving disability payments from their government were psychiatric casualties. In the United States in 1942, 58 percent of the patients in veterans' hospitals were neuropsychiatric casualties of the Great War.

War neurosis increased after the war partly because of the resentment veterans felt toward the government that had placed them in danger. During combat this resentment could be directed toward the enemy, but on returning home, veterans had what Eric Leed calls "an enormous need for care and reassurance, a need combined with anger and hostility toward the society that had placed them in the position of victims."[31] Having idealized home and family in combat, soldiers faced the same everyday problems at home.

Just as doctors have claimed that female hysteria disappeared in the twentieth century, so too they insisted that shell shock faded after the Great War. With more sophisticated psychiatric knowledge, doctors maintained, forewarned and forearmed, they could prevent epidemic hysteria in the trenches. "Shell shock is now nipped in the bud," boasted one German professor of psychiatry at Munich; another at Hamburg explained, "In the Second World War, hysterical symptoms disappeared almost entirely. They simply no longer existed, neither at the fighting front nor at the home front."[32] According to some French doctors, "Hysterical conversion drifted in the direction of somatic pathology."[33]

The U.S. reaction was mixed. In August 1943 General George S. Patton, visiting military hospitals in Italy, lost his temper and assaulted American soldiers who were suffering from nervous symptoms. Patton confronted a bedridden soldier and began to yell: "You are just a goddamned coward, you yellow son of a bitch. You are a disgrace to the Army and you are going back to the front to fight, although that's too good for you. You ought to be lined up against a wall and be shot. In fact, I ought to shoot you myself right now, goddamn you." Patton actually pulled his pistol from its holster, and struck the weeping man in the face with his gloves. Horrified, the doctors tried to stop him as he shoved the soldier out of the ward. In his diary, Patton unapologetically wrote, "One sometimes slaps a baby to bring it to."[34]

A few days later, in another evacuation hospital, he met Private Charles Herman Kuhl, who told the general that he couldn't stand the war anymore. Enraged, Patton slapped and kicked him; doctors afterwards discovered that Kuhl had malaria. Still, Patton was unrepentant.

On August 10, he threatened to shoot Private Paul G. Bennett for cowardice, although Bennett had a distinguished combat record. Eisenhower called Patton's behavior "despicable" and demanded that he apologize to the soldiers, the medical staff, and the Seventh Army. In return Eisenhower urged the press to cover up the incident, but Drew Pearson reported it in a November broadcast, and Patton was almost court-martialed.

Until spring 1943, military censorship had "hampered journalistic coverage of the war neuroses," writes Nathan Hale. But by 1944, medical and journalistic popularizers had "established saving stereotypes to deal with the unappealing psychoneuroses," and to make heroes, rather than cowards, of the neuropsychiatric patients. Anyone, even "big, apparently tough men, with long weeks of continuous fighting against the Japanese on Guadalcanal, or months of combat against the Germans in Europe or North Africa," might break under the terrible conditions of modern warfare. A fictionalized account by John Hersey in *Life* magazine of narcosynthesis (the use of sodium amytal) as treatment for a soldier with hysterical paralysis, sympathetic articles in the news media, and John Huston's *Let There Be Light* (1945), a film about the successful treatment of neuropsychiatric soldiers at a military hospital, helped change public attitudes about the legitimacy of war neurosis and the efficacy of psychiatric treatment.[35]

Male Hysteria Today

War makes people sick; during the past fifty years, mounting evidence has indicated that every war produces psychoneurotic disorders. Even in Israel, where all citizens serve in the army and feel passionately committed to the nation's military defense, war neurosis is common. In *Combat Stress Reaction: The Enduring Toll of War*, Dr. Zahava Solomon describes the psychosomatic effects of combat on Israeli soldiers. After the 1982 Lebanon war, 23 percent of all Israeli medical cases were diagnosed as combat stress reaction. The onset was often delayed. Solomon writes, "A combat stress reaction is the culmination of a process in which the individual is stripped of his sense of safety and mastery and experiences the full thrust of his vulnerability and existential helplessness."[36]

The Vietnam War had clearly observed aftereffects on its troops. According to the National Vietnam Veterans Readjustment Study, 15.2 percent of all male Vietnam theater veterans have suffered from posttraumatic stress disorder, and another 11 percent have had partial symptoms. Over a third of the men and a fourth of the women serving in Vietnam had PTSD. Hispanics had the highest proportion of PTSD, then blacks, then whites. Symptoms often appeared after a "long, seemingly problem-free period, even many years following . . . service in Southeast Asia."[37]

Noncombatants also got involved. One American told his wife and therapist that his psychological problems were caused by traumatic experiences in Vietnam: he had been a navigator on a F-4 fighter jet shot down in the jungle and had been imprisoned in a bamboo cage by the Viet Cong. Diagnosed as a victim of post-traumatic stress disorder, he was unsuccessfully treated for depression, guilt, and anger. After he killed himself by inhaling carbon monoxide, his widow attempted to have his named engraved on the state's war memorial and discovered that he never been to Vietnam.[38]

However, since World War II, and psychoanalysis's days in the 1950s sun, male hysteria has reverted to its status as oxymoron or insult. Both male and female therapists hesitate to call men hysterical, although they may look, sound, and act like textbook examples. At the Menninger Clinic Harriet Lerner observes that she has seen "grave hysterical symptoms," including conversion reactions, dissociative phenomena, and even "male patients in hysterical fits, complete with arching backs, Charcot-style." But despite their symptoms, Lerner denies that the men could be hysterical because they don't exhibit the emotionalism, vanity, or dramatic flair associated with women: "These individuals tend not to manifest the type of cognitive and personality organization that is characteristic of the hysterical individual. It is especially in regard to the hysterical personality, character, or 'style' that the male patient is a rarity."[39]

When men with hysterical symptoms *are* emotional or theatrical, psychiatrists hint that they must be homosexual. Freud argued that hysterical men were sexually passive.[40] Wilhelm Reich described the male hysteric as characterized by "feminine facial expression and feminine behavior."[41] Even the feminist historian Carroll Smith-Rosenberg has written, "It is a truism that hysteria in males is found most frequently among homosexuals."[42] Journalistic taunts of hysterical overreaction directed at women's protest and feminist activism for over a century have expanded to include gay activists and AIDS activists. In December 1989, when ACT-UP and the abortion rights group WHAM staged a demonstration at St. Patrick's Cathedral in New York, interrupting Sunday Mass, the *New York Times* editorialized that "hysterics" would not advance arguments over homosexuality, abortion, and AIDS.[43]

The British therapist Jane Ussher reports that clinicians are quick to apply the term "hysterical" to gay men dealing with AIDS: "In my own clinical work in the field of AIDS, where gay men then formed the majority of the client population, I heard the usually very rare diagnosis of 'hysteria' applied to men—men who were crying and freely expressing their emotions, behaviour which is deemed unacceptable within our present construction of masculinity. Yet, as these men were infected with the HIV virus, and often facing the death of a partner, was crying not an appropriate behaviour? Many of the men I worked with were referred for psychological treatment precisely because of this 'inappropriate affect.' "[44]

For all these reasons, according to Parisian psychoanalyst Lucien Israel, the hysteria diagnosis "became for a man . . . the real injury, a sign of weakness, a castration in a word. To say to a man, 'You are hysterical,' became under these conditions a way of saying to him, 'You are not a man.' "[45] When therapists themselves avoid the topic of male hysteria, how can the rest of us accept and understand it? No wonder Gulf War syndrome has been so frightening and so difficult to cure.

PART TWO

Cultures

6 | *Hysterical Narratives*

I n our own fin de siècle, as medical institutions expel hysteria, literary critics take it up. During the past decade, the "hysterical narrative" has become one of the most popular formulations in literary criticism. It has grown at the busy crossroad where psychoanalytic theory, narratology, feminist criticism, and the history of medicine intersect, drawing both on the vogue for Freud's case studies, especially *Dora*, and the recognition that all medical practice depends on narrative—the "doctor's story," which both shapes the formal case study and determines practical treatment. Freud defined the central task of psychoanalysis as restoring repressed memories and desires in a narrative that is then fully assimilated into the patient's life history. Others see this therapeutic editing and rewriting as manipulative. The novelist Fay Weldon, whose marriage broke up after her husband went into therapy, attacks therapists as "failed novelists, creating nice patterns out of real people's lives for their own satisfaction and for money."[1] Feminist critics, among others, draw attention to the ways doctors' stories tend to dominate medical discourse, while *patients* have to modify their stories. And the decline of "hysteria" as a medical phenomenon reflects its rise as a narrative process.

Hysterical narrative, however, has a literary history that predates Freud. Nineteenth-century French doctors organized their case studies of hysterical women according to the conventions of the French novel, especially its seduction scenes, and writers based their portraits of seductive or unhappy women on medical textbooks. Gustave

Flaubert, the son of a doctor, constructed his portrait of Emma Bovary from the medical literature, and *Madame Bovary* (1855) not only set the style for much subsequent fiction about female hysteria but also molded medical diagnosis and patient behavior. Charcot's assistant Charles Richet called Emma "the most vivid, the truest, the most passionate of hysterics."[2] In the aftermath of *Madame Bovary*, journalists saw a new personality type on the scene: the romantic, emotional, erotic hysterical woman. "One finds hysteria everywhere today," wrote the French theater critic Francisque Sarcey. "These delicious troubles of a young girl who forms only vague desires or cries without knowing why: hysteria. These languors of a the woman of thirty who is bored and who daydreams: hysteria. These tumultuous longings of the woman of forty who flings herself into the future while looking backwards: hysteria. Our doctors have peopled the world with hysterics."[3]

By century's end, literary conventions of hysteria fed into a torrent of new novels, stories, and plays, mainly written by men. French women writers did not seem attracted to the subject of hysteria, which so denigrated their capacities. The fiction of hysteria fed back into the medical literature; for doctors to write case studies, Jann Matlock suggests, required "a *poetics* of hysteria in which doctors articulated the relation of gender, class, sexuality, and heredity to the politically-charged plots they had already become accustomed to telling."[4]

Hysteria entered nineteenth-century English literature too. Tennyson dramatized it in *Maud*; Wilkie Collins and Mary Elizabeth Braddon brought it into the mystery novel; Dickens used it in *Tale of Two Cities*, where Dr. Manette suffers from post-traumatic stress disorder triggered by his incarceration in the Bastille. Split personalities in *Dr. Jekyll and Mr. Hyde*, mesmerism in *Trilby*, and mental breakdowns in *Dracula* and *Jude the Obscure* drew on popular myths of the hysterical personality. Claire Kahane interprets early modernist novels like Henry James's *The Bostonians* (1886) and Virginia Woolf's *The Voyage Out* (1913) as narratives of hysteria, reactions to the gender crisis of the time. "Menaced by a vision of cultural apocalypse, and yet also exhilarated by the possibilities," she writes, "turn-of-the-century writers, both male and female, represented their ambivalence in fictional forms that begin as hysterical articulations of their own labile sexuality and become formalized later as the tenets of literary modernism."[5] In the United States, novelists regarded hysteria as primarily a white middle-class woman's malady, but also as a sign of superior refinement and femininity. In the 1890s, tragic heroines with racially mixed blood displayed nervous and hysterical symptoms as signs of both racial contamination and feminine delicacy.[6]

Not only psychological understanding of hysteria but also the novel changed dramatically in the 1890s. At the time Freud was exploring the unconscious, omniscient narrators of the great Victorian realist novelists like Eliot or Trollope gave way to the unreliable, uncertain narrators of Conrad and James. The leisurely three-volume English novel was abruptly phased out in 1894 because circulating libraries withdrew their subsidies; it was replaced by more intense modern forms like the detective novel, the short story, and the problem play. Freud was fascinated with the psychological subtexts of this new literature, and literary critics have compared his case studies to tales by Conan Doyle or plays by Ibsen.

Both writers and critics in the 1890s saw hysteria as a metaphor for the fin-de-siècle sensibility. To conservative critics, hysteria was the *mal du siècle*, a sign of artistic degeneration. In 1892, Max Nordau, an Austrian doctor and journalist who had attended Charcot's lectures, called hysteria a central motive in avant-garde art: "The physician . . . recognises at a glance, in the *fin-de-siècle* disposition, in the tendencies of contemporary art and poetry, in the life and conduct of the men who write mystic, symbolic and 'decadent' works . . . the conflation of . . . degeneracy and hysteria, of which the minor stages are designated as neurasthenia." By the time Freud described it in his case studies, hysterical narrative had already acquired a negative meaning for readers, a meaning associated with effeminacy and deceitfulness. In his widely read polemic, *Degeneration*, Nordau denounced the elements of fantasy in contemporary writing: "The hysterical subject does not consciously lie. He believes in the truth of his craziest inventions. The morbid mobility of his mind, the excessive excitability of his imagination, conveys to his consciousness all sorts of queer and senseless ideas. . . . A result of the susceptibility of the hysterical subject to suggestion is his irresistible passion for imitation, and the eagerness with which he yields to all the suggestions of writers and artists."[7]

Following Nordau, many critics explored the idea of "hysteria" as the mental disorder responsible for literary experimentation. For male traditionalists, anything called "hysterical" writing was unmanly and incoherent. Thus Walter Pater wrote in "Plato's Esthetics" (1897), "Manliness in art . . . [has to do with] tenacity of intuition and of consequent purpose, the spirit of construction as opposed to what is literally incoherent or ready to fall to pieces, and in opposition to what is

hysteric or works at random." New Women writers in the 1890s, however, such as George Egerton, Olive Schreiner, Victoria Cross,
Charlotte Perkins Gilman, or Rachilde, used the word *hysteria* to
describe the consciousness of heroines expressing their repressed
desires in stories they called "fantasies," "fragments," or "dreams."

Freud may have had such texts in mind when he began his first
full-length case study, Elisabeth von R., with this observation: "It still
strikes me as strange that the case histories I write should read like
short stories and that, as one might say, they lack the serious stamp
of science. I must console myself with the reflection that the nature
of the subject is evidently responsible for this, without any preference of my own. The fact is that local diagnosis and electric reactions
lead nowhere in the study of hysteria, where a detailed description
of mental processes such as we are now accustomed to find in the
works of imaginative writers enables me, with the use of a few psychological formulas, to obtain at least some kind of insight into the
course of that affliction."[8]

Freud believed the nature of the story, rather than the predilections
of the story teller, dictated the form: hysterics were unable to tell a
complete, "smooth and exact" story about themselves; they left out,
distorted, and rearranged information because of sexual repression.
And this incapacity to give an "ordered history of their life" was not
simply characteristic of hysterics—it was the *meaning* of hysteria. The
stories of hysterical girls seemed like "an unnavigable river whose
stream is at one moment choked by masses of rock and at another
divided and lost among shallows and sandbanks." Volubility about one
period of their lives was sure to be followed "by another period in
which their communications run dry, leaving gaps unfilled and rid-
dles unanswered."

If the hysteric could remember what was repressed and lay claim to
"an intelligible, consistent, and unbroken case history," she would be
cured. Thus the therapist's role was to edit or construct such a narrative for the patient. Freud was confident that no matter how elusive
and enigmatic the hysteric's story, the analyst could reconstruct a logical narrative. "Once we have discovered the concealed motives," he
wrote, "which have often remained unconscious, and have taken them
into account, nothing that is puzzling or contrary to rule remains in
hysterical connections of thought, any more than in normal ones."

He compared this process to the archaeologist restoring the mutilated fragments and objects of buried civilizations: "I had no choice

but to follow the example of those discoverers whose good fortune it is to bring to the light of day after their long burial the priceless, though mutilated relics of antiquity."[9] Indeed in his consulting room Freud surrounded himself with a vast collection of mutilated antiquities that seemed illustrative of his self-image as one who collected and repaired broken stories and broken selves.

Freud perfected his definition of hysterical narrative in his work with Dora. While Breuer, in the earlier case of Anna O., had commented on the broken language and multilingual nature of the hysteric's speech, Freud drew attention to the fragmentary and discontinuous nature of the hysteric's narrative and to the physician's responsibility for reorganizing it into a coherent whole. In doing so, he had not only to fill gaps in the hysteric's story but also to overcome her resistance to his narrative interpretations. For this therapy to work, the hysteric had to accept and believe the analyst's story.

Dora, however, was uncooperative. She flatly denied Freud's narrative embellishments of her story, would not accept his version of her activities and feelings, and either contradicted him or fell into stubborn silence. Finally she refused to continue—an act he regarded as the problem of her transference. Dora, he argued, had projected on to him her feelings of erotic attraction for her father and Herr K., and was punishing Freud with her rejection.

If Freud is a reliable narrator, he succeeded in penetrating the mystery of Dora's hysterical symptoms. In his terminology, he unlocked her case and exposed her sexual secrets. Unable to face the truth, Dora ran away from therapy and remained sick for the rest of her life. But if Freud is an unreliable narrator, Dora is a victim of his unconscious erotic feelings, which drove him to dominate and control her. Dora has no voice in Freud's text: we don't hear her part of the dialogue, and her historical and Jewish identity are both suppressed. Freud's interpretations of her problem reflect his own obsessions with masturbation, adultery, and homosexuality. Thus the narrative illustrates the doctor's hysteria rather than the patient's.

In a 1974 *Partisan Review* essay, Steven Marcus described *Dora* as a novel in disguise. Among its resemblances to a modern experimental novel, Marcus argued, were its "plastic, involuted and heterogeneous" organization, its use of what looked like fictional framing devices in Freud's preface and postscript, and its proliferation of such novelistic conventions as "thematic analogies, double plots, reversals, inversions, variations, and betrayals."[10] In addition, Marcus compared the Dora case to Ibsen's plays of the 1880s and 1890s, and suggested connections between Dora and Nora in *A Doll House*.

Other critics have compared Freud and Henry James. To Neil Hertz, the Dora case resembles James's *What Maisie Knew*. To Peter Brooks, "Dora's case history . . . reads like a failed Edwardian novel, one that can never reach a satisfactory denouement, and that can never quite decide what the relations among the cast of characters truly are: as if Freud were one of Henry James's baffled yet inventive narrators . . . but one who must finally give it all up as a bad business."[11] To John Forrester, the Dora case is "an epoch-making narrative, whose flaws, like *The Golden Bowl*, [are] splitting 'on lines and laws of its own.' "[12] For all of them, the deliberate gaps and ambiguities of Freud's hysterical narrative follow the narrative conventions of a new era.

Feminist critics have emphasized other correspondences between Freud's case studies and nineteenth-century fiction. Susan Katz writes, "What remains troubling about the literary form of the case history as a synthesis of clinical observations and fictional devices is that the 'heroines' disguised for anonymity's sake behind pseudonyms and altered circumstances were *real* women; and Freud was trying to direct the course of their lives with his personal and literary values." Katz argues that Freud adopted narrative conventions of nineteenth-century novels; if *Dora* reads like a failed Victorian novel, that's because it invokes obsolete narrative conventions. The conclusion of *Dora* certainly has a familiar ring: "Years have gone by since her visit. In the meantime the girl has married. . . . She had been reclaimed once more by the realities of life."[13]

Hysteria and Feminist Criticism

Recent feminist criticism has been particularly energetic and influential in its examination of hysterical narrative. French feminist theorists such as Hélène Cixous, Julia Kristeva, and Michèle Montrelay define hysteria as a female signifying system outside of language. At the same time, they argue, women are condemned to silence in culture because the representational systems of language, especially a gendered language like French, favor masculinity and logic. French feminists call for an emancipatory *écriture féminine* that could shatter the gendered laws of syntax and grammar. Cixous challenges women writers to create an innovative style that puts the silent discourse of the "admirable hysterics" into words.[14]

To see hysteria as a form of silencing makes clinical and historical sense. Both traditional medical accounts of hysteria and Freud's case histories stressed such symptoms of blocked speech and communication as the *globus hystericus*, or sense of choking; the *tussis nervosa*, or chronic nervous cough; *aphasia*, or inability to use words, and *aphonia*, or loss of voice. Mutism frequently turned up as a symptom of nineteenth-century female hysteria. Anna O. could not speak her native German and instead spoke either Yiddish, which she called "the woman's German," or a jumble of English, Italian, and French.

American and English feminist critics placed an equally important, although very different, emphasis on images of silence and silencing in women's writing. While French feminists regarded hysteria's silence as the essential or natural result of cultural law, American critics attacked the "unnatural silences" that came from deprivation and prejudice. Hysteria or its representation in art was not a glorious female capacity, wrote Elaine Hedges and Shelly Fishkin, but the price of "being born into the wrong class, race, or sex, being denied education, becoming numbed by economic struggles, muffled by censorship, or distracted or impeded by the demands of nurturing."[15]

In her moving book *Silences* (1978), which looked back fifty years to Virginia Woolf's *Room of One's Own*, Tillie Olsen describes the muffling of women's creative voices as the product of social bias, racial struggle, and domestic responsibilities. Class and race as well as gender play a role in Olsen's theory of silence. Woolf testified to the silencing of a female literary genius through her story of Shakespeare's imaginary sister. But Woolf, who came from the intellectual upper class, made her own voice heard. Olsen was different. She came from an immigrant working-class family in Omaha, joined the Young Communist League, and devoted much of her life to the Party. A gifted writer of fiction, she wanted her work to have political meaning. Woolf was childless; Olsen raised four children, taking menial jobs to help support the family. By the time she was in her fifties, she had postponed her writing so long in the interests of family, social commitment, and the stylistic dogmas of American socialist realism that she could not recover her fictional voice.

Tillie Olsen's stories of oppressed women, her testimony to the effects of silencing, and her loving support of other women made her a heroine to an American generation of writers and scholars, including Alice Walker, Ursula LeGuin, Gloria Naylor, Alix Kates Shulman, and Susan Griffin. By 1988, Patricia Yeager called Olsen's "typology of literary silences" a method "indispensable . . . to feminist criticism as a collective enterprise."[16] For feminist critics, the analysis of textual silences in women's writing was one of "the most provocative and liveliest developments in criticism in the past twenty years."[17] It meant a rereading of classic women's writing with attention to spaces or silences that could now be seen to mask forbidden sexual feelings or equally forbidden anger and protest. And then came the poststructuralists, who interpreted gaps and breaks in a text, even blank spaces on the page, as significant contributions to the meaning of a work: marks of repression or resistance that the critic was meant to decipher.

Thus in contrast to Freudian views of hysterical narrative, literary critics could understand Dora's "unreliability and incoherence" as a projection of her social circumstances. Norwegian feminist critic Toril Moi points out, "The *reason* why the neurotic fails to produce coherence is that she lacks the *power* to impose her own connections on her reader/listener."[18] Martha Noel Evans makes a similar point. "If the speech of witches and hysterics was universally discounted as mendacious," she writes, ". . . it is because women did not have the necessary real power to challenge the word of their colonial masters."[19]

In addition, feminist critics believe they have a mission to restore the silenced voices of women writers to literary history. Like other lost cultural histories, feminist literary history is necessarily a process of recovered memory. In their magisterial study *The Madwoman in the Attic* (1979), Sandra Gilbert and Susan Gubar endow this project with mythic significance. They compare the woman artist to "someone suffering from amnesia." In order to recover "her own mother land," the female artist must journey "into what Adrienne Rich has called 'the cratered night of female memory' to revitalize the darkness, to retrieve what has been lost, to regenerate, reconceive, and give birth."[20]

Women writers too have represented past hysterics as artists manqué. When we read about "a witch being ducked, of a woman possessed by devils," wrote Virginia Woolf in *A Room of One's Own* (1928), we are reading about "a lost novelist, a suppressed poet, of some mute and inglorious Jane Austen, some Emily Brontë who dashed her brains out on the moor or mopped and mowed about the highways crazed with the torture her gift had put her to." Alice Walker describes the "Crazy Saints of black culture" as silenced artists, women "who saw visions no one could understand . . . driven to a numb and bleeding madness by the springs of creativity in them for which there was no release."[21]

Feminist therapy and traumatology gave memory new importance. Beginning in the 1980s, some Anglo-American feminist critics and literary biographers joined French theory to the activism of the women's movement by proposing that silences and metaphors in the writing of a number of important women were indeed evidence of childhood sexual abuse. The work of Florence Rush, who posited a marked increase in sexual assault on children during the Victorian era, or E. Sue Blume, who described the symptoms of a "post-incest syndrome" in her book *Secret Survivors: Uncovering Incest and Its Aftereffects in Women* (1990), supported critics' effort to find such a syndrome in the work of Victorian women writers or activists born during the Victorian era. With the writer dead, the critic herself performed the work of remembering, often arguing that clues had deliberately been left behind to point the way. Feminist critics saw themselves as loving sisterly collaborators in the twofold task of recovery—both recovery of the lost artist's full stature and retroactive recovery of her sexual trauma.

Virginia Woolf played an important role in this process. In the 1970s Quentin Bell's biography and Woolf's own letters and diaries made readers aware that as a child and adolescent she had been molested by her half-brothers, George and Gerald Duckworth. But Woolf's early biographers, including Jean Love, Phyllis Rose, and Lyndall Gordon, thought it impossible to know exactly what had gone on. "It cannot be determined that the alleged offenses actually took place," writes Rose. "Nor can it be determined that they did not."[22]

In 1989, however, Louise DeSalvo wrote without equivocation that Woolf was "an incest survivor." In DeSalvo's view, childhood abuse shaped Woolf as woman and writer: "Virginia Woolf was surely traumatized by the events and experience she had been subjected to within her family. Her reports of illness, disorientation, and feelings of worthlessness coincide with those of other incest survivors; her suicide is surely linked to it."

DeSalvo sees evidence of the trauma in Woolf's writing as well as in her dysfunctional family and disappointing married life. "Every one of her novels describes a child abandoned, a child ignored, a child at risk, a child abused, a child betrayed." Moreover, "Woolf devoted a considerable amount of her writing energy to describing the common experience of sexual assault in women's lives." Writing, in fact, was Woolf's form of therapy: "Through language, through her diary, Virginia rebuilt her life, rebuilt her psyche, through all the days of 1897, painstakingly, slowly, one day at a time."[23]

Following DeSalvo's book, other feminist critics proposed childhood sexual abuse to explain mysteries, gaps, and ambiguities in the
lives of women writers. Unlike Woolf, Christina Rossetti left no mem-
oirs accusing her male relatives of molestation. But Jan Marsh speculates on the basis of internal literary evidence that it may have
occurred: "Throughout Christina's verse, ghostly lovers return in the
dark, frighteningly intent on reclaiming their loved ones. . . . Secrets
must be kept or cannot be told." To Marsh, this gothic imagery
strongly suggests sexual trauma. "Once raised, the suspicion that
Christina was the victim of sexual trauma has to be explored and
defended. Is it likely that her nightmares, morbid fancies, neuralgic
migraine and recurrent depressions had a psychological origin in some
such experience? If so, how was this related to her breakdown at age
fourteen? . . . Did Christina's father . . . make sexual advances or
requests she could not refuse?"[24]

Marsh believes the answer is "yes": a secret trauma of abuse must be
the source for Rossetti's violent, even sadistic, images and children's
stories. Apparently some feminist literary critics still find it hard to
accept that women can have cruel fantasies or visions, even though
they live outwardly pious lives. Critics seeking an explanation for
anomalies or contradictions in women's writing have found the sexual abuse model irresistible. Edith Wharton is the most recent subject
of biographical bombshells. We have learned of her passionate affair
with the bisexual journalist Morton Fullerton. We've read her erotic,
graphic, semipornographic short story about father-daughter incest,
"Beatrice Palmato." And we know that Wharton was an unhappy adolescent and young woman who suffered from what she called "an
intense and unreasoning physical timidity." Wharton too was treated
by Silas Weir Mitchell for neurasthenic symptoms. She had a phobia
about thresholds, and was afraid of the dark.

Barbara White perceives clear evidence of incest and trauma: "It was
not only the strange father-daughter stories that led me to the incest
theory but also the obsessive themes of hidden male corruption and
revelation of past crimes and secrets. (Survivors of childhood sexual
abuse, having been almost universally threatened not to tell, are usually preoccupied with secrets.)" White concludes: "For Edith Wharton,
then, writing was in many ways an act of courage."[25] In her footnotes
she cites well-known survivors and therapists: Maya Angelou, Sylvia
Fraser, Florence Rush, E. Sue Blume, Judith Herman, Ellen Bass and
Laura Davis, and of course Louise DeSalvo. Obviously Wharton did

know about incest. She had seen it at close hand in New England, and wrote about households in rural Massachusetts where the daughter was known to be pregnant with her father's child. She had read about it. But the leap to assumptions about her personal experience is symptomatically speculative.

Incest in the lives of women writers has become an open secret, a secret everyone knows. Ironically, incest has also become the standard plot twist in women's pulp fiction. Reviewing the latest batch of Black Lace offerings—pornography for women—Maureen Freely notes that "the deep, dark secret that you have to plow through hundreds of pages to discover is always—but *always*—what the blurb writers like to call 'society's last taboo.' So it's not much of a surprise anymore."[26]

The Female Gothic

Feminist critics in the 1980s applied their analysis of hysteria to genres of women's writing as well as to its conventions and images. Julia Kristeva proclaimed that "Freud's statement 'the hysteric suffers from reminiscences' sums up the large majority of novels produced by women";[27] Juliet Mitchell declared that "the woman novelist must be an hysteric";[28] and Mary Jacobus asked whether "women's writing [can] ever be anything other than hysterical?"[29] The end of the nineteenth century, as Foucault argued, produced the widespread medical hysterization of women's bodies; with the rise of literary theory, the end of the twentieth century has produced a widespread critical hysterization of women's stories. Sometimes referring to *all* fiction by women, sometimes to fiction *about* hysterical women, sometimes to fiction that is fragmented, evasive, and ambiguous, poststructuralist critics equated hysteria with the incoherent female imagination, just as pre-Freudian doctors had equated hysteria with the disorderly female body.

In fact, after centuries of serving as the wastebasket diagnosis of psychiatry and medicine, hysteria has now become the wastebasket category of literary criticism, into which any excitable heroine from Jane Eyre to Blanche DuBois can be tossed. The label has been applied not only to stories in which heroines become mute or nervous invalids but also to stories in which they are merely unhappy, histrionic, rebellious, or shaky. Critics see George Eliot's sexually repressed heroines as the paradigmatic nineteenth-century hysterics: the jumpy Maggy T., the "incipiently hysterical" Dorothea B.,[30] or the frigid Gwendolen H.

(Peter Brooks observes that she "seems by now to be well established in criticism as a hysteric").[31]

Feminist critics in the 1980s also defined the female gothic as the paradigmatic genre of hysterical narrative. In its classic form, created in the late eighteenth century by novelists like Ann Radcliffe, a young woman is trapped in an enclosure, a haunted castle or dungeon. She believes that a sinister older man is holding her captive, but invariably the mystery turns out to have as much to do with her mother and with anxieties about female sexual maturity. Eve Kosofsky Sedgwick describes the heroine of the Gothic novel as a "classic hysteric" whose anxieties and desires are projected onto her environment.[32] Mary Jacobus also links Freudian hysteria with elements of the romantic, unconscious, and gothic in women's writing.[33]

Charlotte Perkins Gilman's 1892 gothic short story "The Yellow Wallpaper" is, according to Diane Price Herndl, "the most famous narrative of hysteria."[34] It's about a woman with postpartum depression, "a slight hysterical tendency," who is taken to the country for a rest cure by her physician-husband. Deprived of social outlets, forbidden to write—though she does so secretly—the heroine begins to lose her mind and to have hallucinations of women trapped behind the yellow Art Nouveau wallpaper in her bedroom. By the end of the story, she has had a complete breakdown; when her husband finally forces his way into the room where she has barricaded herself, she has torn the paper off the wall and is creeping around the floor: " 'I've got out at last,' said I . . . 'and I've pulled off most of the paper, so you can't put me back!' "

According to Jacobus, "The Yellow Wallpaper" could be one of Freud's case studies. Gilman's unnamed heroine embodies turn-of-the-century male fears of women as crazy and devious. Jacobus encourages other critics to explore the parallels between hysterical narrative and the Female Gothic: "Where hysteria is concerned, it is impossible to overread."[35] Barbara Johnson writes that both "The Yellow Wallpaper" and *Dora* are stories "of a failed cure" in which "a female patient [is] subject to the therapeutic ambitions of a male doctor." Johnson defines "The Yellow Wallpaper" as "an allegory of psychoanalysis."[36] Gillian Brown reads Gilman's story as a narrative in which "hysteria . . . the disease of the Victorian bourgeois family, caricatures domesticity [and] . . . . the hysteric suffers mainly from reminiscences of that domesticity."[37]

What these feminist critics do not always make clear, however, is the distinction between Gilman's representation of a metaphorical feminine "hysteria" and the innately "hysterical" qualities of her writing and of the Female Gothic as a genre. Comparisons of the Gothic novel and hysterical discourse are circular, since *Dora*—the "context"—can also be read as a Gothic "text." In her analysis of women and the Gothic genre, for example, Michelle Massé writes:

> The comparison of *Dora* and the heroine gives us a startling, if partial, plot similarity. A young girl who dotes on her father is much impressed in her early reading about love. She is somewhat interested in a man, but is repelled when he reveals a sinister side to his character. She attempts to flee, but time and again finds herself in an isolated setting with him. She locks herself in a room, but the key is taken from her; she tries to get help by telling someone what has happened to her, but she is told she imagined her danger. Her mother is herself helpless, and the one woman she thought she could trust betrays her. She suspects a dark secret in her family that curses each generation and that would explain much of what has happened to her. She refuses to do what her parents want and is brought, not to a cell to con- template her sins and the virtues of obedience, but to Freud to analyze her own desire as precipitant for her story.[38]

In my view, some feminist critics have overread women's stories and underread doctors' studies. They have reduced the vast medical liter- ature on hysteria to a few canonical case studies of the great hysteri- cal stars, chiefly Dora and Anna O. They have disregarded the history of hysteria or treated it as a metaphor. They have underestimated the difference between novels about sick women and novels about sad women.

Then, too, although women writing about hysteria may be con- structing fragmented narratives or inventing a potent symbolism of Gothic spaces and images, novelists are the very opposite of silenced hysterics compelled to express their protest or desire through the body. Indeed, "The Yellow Wallpaper" is one of our clearest examples of the *antithesis* of writing and hysteria. The heroine's hallucinations begin after she is deprived of the freedom to write. Gilman herself wrote the story as a protest against the rest cure that had restricted her intellectual and creative life. As Diane Price Herndl has argued, the story was Gilman's "writing cure," for "in creating a narrative of her hysterical condition, she no longer had to embody illness directly but could represent it in her text."[39]

Male Hysterical Narratives

Basing their theories on case studies in which the hysteric is invariably a woman and the doctor a man, literary critics tend to equate "hysteria" and "femininity." What happens when the roles in this scenario are switched, when the hysteric is a man and the doctor a woman? In an important essay, the psychologist Lisa Gornick has discussed the potential for a "new narrative" in interactions between female therapists and male patients. Gornick suggests some of the directions our thinking might take: "When the tables are turned so that a woman looks at, interprets, and (to borrow Freud's metaphor) 'penetrates' a man, the treatment will differ in significant ways from the treatment of women patients by male therapists, and . . . in order to capture this difference, it will be necessary to develop a new narrative line that specifically addresses the relationship of boys to their mothers and the quite different meanings of power and sexuality for men and women in our culture." In this dyad, she suggests, "The impact of the gender of the participants on the therapeutic dialogue becomes more salient."

But cultural resistance to female therapeutic rationality is strong, as we see in films like *Zelig*, *Spellbound*, and *The Prince of Tides*, where the woman therapist falls in love with her hysterical male patient and becomes hysterical herself. Gornick writes, "These male fantasies of psychotherapeutic treatment by a woman clinician as a love-cure . . . invert the reality about sexual contact between therapists and patients." In reality male therapist are four times more likely than female therapists to have sexual contact with their patients. But the male hysteric's fantasy of erotic contact undoes the woman analyst's authority and "restores the man to the dominant position." Gornick argues that the master narratives of psychoanalysis, including hysterical narrative, should be reexamined in the light of other gender configurations.[40]

On the whole, feminist critics have been less interested in analyzing male hysteria and its narrative representations than in studying hysterical narratives by or about women. Since "hysteria" has long been used to denigrate women's political discontents, Juli Loesch, an organizer for the United Farm Workers, coined the term "testeria" to describe a "crippled emotional condition found in males," a fear of feminism.[41] Some feminist critics have put these theories into action by labeling their male critical opponents "testerical" men.

When Duke University professor Frank Lentricchia attacked the work of Sandra Gilbert and Susan Gubar, they countered that his over-heated rhetoric and macho muscle-shirt jacket photo reveal his tester-ical fear of the "feminization of the literary critical life." They com-pared Lentricchia to the male modernist poets he writes about; their techniques and values were part envy, part rebellion against the "fem-inization" of poetry. Lentricchia, Gilbert and Gubar wrote, "may want to be a feminist, but . . . he certainly doesn't want to be thought effem-inate."[42] These slanging matches do enliven the pages of literary jour-nals, but they leave the stigma and stereotypes of hysteria untouched. After all, Gilbert and Gubar may want to be feminists but they cer-tainly don't want to be thought hysterical.

Surprisingly, male writers and critics have long been fascinated by hysteria. In the nineteenth century, French male artists and writers, including Baudelaire, Flaubert, and Mallarmé, claimed "hysteria" as a metaphor for writing, and for the androgynous nature of the creative process. Jan Goldstein argues, "Given the analogy and the pervasive unconscious associations between literary creativity and female bio-logical procreativity," writing was "the logical area of discussion in which male appropriation of the hysteria concept could take place during the nineteenth century. From hysteria as a malfunction of the organs of female procreativity . . . there was only a short step to hyste-ria as a malfunction of the organs of male artistic creativity."[43]

Emma Bovary became a prototype for the female hysteric in nineteenth-century French literature, and Flaubert became the pro-totype of the male writer whose hysteria allows him to understand both femininity and his writing blocks. In 1867, Flaubert wrote to George Sand that he was working on his new novel and experienc-ing "flutterings of the heart for no reason at all—an understandable thing in an old hysteric like me." He interpreted his hysterical symp-toms as resistances to writing, but they seem also to have been a stim-ulus, a sense of excitement and empathy.

Though the classic case histories of hysterical women are structured like Victorian novels that end with marriage, madness, or death, the case histories of Freud's male patients, such as the Wolf Man, read more like open-ended modernist fictions. Here, Susan Katz points out, closed marriage plots are significantly absent: "The forms of Freud's case histories reflect his ideological positions toward women and men: the univocal, conventionally 'Victorian' narratives of Freud's female patients become inadequate in the later case histories because Freud does not want to cement his male patients into a closed plot like that of marriage. Freud's male patients get more play in narrative because men get more play in life."[44]

Male Hysterical Fictions

After World War I, several novels about shell-shocked veterans were published, including Rebecca West's *The Return of the Soldier* (1918) and Virginia Woolf's *Mrs. Dalloway* (1925). Pat Barker's prize-winning trilogy—*Regeneration* (1991), *The Eye in the Door* (1993), and *The Ghost Road* (1995)—revisits World War I to explore the connections between male hysteria, sexuality, and the doctor-patient relationship. The hero of the series is Dr. W. H. R. Rivers (1864–1922), a real neurologist and anthropologist who served with the British army during the war and treated a number of shell-shock patients, including the poets Wilfred Owen and Siegfried Sassoon. Barker describes her project as a form of writing about trauma and recovery. In her view, "What made the treatment of the male hysteric during wartime so hostile was precisely that it was thought of as a female way of responding to stress, so the feeling was that he wasn't just shirking or being cowardly, he was also being effeminate."[45]

A little-known American novel about male hysteria, Dorothy Canfield's *The Home-Maker* (1924), took the insights of shell shock to the domestic front. Both Evangeline Knapp and her husband, Lester, have nearly destroyed themselves in the effort to obey standards of proper female and male behavior which suit neither. The ambitious, highly organized Evangeline is becoming hysterical and making her children sick as she tries to channel her energy into running a perfect household. She has painful eczema, the pustulant eruption of her pent-up anger and frustration. At one point, Evangeline begins sobbing, in "the terrifying sounds of an hysteric breakdown," when her son Henry accidentally spills grease from the meat platter onto the floor. Henry, predictably, has bouts of vomiting. Helen, the daughter, is cowed and miserable. The smallest child, Stephen, is a violent hellraiser. Evangeline gets her only pleasure from thinking of her cleverness in furnishing the house and making the children stylish clothes on a tight budget. But these moments of satisfaction are brief. "The clock behind her struck half-past nine, and she became aware of its ticking once more, its insistent whisper: '*So much to do! So much to do! So much to do!*'"

Evangeline hates her life of domestic duty and solitary confinement. "How she *loathed* housework! the sight of a dishpan full of dishes made her feel like screaming out. And what else did she have? Loneliness; never-ending monotony; blank, gray days, one after another, full of drudgery." Meanwhile her husband, by nature a poet and intellectual, hates his drudgery too. He dreads getting out of bed in the morning to face the hustling and competition of his job as a department store manager. Like Weir Mitchell's patient Robert Conolly, Lester feels like a clockwork automaton: "How he loathed his life-long slavery to the clock, that pervasive intimate negative opposed to every spontaneous impulse." In particular, he misses spending time with his children. "He never had *time* to know his children, to stalk and catch that exquisitely elusive bird-of-paradise, their confidence."

Lester resents Evangeline's pride in shopping for their children rather than nurturing them. "Did anybody suggest to women that they give to understanding their children a tenth part of the time and real intelligence and real purposefulness they put into getting the right clothes for them?" A failure in his job, he is finally sacked, and succumbs to despair. On an icy winter day, trying to make it look like an accident, he goes up on his roof determined to kill himself so that the family can have the insurance.

But Lester fails even in his suicide attempt. His legs are paralyzed and he's confined to a wheelchair. This emergency gives both partners sanction to reshape their lives. Evangeline applies for a sales job in her husband's store and is hired out of charity; it quickly turns out to be a perfect match. Her fashion sense and management skills blossom in this setting. She loves her work and even develops a sense of humor. Her husband is blooming too. He begins by talking to his children and discovering their secret anxieties. He takes over the homemaking, learns to cook, and manages the house even better than his wife had. Above all, he learns to be a successful parent.

Inevitably, the idyll faces a crisis: watching her husband sleep one night, Evangeline sees him move his legs and realizes that the paralysis is psychological rather than organic. What ought she to do? If he is "cured," they must return to their soul-destroying former life. Yet her conscience demands that she seek a cure. In the end, the Knapps are freed from their agony by a wise family doctor, who gives his judgment: "It would be very dangerous for Mr. Knapp ever to use his legs."

Canfield's sardonic conclusion is that hysterical paralysis is a cheap price to pay for release from suffocating sexual conventions.

In the fiction of the 1990s, the male hysteric suffering from sexual anxiety, angst, and fears of aging has become a central figure. Martin Amis's *The Information* (1994) and Philip Roth's *Sabbath's Theatre* (1995) feature hysterical heroes. "What *Sabbath's Theatre* involves you in is a 450-page spasm of hysteria," wrote Amis in his review of Roth's book. "It is a hysterical novel about the hysteria of an hysterical man, and it leaves you feeling—hysterical."[46] David Lodge's *Therapy* (1995) is another seriocomic novel of male hysteria. The hero, Laurence Passmore or Tubby, a successful sitcom writer in his late fifties, has a heavy-duty midlife crisis, accompanied by sexual impotence and a mysterious pain in the knee that persists through several operations. Tubby is bewildered by the signals from his unconscious: "I have depression, anxiety, panic attacks, night sweats, insomnia, but not nightmares." He speculates on the possible reasons for his malaise. Could it be "compassion fatigue," a numbness to human misery? Could it be "idiopathic patella chondromalacia," "internal derangement of the knee," or "internal derangement of the hormones"? Tubby's cognitive psychotherapist, Dr. Alexandra Marples, thinks he suffers from a lack of self-esteem: "There's something like an epidemic of lack of self-esteem in Britain at the current moment."

Tubby looks back nostalgically to the day of the World Cup Final in June 1966 as the last moment of England's national self-esteem. Yet the cure for his hysteria is not political or athletic, but rather spiritual and regressive. Convinced that he has betrayed his first love, a simple Catholic girl, in adolescence, he locates her on a pilgrimage in Spain and seeks her forgiveness, absolution, and warm maternal sexual comfort. "I seem," he concludes, "to have abandoned cognitive therapy in favour of the old-fashioned analytical kind, finding the source of my troubles in a long-repressed memory." For many of Lodge's English readers, the resurgence of national self-esteem during the Euro 96 football finals may have had the same curative effect.

Literary critics have been astute in seeing that hysteria cannot be understood apart from its historical and social contexts. They have shown again and again how the hysterical emotionalism of an Emma Bovary in nineteenth-century Rouen, the neurasthenic symptoms of Charlotte Perkins Gilman in Victorian New England, and the limps and coughs of Ida Bauer in fin-de-siècle Vienna were produced by the social expectations and cultural givens of the moments in which these women live. Critics have also become sensitive to the symbolic meaning of a wide range of sicknesses, breakdowns, and invalid episodes in stories and novels. But when it comes to contemporary texts, to stories close to home, literary critics have too often overlooked metaphor, convention, context, and intertextuality. Literature spreads hysteria, but it can also help us understand it. In that sense, the hysterical narratives of fiction can tell us a lot more about the causes and cures of hysteria than most of the self-help books on the market.

7

Hysteria and the Histrionic

Today the theater, movies, and television play an even more important role than literature in publicizing and circulating views of hysteria. Metaphors of the histrionic have long influenced clinical discussion: nineteenth-century physician Jules Falret regarded hysterical women as "veritable actresses," who "know no greater pleasure than to deceive."[1] With Charcot as the producer and director of a great hysterical theater at the Salpêtrière, Paris became the capital of histrionic hysteria. According to the historian Jacqueline Carroy-Thiraud, Charcot and his interns were puppet masters using "human marionettes."[2] Georgette Déga, a female intern who studied with Charcot, compared the histrionic qualities of hysteria to the artificiality of women's normal roles: "Theatricality," according to Déga, "is part and parcel of all women's lives and originates . . . in the dissonance produced in women's psychic lives by their being assigned, in all social classes, inferior roles to play."[3] In the 1890s hysterical performance influenced both the representation of women and a coded representation of homosexual men. Like femininity, decadent male artists at the end of the century believed, homosexuality was a form of hysterical posing and a thrilling secret performance.

As Charcot's clinic achieved celebrity in the 1890s, images of hysteria crossed over to theater and cabaret. At the Chat Noir and Folies Bergères, performers, singers, and mimes who called themselves "Harengs Saurs Épileptiques (The Epileptic Sour Herrings)" or "Hydropathes" mimicked the jerky, zigzag movements of the hysterical seizure.[4] Theater critics like Hélène Zimmern described some of the most famous French actresses as hysterical women who had found an appropriate outlet for their histrionic personalities. Eleanor Duse was "the *fin-de-siècle* woman par excellence, with her hysterical maladies"; Aimée Desclée's performances were "worldly hysteria"; Réjane was "the muse of hystero-epilepsy."[5] In May 1908, Charcot's disciple André de Lorde wrote a play called *A Lesson at the Salpêtrière*, produced at the Grand-Guignol theater of horrors, in which one hysterical patient of the tyrannical Professor Marbois exacts her revenge by throwing acid at an intern.

The poses of *grande hystérie* enacted at the Friday *spectacles* of the Salpêtrière closely resembled the stylized movements of French classical acting. Indeed, hysterical women at the clinic and fallen women in melodrama were virtually indistinguishable; the theater historian Elin Diamond comments that both displayed "eye rolling, facial grimaces, gnashing teeth, heavy sighs, fainting, shrieking, choking; 'hysterical laughter' was a frequent stage direction as well as a common occurrence in medical asylums."[6] In folklore and in medicine, dance, too, whether the violent *chorea* of the asylum or the tarantella of legend, imitated female hysteria. As Dr. Harry Campbell wrote in 1891, "The movements of these wild dances imperceptibly shade off into the co-ordinate movements of the hysterical fit. . . . Hence it is possible that the love of dancing, so peculiarly strong among women, is the outcome of a nervous organization affording a suitable soil for hysteria."[7] Arthur Symons regarded the Moulin Rouge dancer Jane Avril as the embodiment of the age's "pathological choreography." These resemblances were not coincidental: writers, actresses, cabaret performers, and dancers like Avril attended Charcot's matinees and then worked the Salpêtrière style into their own performances.[8]

Psychoanalysis, famously called "the talking cure," was in another sense an acting cure. Breuer and Freud stressed the importance of reliving and dramatizing feelings while remembering and telling. As they wrote in *Studies on Hysteria*, "Recollection without affect almost invariably produces no result. The psychical process which originally took place must be repeated as vividly as possible." Anna O. called her therapy a "private theatre."[9] Of course, the private theater of psychoanalysis differed from the spectacular follies of Charcot; Freud's office in Vienna, with its many doors for entrances and exits, may have resembled a set from a French farce, but he specialized in intimate dialogue—what theater people call a "two-hander." These subdued but intense exchanges made their mark on theater, through realists who were keeping up with the new psychology and writing about the woman with a past.

By the twentieth century, metaphors of the hysterical woman as actress had become formalized in medical literature. In *Hysterical Personality* (1977), psychiatrists Kay H. Blacker and Joe P. Tupin recommended acting as the ideal career choice for the hysteric, who may find in the theater a way to satisfy "her exhibitionistic needs."[10] Obviously, such advice mingled traditional hostility toward hysterics with a puritanical view of the actress as narcissist rather than artist. The theatrical subtext of hysteria was codified in 1987 when the *Diagnostic and Statistical Manual of Mental Disorders* officially renamed what had previously been "hysterical personality disorder" as "histrionic personality disorder":

> The essential feature of this disorder is a pervasive pattern of excessive emotionality and attention-seeking, beginning by early adulthood. . . . People with this disorder constantly seek or demand reassurance, approval, or praise from others and are uncomfortable in situations in which they are not the center of attention. They characteristically display rapidly shifting and shallow expression of emotions. . . . These people are typically attractive and seductive, often to the point of looking flamboyant and acting inappropriately. They . . . are lively and dramatic and always drawing attention to themselves.

Hedda and Hysteria: Ibsen

For more than a century, Ibsen has provided scripts for psychoanalysts who want to define hysteria. Ibsen's popularity in Germany and Austria reached its height in the 1890s. Freud, who may well have taken the model of the psychoanalytic method from him, was especially influenced by the way his plays built to revelations of the protagonists' secret pasts.[11] For Max Nordau, who had studied with Charcot in Paris, "Ibsenism" was actually a synonym for "hysteria." "Ibsen's feminine clientele," he wrote, "is not composed merely of hysterical and degenerate characters" who enjoyed seeing themselves mirrored on the stage but also of frustrated feminists and unhappily married women.[12]

Literary critics in the twentieth century have regarded Hedda Gabler, with her phallic pistols, her inexplicable horror of pregnancy, and her ability to manipulate, deceive, and seduce, as the paradigmatic hysterical heroine in Ibsen's dramatic canon. Ibsen himself wrote, "It is Hedda's repression, her hysteria that motivates everything she does."[13] Although Hedda plays the role of respectable wife, behind the facade she is seething with jealousy, sexual instability, and violence. She hates her woman's body, her pregnancy, the femininity that enslaves her to conventional roles and puts her at the mercy of obtuse pedants like her husband or sophisticated blackmailers like Judge Brack. Above all, she sees herself as an actress in a romantic melodrama. But the people around Hedda cannot live up to her expectations of noble dramatic behavior. She is a histrionic performer who has believed herself to be the heroine of a tragic epic; she must finally realize that she is living a farce.

In a brilliant 1991 production that originated at the Abbey Theatre in Dublin and then moved to London, the Irish actress Fiona Shaw and the English director Deborah Warner decided to foreground the play's hysterical subtexts, in a production influenced by feminist interpretations of hysteria as the body language of powerlessness. The set was a stylized barren interior rather than the overstuffed drawing room of Scandinavian realism. Warner and Shaw invented a wordless prologue: Hedda has an anxiety attack in the house at night before we ever see her with her husband. Charles Spenser wrote in the *Daily Telegraph*, "These first few minutes set the tone. Fiona Shaw's Hedda is no suburban Lady Macbeth, no vengeful maiden, but a woman on the verge of a nervous breakdown. There is a hint of hysteria in her every utterance, her voice wavering precariously between tears and laughter, the words tumbling out in ugly cascades. She wears a smile like a mask, as if it were the last token of her sanity, and she sniffs and grunts like a caged animal in the prison of her marital home."[14] John Peter in the *Sunday Times* commented on the way Shaw constantly moves furniture around, "turning the large drawing room into an arena for complete freedom of movement. This creates an emptiness which vibrates with a sense of futile, misused power."[15] Hedda's repressed hysteria had broken loose from its bonds.

In a discussion at the National Theatre in August 1993, Fiona Shaw explained that her performance of Hedda was partly based on her own grandmother, who "used to get hysteria when she was strapped into these fantastic corsets." Hedda's reaction to her environment mirrored the repressive upbringing and lives of Irish women of an older generation. In Shaw's view, while the Heddas of Glenda Jackson and Janet Suzman were "valid for that time," she and Warner had been "ruthlessly true to the text" and had found the rhythm of the play "through rigorous exercise and rigorous thought": she felt certain that "Ibsen would have approved their interpretation of Hedda as "someone who has no courage," who has "come to this dry edge" of loneliness and desperation.[16] As Shaw commented during a symposium on women and theater, "The reason we put in the short tableau scene at the beginning . . . was that I wanted something before the play started, partly to avoid the entrance of Hedda Gabler, because historically that's so associated with . . . looking suitably evil."[17]

Some reviewers found Hedda's performance "eye-opening" and admired the "stern feminist interpretation which turns Hedda into a victim of a stifling patriarchal society," but others found it "far too hysterical," reminding them of "Virginia Woolf on a particularly bad day." Milton Shulman wrote in the *Evening Standard* that Fiona Shaw is "an incurable psychotic case with a straitjacket waiting in her wardrobe." Yet, as Christopher Edwards wrote in *The Spectator*, Shaw's Hedda was supremely histrionic: "She is always striking mock-melodramatic theatrical poses, as if poking fun at her own absurd lot."[18]

Salome: The Movement Cure

Since its earliest productions, Oscar Wilde's *Salome* (1893) has also been associated with hysteria. Wilde admired Ibsen's Hedda, and Ibsen's English translator William Archer pointed out that Salome is "an oriental Hedda Gabler."[19] Productions of Wilde's play and the Strauss opera based on it have emphasized their hysterical elements, and critics have interpreted both play and opera in line with the dominant psychological theories of the day, from lesbianism to nymphomania to fetishism to sexual abuse. In 1964, in the wake of Nabokov's *Lolita,* William Mann called Salome "a hysterical nymphet" looking for a father during an adolescent crisis.[20] In 1988, Sander Gilman described Salome as a hysteric whose neurosis was the result of childhood abuse. "The symptom, Salome's sadism—manifested by her desire to possess a fetish, the severed head of a man who has rejected her—had its origin in the trauma of her attempted seduction by her stepfather, Herod. . . . A simple case for the master solver of cases of hysteria, Sigmund Freud, Salome suffers from memories, memories acted out for the audience in Herod's attempts to seduce her. This was certainly not Herod's first attempt, as the text documents. Is Salome then perverted because she is a victim who in turn victimizes? Is she perverted because she is presented as mentally ill, as a hysteric, where the signs, symptoms, and etiology are clearly present for the audience to see?"[21]

The legend of Salome and her dance of the seven veils has resonance as a cinematic metaphor of the multilayered female psyche. In the British film *The Seventh Veil* (1945), a psychiatrist explains that hypnosis will help a hysterical woman patient understand herself: "The human mind is like Salome—hidden by a series of veils . . . five minutes under narcosis and down comes the seventh veil."[22] Hollywood went from Wilde to Wilder in *Sunset Boulevard* (1950), which satirized the hysteria of Norma Desmond, an aging film star obsessed with playing Salome. In Andrew Lloyd Webber's 1990 musical version, Salome is Norma's alter ago, the histrionic personality unable to survive without the adoration of an audience:

> Salome, what a woman, what a part!
> Innocent body and a sinful heart,
> Inflaming Herod's lust,
> But secretly loving a holy man,
> No one could play her like I can![23]

Salome plays another role in the history of hysteria: Charcot called some of his hysterics' exhibitions choreas because they resembled dance, and the story of Salome has inspired many choreographers and dancers. Though the treatment for neurasthenia sentenced women to immobility, late nineteenth-century pioneers of modern dance, such as Loie Fuller and Maude Allen, composed dances based on Salome that mimed hypnosis and incorporated hysterical gesture and electricity to produce a metaphorical "movement cure"; these ballets, argues dance historian Felicia McCarren, allowed "the dancer the very freedom of movement, the mobile subjectivity, that in other contexts develops as malady."[24]

Staging Hysteria Today

Several women artists and directors have recently attempted to reappropriate the histrionic, aesthetic, and choreographic elements of hysteria. Charcot's clinic has been the subject of several revisionary feminist works. Mary Kelley has used his photographs of Augustine in an art installation called "Corpus," which translates the iconography of hysteria into contemporary fashion images, such as the black leather jacket for "menace." One of the most successful feminist plays about hysteria, *Augustine or Big Hysteria* by the English director Anna Furse, takes the poetic license of bringing Augustine, Charcot, and Freud together in the asylum: Freud begins to *listen* to hysterics and interpret their gestures as a private body theater of the unconscious. This play was produced in London by the Paines Plough repertory group, and toured throughout Europe.

Dr. Charcot's Hysteria Shows, produced in Hartford and New York in 1989, is a theater and dance performance written by Dianne Hunter, who teaches at Trinity College in Hartford, Connecticut, and has written an influential essay on Anna O. Working with colleagues in the dance department, Hunter analyzed the Salpêtrière artist Paul Richer's sketches of the sequence of gestures in *grande hystérie* as if they were choreographic notation. "As a basis for our work," she explained, "we assumed that Salpêtrière hysteria was a kind of angry, coquettish, self-repressed dance; that this dance was dominated by an attractive male figure; that this figure objectified what he saw and reserved to himself the privilege of naming it; and that he took great satisfaction in displaying his hypnotic magnetism, power to domi-nate, emotional distance and verbal fluency."[25] In short, Charcot is a nineteenth-century psychiatric Balanchine. In the *Hysteria Shows*, didactic speeches by nineteenth-century feminists like Florence Nightingale and dance scenarios based on the Richer drawings alter-nate with or overlap ironic recreations of the Salpêtrière theater. The performance ends with a monologue by a modern Cassandra who speaks to an image of Jacques Lacan projected over Charcot's emp-ty chair.

But despite its feminist framing, *Hysteria Shows* did not entirely suc-ceed. The satisfactions of watching the performance were offset by the anxieties of colluding in its images. Mady Schutzman's review in the journal *Women and Performance* highlighted the problems inherent in the theatrical representation of hysteria, especially the contrast between men and women, as actors and as spectators: "To observe on the one hand the convulsive contortions, animalistic sexuality, and innocent rage of the hysterics, and, on the other hand, . . . the note-taking and balletic refinement of the black-tuxedoed, white-aproned, psychic surgeons, is to participate within a painfully self-denigrating reality. . . . Watching these primitive female grotesques amidst the civ-ilized male aesthetes incites . . . two antagonistic sensations in the female spectator: first, a disturbing personal/historical recall of hyster-ical objectification that triggers a re-traumatization filled with inexpressible anger, terror, fear, and depression. . . . Second, the internalized stance of the male gazer that accompanies, perhaps propagates, the very despair and rage that hysteria is made of."[26]

The Acting Cure

Feminist and commercial theater has also dramatized Freud's treatment of hysteria. Most of these plays are hostile to him: they present hysterical women deliberately appropriating the histrionic in an acting cure that displaces the therapist as director of women's emotional theater. Among the earliest and most influential theater pieces was Hélène Cixous's *Portrait de Dora*, presented in 1976 at the Théâtre d'honneur in Paris under the direction of Simone Benmussa; Marguerite Duras directed filmed sequences within the play. Cixous wrote *Portrait de Dora* in the "incoherent" style of hysteria, as a collage of "events, memories, fantasies and dreams." This lyrical drama attempts to restore Dora's words and thoughts to the Freudian script and to present both femininity and hysteria as valid ways "of thinking, feeling, and acting."[27] In an effort to speak for the silenced Dora, Cixous uses doubled characters, off-stage voices, and simultaneous or overlapping speeches.[28]

By contrast, Canadian Kim Morrissey's *Dora: A Case of Hysteria* (1994) presents Freud as an unreliable narrator, very much influenced by Ibsen—he often says "Nora" when he means "Dora"—and uses the language of the case study itself, but with satiric intent. When he presents Dora with his explanation of her hysterical symptoms, she tells him off before she slams the door on him: "Herr Freud, I loathe you. You are like a fetid lump of cheese; you leave your trail of filth and sex and slime like a great snotty slug, across everything you touch. I hate you." Her exit is marked by an "Ibsenite sound of door closing."[29] These are the cliches of the Dora case for our fin de siècle.

Nicholas Wright's *Mrs. Klein* and Terry Johnson's *Hysteria* imagine psychoanalysis in the context of Hampstead houses and English gardens; they adapt hysteria to the modes of English theater from farce to drawing room comedy. Melanie Klein arrived in London in 1926 to analyze the children of Ernest Jones. She rented flats in Gloucester Place, Notting Hill, and finally St. Johns Wood, in a house designed by Freud's architect son, Ernst. But Klein's own version of child analysis soon alienated the Freudians. Wright's play is set in 1934, shortly after Klein's son Hans died in a climbing accident near Budapest. It brilliantly dramatizes the three-way power struggle among Klein, her analyst daughter Melitta, and the German refugee analyst Paula Heimann, who became Klein's disciple and surrogate daughter. When *Mrs. Klein* was first produced in London in August 1988, audiences at the Cottesloe Theatre laughed appreciatively at the play's Freudian in-jokes; reviews were almost universally enthusiastic, although many of them expressed amazement that a play about a psychoanalyst—a *Jewish* psychoanalyst—a WOMAN psychoanalyst—could yield such intellectu-ally stimulating and emotionally engaging theater.[30]

By far the most ambitious, ingenious, and entertaining of these 1990s plays is Terry Johnson's *Hysteria*, first presented in London at the Royal Court in 1993. The play is set in Hampstead in 1939, where a dying Freud, in exile from the Nazis, is writing *Moses and Monotheism*, his controversial study of the origins of Judaism. The morphine he takes for the pain of terminal cancer causes Freud to hallucinate. He encounters real and conflated characters from his life—his physician, the Judaic scholar Abraham Yahudah, the surrealist Salvador Dali, and the vengeful daughter of one of his hysterical patients. Freud feels guilty about relatives left behind in Vienna, and he broods about the approach of death. Using the techniques of classic British farce and the imagery of surrealism, Johnson puts Freud's theories of hysteria on trial in a wild black comedy, and the play puts the anxious, traumatized contents of his unconscious on stage. Johnson takes the position that Freud abandoned the seduction theory of hysteria to avoid offending his prosperous Viennese clients and confronting his suspicions that his own father may have molested one of his sisters.

Johnson's *Dead Funny* (1994) also plays with the idea of laughter and joking as a hysterical symptom in British men. A group of dysfunc-tional men have organized a club dedicated to the great British come-dians, including Sid James and Benny Hill, whose routines they know by heart and imitate at the drop of a hat. The men use jokes and stand-up monologues as rituals to stave off responsibilities to women, recog-nitions of failure, and troubling emotions. Farce becomes tragedy, in a device central to contemporary British theater, as in Trevor Griffiths's *Comedians* or the increasingly dark plays of Alan Ayckbourn. The hys-terical laughter of the men, Johnson commented in an interview, was "the breaking of some kind of mental block," one "triggered much more easily in men who as a sex are more fucked-up, up-tight, and defended in their own self-image."[31]

Why so many plays now about Freud, hysteria, and the genealogy of psychoanalysis? Playwrights understand that the gap between theory and therapist is inherently dramatic. Dramatizing the psychoanalyst's hysteria, reducing his theories to performance or farce, is another way of fending off the specter of the unconscious.

Screening Hysteria

Movies, television, video, and the Internet have increasingly exploited and exported hysteria's links with the histrionic. Charcot was certainly not the last to take advantage of the photogenic appeal of the hysteric. One film critic, Lizzie Francke in *The Guardian*, writes, "There is a tendency in films about female madness to indulge in the spectacle of . . . disintegration as if there were something inherently cinematic about the woman hysteric."[32] Hélène Cixous and Catherine Clément have pointed out that cinema was invented in the 1890s, at the time the hysterical woman became a cultural icon. They see "the institutionalization of hysteria" in "the expressive, expressionistic women of the silent films, their mouths open wide in unformulated cries, which florid subtitles repeat."[33]

The spectacle of hysteria is depicted in Jane Campion's Oscar-winning film *The Piano* (1993). The heroine, Ada, has been mysteriously mute since the age of six: "No one knows why, not even me." Now a woman with a young daughter, she arrives on a remote New Zealand island to be married to a planter. Instead of speech, Ada relies for self-expression on the passionate piano music she plays and on an idiosyncratic sign language she uses to communicate with her daughter, Flora. In other words, music is her sexual language; signs are her maternal language. Through their gestures and signals, as if they were wild creatures, mother and daughter are uncannily allied in the film's cinematography to the island's wild tropical forest.

Campion evidently intends Ada's muteness to be read as protest against a patriarchy represented by the father who has sold her into marriage and the husband who tries to break her will. (One feminist reading might argue that Ada is probably a victim of childhood sexual abuse.) Ada's sexual history is bound up with the piano, and when her husband, Stewart, refuses to have it moved from the beach to their house, she cannot feel, in the film's terms, "affectionate" to him. Instead, the illiterate steward Baines, who has a hysterical body language of his own made up of the tattooed signs of Maori culture, arranges to move the piano to his hut and sells it back to her, key by key, in exchange for sexual favors. He is giving her the keys to her own story, much as Freud claimed to own the keys that could unlock Dora's case.

While Ada's husband makes every effort, even chopping off her finger—a symbolic castration?—to silence her sexual and psychic expression, Baines allows her to make her own sexual choices. In so doing, he cures her "hysteria" and allows her to return to the normal, speaking world. At first she voluntarily cuts out a key from the piano to send him a message; later she decides that the piano must be jettisoned entirely; finally, she is regaining her voice. However, Ada's musical genius is bound up with her hysterical repression. When she becomes normal, she also becomes ordinary and domestic, speaking her words beneath a veil. *The Piano* seems to say that the hysteric within women is creative, for dutiful daughters can only give piano lessons.

Modern cinematic mythologies like *The Piano* promote a romantic view of female hysteria and define domestic normality as taming and sacrifice. But the silent or mute woman is also a convenient figure of helplessness and passivity. We need to recognize the risks of making her a heroine.

Screening Male Hysteria

Film theorists have applied the adjective "hysterical" to movie heroes from Buster Keaton, Jerry Lewis, and Pee Wee Herman to Jeremy Irons and Clint Eastwood.[34] Sometimes, they argue, these actors are comedians using a particularly expressive body language; sometimes they represent male bodies that are stoic, repressed, and subjected to punishment. According to Barbara Creed, "The representation of male hysteria in Hollywood cinema has taken various forms and differs from genre to genre. In the woman's film . . . and the suspense thriller, male hysteria is represented in terms of a mental problem, such as a loss of memory. . . . The representation of male hysteria as arising from a disturbance of gender occurs most frequently in comedy; hysteria is displayed not only in scenes of cross-dressing, but also in the breakneck speed of these films."[35] A comic actor like Robin Williams is allowed to be over-the-top emotional, volatile, and mobile; in *Mrs. Doubtfire*, he can also dress like a woman.

Lynne Kirby relates male hysteria to early cinema's central metaphor of the train. Reminding us that male hysteria first drew serious medical attention in the context of the railway accident, she argues that railway-assisted "nineteenth-century mechanization . . . made of its traumatized victims something like female hysterics." In the actor responding to an oncoming train, Kirby sees an image of a "technological seduction fantasy—imagining oneself aggressed, raped, seduced and destroyed by the train, hysteria as a fantasy of the *corps morcelé*, the regression to infantile scenarios of . . . mutilated body parts, mechanically constituted as such." Practically speaking, or clinically speaking, such a fantasy might produce a patient like Robert Conolly. In cinematic terms, "The assaulted spectator is the hysterical spectator. The fantasies of being run over and assaulted, penetrated, produce a certain pleasure of pain—beyond the pleasure principle and in the realm of repetition compulsion—which is as much about will-to-submission, to loss of mastery, as it is about will to mastery/control."[36]

In *Laughing Hysterically: American Screen Comedy of the 1950s* (1994), Ed Sikov compares 1950s Hollywood comedies, with their sexually uncertain and manic heroes, to the political witch-hunts and social hysterias, especially over homosexuality, of the McCarthy era. "When we look back at the 1950s," writes Sikov, "we see a culture of extreme neurosis and paranoia, an age that was defined by inner turmoil and external threat, but that nonetheless had the relaxing benefit of a full-fledged breakdown." The Hollywood symbols of these breakdowns were the conversion hysterias and anxiety hysterias in the films of Jerry Lewis ("a jester in a court of sexual panic . . . the hysterical manifestation of his culture's failed repression") and the overwrought melodramas of Douglas Sirk.[37]

Dracula Lite: Crisis and Conspiracy

One of the best-known hysterical heroes in contemporary popular culture is Batman, an Americanized version of Dracula who made his 1939 debut in the comic book *Detective*. Batman is a benign prince of darkness transported to Gotham City, where he lives in Depression-fantasy splendor by day as billionaire philanthropist Bruce Wayne and by night battles an endless series of mutant and schizoid criminals. In the latest Hollywood installment, *Batman Forever* (1995), Bela Lugosi's caped and campy 1931 performance as Dracula provides some of the gothic imagery that surrounds Batman and his tormented villains. In the German "Nosferatu" versions of the Dracula story, the courageous young solicitor Jonathan Harker, who pursues the vampire, gradually turns into him; Batman too seems to generate obsessive transferential attachments among his enemies, while his own psychic divisions are mirrored and projected onto them like the Batsignal that summons him into the night. Despite his wealth, Bruce Wayne is a loner, a guy "with a thing for bats," unable to find love or peace, compulsively driven to search for other children of the night.

In *Batman Forever*, producer Tim Burton and director Joel Schumacher picked up on contemporary trends to throw a crew of male hysterics on the screen: Harvey Dent/Two-Face, Ed Nygma/ The Riddler, and Dick Grayson/Robin, a circus brat driven by revenge because his family has been gunned down by Two-Face. All three of these split personalities are fixated on Batman, with an unrequited love that finds an outlet in imitation, stalking, and dreams of violent consummation. Moreover, as Peter David's novelization of *Batman Forever* makes clear, all these male characters have been shaped by childhood traumas, from domineering dads to hinted sexual abuse.

As always, the plot of the film revolves around the villains' effort to destroy Batman and take over Gotham City, not to mention the world, but this time out, Batman is having a '90s-style identity crisis, with nightmares about his parents' death and waking flashbacks of a childhood trauma at their funeral. Enter Nicole Kidman as Dr. Meridian, who specializes in treating multiple personalities and recovering repressed memories. The film comes close to revealing the secret of Batman's hysteria but holds back at the end; maybe they're saving stuff like hypnosis, memory drugs, and satanic ritual abuse for *Batman IV*.

In most respects, however, *Batman Forever* is in tune with American millenarian paranoia. The authorities are corrupt or impotent; vast conspiracies of a New World Order take place behind the closed doors of Wall Street and in television studios, where "GNN" rules the airwaves; citizens are at the mercy of Manichean forces—an uneven clash in which the villains are large, exciting, and purposeful and the heroes are flawed, hysterical, and self-questioning. In the 1990s, the cinema of hysteria has evolved from theories of theatricality to theories of conspiracy. Individual trauma has given way to social disorder. As in Salem three centuries ago, the culture has prepared us for hysterical epidemics. And if we need them, they will come.

PART THREE

Epidemics

8

Chronic Fatigue Syndrome

In 1993, Jo Gerzimbke, a young English woman rendered almost helpless by chronic fatigue syndrome, was miraculously cured by a faith healer. After a year of progressive deterioration, during which she couldn't walk, go to work, or even brush her teeth, Jo heard about the healing powers of a man called Reverend Bill Isaacs-Sodeye. Her fiancé, Nick, carried her to the car and they drove to Reverend Bill's home in Impington, Cambridgeshire. "Ask Jesus to forgive your sins," he told her, and she thought of "swearing, sleeping with people, and lying." "Jesus loves you," said Reverend Bill. "Get up and do aerobics." Jo immediately did several jumping jacks and now cycles three miles to work each day. "I used to be insecure," she told a sympathetic reporter from *The Independent*. "I was always anxious, but I feel whole now for the first time in my life."[1]

But there was no faith healer around to help an entire family with chronic fatigue in Dundee, Scotland. Since 1989, Eiledh Hewitt and three of her children have become virtually housebound. "They may read for half an hour or so until they get tired; or listen to music that would be barely audible to most people—their ears are particularly sensitive." The children spend much of their time playing with an enormous doll's house. "From attics to cellar, they have recreated every detail of a Victorian mansion in perfect miniature—and now they are living out their lives through those of the doll house family."

All the Hewitts, including the unaffected father and the eldest son, who was away at college, deny the possibility of psychological causes. "I have a total belief that this isn't a mental thing," the father told journalist Liz Hunt. "I know what Eiledh is like. I trust her completely." Psychological conflicts, a "mental thing," would be a betrayal of trust, a breach in the marital contract; debilitating illness must be accepted. Hunt notes that mother and children "appear curiously unconcerned about their future—or lack of it. They talk about being ill, but they do not talk about getting well." "I'm not into the future at all," says one of the children. "I sometimes think that it is just as well that the rest of the family got ill too, because at least they understand."[2]

The Hewitt family's story cries out for Ibsen, but such dramatic hystories of illness have helped chronic fatigue syndrome, according to *Newsweek*, become the "malaise of the Eighties."[3] Fatigue in itself is a standard complaint in doctors' offices; indeed, according to Harvard Medical School professor Anthony L. Komaroff, it accounts for ten to fifteen million office visits a year in the U.S. In England, writes Dr. Luisa Dillner, "tired all the time" or TATT, is "the medical syndrome of the '90s, and the second commonest cause for a trip to the GP."[4] But in the 1980s, this perennial symptom took on new meanings. Arthur Kleinman and Stephen Straus speculate that both the fast-track lifestyles promoted in the 1980s and the AIDS panic contributed to the media's interest in a new epidemic of fatigue: "In our times, the metaphor of being exhausted by the multiple, competing demands of work, family and play is a badge of success and achievement, a lifestyle that demonstrates that one has prestige, position, and power. Clearly, it is not entirely coincidence that CFS has achieved prominence in the media in the era of AIDS, with its recrudescence of interest in viruses and immunology, including psychoneuroimmunological relationships."[5]

No one really knows how many cases of chronic fatigue there have been around the world, but while medical accounts of CFS describe it in a social context, patients' metaphors cast it as a force of nature, an uncontrollable catastrophe. "Unexpected as a tornado and almost as devastating," according to *Hope and Help for Chronic Fatigue Syndrome*, the official American handbook of the patient network, "CFS rips apart the lives of its victims, often incapacitating them in the prime of life while shattering personal relationships and destroying careers. The illness is causing alarm within the scientific community and hardship and heartbreak among the afflicted."[6]

I do not disparage the suffering of patients with CFS. Their symptoms are genuine, whether psychologically or organically caused, or both. Indeed, as Harvard Medical School researcher Dr. Anthony Komaroff suggests, CFS "may become a paradigmatic illness that leads us away from being trapped by the rigidity of the conventional bio-medical model and leads us toward a fuller understanding of suffer-ing."[7] Some CFS patients continue to go about their routines, but many others spend their time in bed, become progressively weaker, and give up work and school. The syndrome is a reality that undoubt-edly has a devastating effect on their lives, marriages, and families. Chronic fatigue syndrome has interrupted people's careers and destroyed their dreams.

As Dr. Simon Wessely, a London historian of psychiatry who has written extensively on CFS and mass hysteria, wisely observes, "Worrying about whether or not CFS exists . . . is hardly the issue. It exists in the real world. . . . What lies behind CFS is neither a virus, nor psychiatry, but our idea of what constitutes a real illness, what doesn't, and what we do to make something real."[8] In other words, patients with chronic fatigue live in a culture that still looks down on psy-chogenic illness, that does not recognize or respect its reality. The self-esteem of the patient depends on having the physiological nature of the illness accepted. The culture forces people to deny the psycholog-ical, circumstantial, or emotional sources of their symptoms and to insist that they must be biological and beyond their control in order for them to view themselves as legitimately ill and entitled to the priv-ileges of the sick role. Arthur Kleinman and Stephen Straus, editors of a symposium on CFS, conclude: "In much of biomedicine, only a tan-gible or laboratory abnormality justifies the imprimatur of a 'real' dis-ease. . . . Patients sense this . . . so they are driven to find a practitioner who would document their illness."[9]

The media history of chronic fatigue, however, does not attempt to educate readers and to change the cultural climate so that people bet-ter understand how much power emotions have over the body. Instead the CFS hystory is incorporating the conspiracy theories of fin-de-siècle American society. Until recently, frustrated CFS sufferers blamed the medical establishment for ignorance or inertia. Now Hillary Johnson, an American journalist, has upped the ante. In 1996 Johnson merged rumors, anxieties, theories, and suspicions in *Osler's Web: Inside the Laby-rinth of the Chronic Fatigue Syndrome Epidemic.* The book likened gov-ernment attitudes toward chronic fatigue to those during the early stages of the AIDS epidemic and charged that many doctors and gov-ernment officials had refused to take CFS seriously. At the same time,

Osler's Web gave the most complete and precise account of the history of CFS. With innuendo, inflammatory rhetoric, and a detailed history of medical investigations and dead ends, Johnson brought chronic fatigue into the spectrum of epidemic conspiracies.[10] In a full-page *New York Times Book Review* ad, Johnson's publisher, Crown, announced: "This book reveals that a devastating infectious disease is reaching epidemic proportions while government researchers ignore the evidence and the shocking statistics."[11]

Alarming statements like that one, filled with loose terminology, add to the public's confusion. We need to remember that chronic fatigue is recognized as a *syndrome*, not a disease, much less an infectious disease. A *syndrome*, as Johnson herself writes, "is a collection of uniquely presented symptoms and physical signs for which a cause has yet to be found." A *disease* is "a manifestation of illness for which medicine has an explanation—for example, the identity of the bacterium—as well as a scientifically sound explanation of the patho-physiology."[12] Scientists eventually identify some symptom clusters as diseases, such as acquired immunodeficiency syndrome, now known as HIV infection. AIDS may have started as a syndrome with an unknown cause, but its symptoms were clearly observable and measurable in scientific terms. People with AIDS developed skin lesions, pneumonia, dementia; inevitably they died.

The syndrome of chronic fatigue is very different from that of AIDS. Symptoms are largely subjective; patients feel tired, achy, and ill but, apart from sporadic low-grade fevers or swollen lymph nodes, have no objective clinical signs of disease. Neurological, cardiovascular, and endocrinological tests show no consistent abnormalities. Sometimes the syndrome follows a viral illness, but the viruses are quite varied, and usually they do not produce chronic fatigue. Symptoms come and go but linger for months, even years. Although many say they never recover from CFS, no one has died from it. Johnson frequently describes chronic fatigue patients as "desperately ill," but she refers to the way patients feel and the extent of changes in their habits and responsibilities rather than to any life-threatening physical signs. In addition, the symptom of fatigue can neither be scientifically measured nor scientifically disproved. If I say I feel very tired, is there any way to prove I'm wrong?

Another difficulty in pinning down chronic fatigue is the way the symptoms mutate. "What is really so extraordinary is that the symptoms constantly change," explained a thirty-two-year-old woman from Georgia. "I'll go through one month of intense body pains and that will be my main problem. The next month it is the intense headaches that overwhelm me. And the month after that I'll feel physically better but I'll be so panic-stricken that I just want to curl up under the covers and hide."[13]

From American Nervousness to Epidemic Fatigue: How It Began

How did it all start? In 1984, some patients at the Nevada clinic of Paul Cheney and Dan Peterson began turning up with odd symptoms—dizziness, rashes, abdominal pain, sore throats, headaches, diarrhea, rapid heartbeat, shortness of breath, blurred vision, aching joints, light sensitivity, ringing in their ears, weight fluctuations, loss of libido, loss of sensation in their fingertips, facial numbness, swelling, sensitivity to alcohol, cold sores, overall weakness, and allergic reactions to foods. Several complained that they were losing their hair. Incline Village, where Cheney and Peterson practiced, was a town of 6,000 near Lake Tahoe, with many well-off retirees in their forties or fifties. By February 1985, Cheney and Peterson had identified twenty cases of the mysterious illness. By June, the number was over ninety. By the time they notified the Centers for Disease Control in July, it had topped one hundred and twenty.[14] By late November, when it came to an end, the number had reached one hundred and sixty. Jon Kaplan, who works at the Centers for Disease Control in Atlanta, and was a member of the team that investigated the outbreak, was struck by the huge range of symptoms: "It wasn't like an epidemic of shigella [dysentery], where everybody comes in and they've got exactly the same thing. These people were coming in with very different stories. It wasn't as if everybody had fatigue, sore throat, and a cough. This patient might have fatigue, sore throat, and itchy feet and scratchy legs. And another patient might have fatigue that's only half as much, and a headache, and can't fall asleep. All different things. And yet they were coming in and saying they had the same disease."[15]

The epidemic in Incline Village was not unique. In fact, doctors had seen similar symptom clusters as far back as the neurasthenia, American nervousness, or Nervous Exhaustion epidemic of the nineteenth century. In many respects, chronic fatigue is a new form of "effort syndrome," a disorder with a long history; Simon Wessely calls it "new wine in old bottles."[16] In the journal *Psychological Medicine*, Wessely argues that neurasthenia, chronic fatigue syndrome, and "postviral fatigue syndrome" share numerous ailments, symptoms, and signs. George M. Beard, the American neurologist who wrote the major texts *Nervous Exhaustion* (1880) and *American Nervousness* (1881), listed over seventy possible symptoms, especially extreme physical fatigue and mental exhaustion. In the *Doctor's Guide to Chronic Fatigue Syndrome* (1993), David S. Bell lists forty-three. Like CFS, neurasthenia was most commonly seen among the upper social classes; Beard suggested that it came from the stresses and pace of urban American life in the 1880s and the stimulation of sensational newspapers, the steam engine, and the telegraph. He advised both men and women with the disorder to take a break from the pressures of their work and domestic lives.

In the early years of this century, medical researchers investigated a "fatigue toxin," or viral cause, for neurasthenia, without success. When they could find no organic explanation for the symptoms, doctors sought psychological causes, especially in depression. In 1909, the *British Medical Journal* editorialized that neurasthenia was an imaginary disorder that "breeds the almost universal anxiety about health which is one of the signs of the times. This leads to a corresponding prevalence of quackery of every kind."[17] Wessely analyzes the rapid decline in diagnoses of neurasthenia during the early decades of this century. Medical skeptics redefined it as a psychological rather than neurological disorder. Freud blamed neurasthenia on excessive masturbation and nocturnal emission; he wrote that the syndrome included headaches, spinal irritation, indigestion, flatulence, and constipation. By 1930, in a *Lancet* article called "The dumping ground of neuralgic," the English neurologist Falret Buzzard maintained that "the label of neuralgic is often in order to evade a duty—the duty imposed on us to declare a correct diagnosis." By 1970, Wessely reports, from being "one of the most frequently diagnosed conditions in medical practice," neurasthenia had virtually disappeared.[18]

To be sure, there were scattered outbreaks of mysterious neurasthenic symptoms. In July 1955 at the Royal Free Hospital, over two hundred people from North London were admitted with symptoms of exhaustion, headache, nausea, and muscle aches. In the hospital, some later developed dizziness, blurred vision, and extreme muscle weakness. During the two weeks after the outbreak, seventy doctors and nurses at the hospital were also taken ill, and the hospital had to close for two months. Dr. Melvyn Ramsay, a physician at the hospital, called the outbreak a new clinical entity. No cause has ever been found, despite extensive tests. In 1970 two psychiatrists writing in the

British Medical Journal concluded that it was mass hysteria, although CFS advocates bitterly dispute this allegation.

But in the fast-track 1980s, a century after George Beard had first identified neurasthenia, chronic fatigue symptoms reappeared. In 1984, following the identification of the Epstein-Barr virus, one of the herpes viruses, and its popularization by the press, patients with flulike symptoms—sore throat, fatigue, memory loss, muscle aches, headaches, insomnia—began making appointments with doctors and at clinics around the United States. Stephen Straus, a medical virologist at the National Institutes of Health in Bethesda, Maryland, studied twenty-three cases from eleven states and wrote them up for the *Annals of Internal Medicine* in January 1985. In the same issue, a companion study by research clinician James Jones suggested that the disease might be related to the Epstein-Barr virus. Epstein-Barr virus was soon to become a virtual fad in fast-track, high-stress Hollywood. In *New York* magazine, Steve Pond warned that "a mysterious epidemic is sweeping Hollywood. Screenwriters, actors, producers, and studio executives alike are coming down with Epstein-Barr, a nonfatal viral syndrome that causes deep fatigue and has no known cure." Southern California clinics for the treatment of Epstein-Barr sprang up, offering exercise, acupuncture, biofeedback, and vitamins.[19] Peterson and Cheney tested their Nevada patients for EBV and found that almost 75 percent had raised antibodies, but these findings proved nothing since nearly 90 percent of all adults over thirty have developed antibodies to EBV from childhood exposure.

Many of these early patients were young professionals—leading to the nickname "Yuppie Flu"; they also included athletes, runners, and frequent travelers, such as an airline pilot and touring musicians. Perhaps, doctors speculated, the illness was caused by overexertion. Scientists tested patients for mononucleosis, herpes, and environmental poisons; but results could not be verified. As cases showed up in Europe as well, physicians in several countries proposed local explanations, as Simon Wessely observes: "In France, it can be due to educational practice; in Scandinavia, leakage from dental amalgam . . . in the United States, viral agents remain very popular."[20] These explanations reflected national medical cultures and obsessions.

Meanwhile, in Incline Village, epidemiologists Jon Kaplan and Gary Holmes of the Centers for Disease Control arrived in September 1985 to carry out an investigation of Peterson and Cheney's outbreak. They examined about ten patients—fewer than Peterson and Cheney

wished—and interviewed over a hundred more; primarily they studied the records and charts, and devised a control study on the basis of
the central symptom of fatigue. Out of the clinicians' roster of over one
hundred and fifty cases they winnowed the number to fifteen with
longterm fatigue and no explanatory medical conditions. Thirteen of
the group were women, and all the patients were white. Blood from
these patients was tested for EBV antibodies, and compared to blood
from a control group in the community.

Kaplan was struck by the affluence of Incline Village, and skeptical
about the symptoms: "There definitely seemed to be some people
who had some kind of emotional overlay," he told Hillary Johnson.
"They had some symptoms, and they wanted to make the most of
them and were looking for some credibility. And all of a sudden here
come these two doctors who not only listen to them but give them
credibility. They give a label to their disease. They do a test and say,
'You've got this.' And the doctors like doing it, and the patients like
hearing it. And so it's a collusion."

The media soon picked up the story. On October 11, 1985, soon
after the team had returned to Atlanta, the *Sacramento Bee* published an
article titled "Mysterious Sickness Plagues North Tahoe." The story
went out over the Associated Press national wire, and TV reporters,
who suspected that the malady might be AIDS, descended on the town.
The publicity horrified the community, and a hasty press conference
organized by Cheney and Peterson on October 15 made matters
worse. However bad for Nevada tourism, the publicity alerted many
Americans to the possibility of a new disease. Within days, Johnson
reports, "emotional pleas for help poured in . . . from as far away as
Florida, New York, and Canada. For those who had been suffering in
isolation, particularly those who had been written off by their doctors
and families as hypochondriacs or malingerers or lunatics, news of the
Nevada outbreak crystallized their problem." The number of new cases
in Incline had dwindled, but Cheney and Peterson did not lack
patients: "Like pilgrims journeying to Lourdes, ailing patients from
every state were flying to Reno." By late November they hypothesized
that a mysterious contagion—"Agent X"—was targeting the human
immune system and causing neurological complications. They suspected it might be a retrovirus.

On May 30, 1986, the Centers for Disease Control issued its first
public report about the Incline Village epidemic—a brief monograph
by Holmes and Kaplan in the *Morbidity and Mortality Weekly Report*—

which concluded that chronic Epstein-Barr virus could not be proven to be the cause. Cheney and Peterson were indignant; and CFS advocates like Hillary Johnson view the report as a turning point in the battle among patients, doctors, epidemiologists, and the government. The CDC's "equivocation," writes Johnson, "served to keep panic at bay but it also isolated sufferers in a Kafkaesque universe where what they knew to be real was reported by the authorities to be patently false and where their testimony carried no weight at all."[21] Into the space left by the breach between individuals and the official statement came patient self-help groups, which rapidly enrolled thousands of members.

The press also continued to generate interest in chronic fatigue. In 1987, Johnson published a widely-read story in *Rolling Stone* entitled "Journey into Fear: The Growing Nightmare of Epstein-Barr Virus." In the story, she told how she had been incapacitated by an "enigmatic disease" that left her "unable to lift my toothbrush or remember my phone number." When her own doctors could find nothing wrong, Johnson read about the "epidemic" at Cheney and Peterson's clinic, and brought her blood reports to a doctor who told her that she had the Lake Tahoe disease.[22]

In 1988, after several years of fruitless investigation, the Centers for Disease Control classified chronic fatigue as a syndrome. To qualify for the CFS diagnosis, the CDC announced, a case had to fulfill two major criteria: persistent and debilitating fatigue of at least six months' duration, with at least 50 percent reduction of normal activity; and the elimination of other clinical conditions, including cancer, AIDS, multiple sclerosis, or chronic psychiatric disorder. In addition, patients had to report at least six of eleven symptoms: mild fever, sore throat, painful lymph nodes, muscle weakness, excessive fatigue after normal exercise, headaches, joint pain, forgetfulness, sleep disturbances, and rapid onset of these symptoms. Finally, a physician had to confirm at least two instances, a month or more apart, of low-grade fever, inflammation of the throat, mucous membranes, or upper respiratory tract, and palpable or tender lymph nodes. By December 1994, these guidelines had been modified and simplified; now patients had to meet just four criteria of persistent symptoms out of a list of eight.

Publication of the guidelines seemed like a victory to the doctors and patients fighting to have chronic fatigue legitimized, although they were unhappy with the name itself. According to Dr. David Bell, "It implies a benign condition of almost no importance in which people are tired, maybe bored, probably because they work too hard or are depressed." Dr. Bell prefers "chronic fatigue/immune dysfunction syndrome," "fibromyalgia," "Tapanui flu," or the term "myalgic encephalomyelitis," or ME, which is used in the United Kingdom. "There can be no doubt that it [ME] represents a real disease," he wrote in *The Doctor's Guide to Chronic Fatigue Syndrome*. "It sounds as if it could be fatal."[23]

That myalgic encephalomyelitis *sounds* impressively medical, serious, and possibly even fatal does not, of course, change the disorder itself. ME is no more life-threatening or lethal than CFS. The acronym ME also ironically emphasizes the patient's self-absorption. Whatever the official definition or name of the syndrome, doctors use it in lax and general ways. Officially, CFS, as Karyn Feiden explains, is a "diagnosis of exclusion, bestowed on a patient only after illnesses with a similar pattern of symptoms have been ruled out." But patients feeling acute anxiety about their symptoms demand a name for their disorder. "They need a name, they need to know the ballpark they are playing in," says Paul Cheney. "The name isn't terribly comforting but at least it focuses them a little bit."[24] In a 1993 study of 13,500 people who had been diagnosed with CFS, for example, Rumi K. Price and Carol S. North of Washington University School of Medicine found only *one* person who met the CDC's criteria. Medical problems, psychiatric complications, or side effects of medication could have accounted for the others. The researchers were cautious in their conclusions. "We don't want to say there is no chronic fatigue syndrome," Price said, "but we didn't find the kind as defined by the Centers for Disease Control."[25]

Meanwhile, CFS has continued to be a media sensation. In England, Sue Finley's *Observer* article "An Illness Doctors Don't Recognize" brought in six thousand letters and led to the formation of an ME Action Campaign in 1986. Women's magazines publicized chronic fatigue, and celebrities confessed that they suffered from the disorder. Neenyah Ostrom asked whether CFS, rather than ovarian cancer, had killed Gilda Radner.[26] *McCall's* reported that for three years Cher had used holistic treatments to battle CFS.[27] By the late 1980s, chronic fatigue began to show up on TV sitcoms like *The Golden Girls*: Dorothy develops mysterious symptoms; unsympathetic doctors recommend hypnosis or a cruise, but a virologist named Dr. Chang reassures her that she "really is sick and not merely depressed." Dorothy is relieved to discover that she has "something real."

Patient support groups started up in the United States, England, Australia, New Zealand, Belgium, Denmark, Italy, Norway, and South Africa. Bookstores devoted whole sections to self-help, with titles ranging from *Chronic Fatigue Syndrome: The Hidden Epidemic* to *The Chronic Fatigue Syndrome Cookbook*. Betsy Kraus, in *Library Journal*, advised consumers: "If your library's newest item on it is more than two years old, it is already out of date."[28] By 1990, the Centers for Disease Control were getting more than two thousand calls a months about chronic fatigue.[29] In 1995, a *New Yorker* cartoon captured the spirit of déjà vu: a mother at the bedside of her droopy-eyed tot declares, "It's just exhaustion, sweetie. Everybody's got it." In 1996, Johnson claimed that two million Americans were afflicted and that the epidemic was moving worldwide. CFS organizations for patients sponsored social activities that made chronic fatigue almost a way of life—outings, coffee hours, self-help groups.

Research into the causes of CFS is a way of life for many people as well. Although hundreds of costly studies have failed to find convincing evidence of the bacteria, chemicals, and viruses hypothesized as the causes of CFS, the possibilities seem endless because every new virus or chemical must be investigated in its turn. The failure to discover a cause for CFS after millions of dollars of experimental funding doesn't rule out the possibility that there may yet be a cause beyond current medical knowledge. For the past two decades at least, medical researchers have moved to new hypotheses as old ones prove untenable. Among those candidates already abandoned are malaria, flu, typhoid, vaccinations, brucellosis, mononucleosis, encephalitis, Epstein-Barr, Coxsackie B virus, Lyme disease, and rickettsae.[30] Candidiasis and African swine fever have also been proposed. In September 1995, researchers at Johns Hopkins found an overlap between low blood pressure and CFS.[31] Current research focuses on immunology, the retroviruses, nucleic acids, and cytokines.

No doubt as you read this book, headlines are proclaiming another breakthrough. The CFS researcher, writes David Bell, repeatedly "experiences excitement that medical progress is about to make the greatest leap it has ever known."[32] In *Living With M.E.* Dr. Charles Shepherd lists ongoing research into pesticides, hormones, and neurotransmitters. Hillary Johnson charges that powerful members of the scientific establishment and Centers for Disease Control are biased against patient accounts or have their own turf to protect. She argues that medical and scientific explanation is a fetishized worship of method and laboratory evidence. When doctors at the Mayo Clinic suggested that CFS could be caused by stress reactions or emotional problems, Marc Iverson, a young banker with severe CFS symptoms, who had spent thousands of dollars at the clinic, was indignant: "Everything is black or white for them," he said. "There can't be anything in the world they don't understand—because they understand everything! They don't believe in their patients—they believe in their orthodoxy. They read their printouts, but they never really listen to what you're saying. It's the worst of modern medicine."[33]

Many well-informed, thoughtful, educated people in the U.S. and Europe are convinced they've read that an organic basis for CFS has been firmly established. Announcements of breakthroughs prematurely cited in the mass media add to the confusion. The London *Times*, for example, printed a story in 1995 claiming that chronic fatigue syndrome had been defined by the World Health Organization as "an organic disorder of the brain,"[34] but WHO officials in Geneva deny ever making such an announcement.

The reality is a good illustration of the way the same story may be differently interpreted by different readers. On September 29, 1992, the World Health Organization had disappointed CFS sufferers when it concluded that there was no evidence of a new virus causing immunosuppression. But in early 1993, WHO published the tenth edition of the *International Statistical Classification of Diseases and Related Health Problems*, or ICD-10. This included a postviral fatigue syndrome, or benign myalgic encephalomyelitis, with the designation G93.3. In this classification system, G90–99 refer to disorders of the central nervous system, with G93 representing brain disorders. ME and CFS advocates seized on the classification as a scientific finding, while, to skeptics, it was no more than a recognition of the symptom reports.[35]

Journalistic and medical refusal to investigate the most extreme claims and melodramatic scenarios of CFS and ME have increased public awareness of symptoms and fueled the epidemic. Reviewing an autobiographical account of living with CFS, a writer for *Publishers Weekly* criticized its messy chronology, poor writing, and muddled science, including a claim that 15 percent of the patients thought their fingerprints were fading, but then added kindly that "CFS tends to undermine one's ability to communicate clearly."[36] With this sort of special pleading and suspension of critical attention, how can readers assess claims or differentiate between contradictory narratives of the CFS epidemic?

Indeed, in an eye-opening study of all the articles on CFS published in the British scientific, medical, and popular press between 1980 and 1994, Gail MacLean and Simon Wessely reported that while only 31 percent of articles in medical journals favored organic over psychological cause for the syndrome, 69 percent of the articles in newspapers and women's magazines supported organic explanations. MacLean and Wessely interviewed six medical journalists who agreed that "there is no middle ground when it comes to CFS." Journalists were inclined to sympathize with patients who told them about arrogant doctors and to view CFS as part of the "modern reaction against medical authority and paternalism, and hence a valid subject for reporting." MacLean and Wessely concluded, "Press coverage of chronic fatigue syndrome usually reflects a disease model in which the pathogenic agent causes a specific pathological event that will, in time, be cured by a single magic bullet. . . . Many stories were fuelled by, but also contributed to, the stigma of psychological disorder. Several journalists spoke of the anger provoked by articles which did refer to psychological causes. In consequence, two journalists said they did not want to write any further articles on the subject."[37]

CFS: The Patients

Most of us know someone, someone we respect, who has chronic fatigue syndrome. On the whole, because the chief sufferers are our relatives, neighbors, colleagues, or friends, we believe them. They're not, after all, describing supernatural experiences or bizarre rituals—just symptoms we've all endured. In the course of writing this book, I have met many impressive men and women in the United States and Europe with CFS who are certain that whatever others may say, they themselves have been exposed to an unknown, disease-causing agent. I have also heard tragic stories of lives and careers destroyed by CFS.

The patient population of CFS nonetheless exhibits some dramatic and distinctive features. More than 90 percent of CFS patients are white; Simon Wessely points out that it "seems not to be diagnosed among ethnic minorities."[38] Women outnumber men three or four to one. In a study carried out at Harvard Medical School, women CFS patients reported frantic lives with multiple responsibilities: jobs, child-rearing, volunteer work, exercise, and social activity. "I wouldn't do just *one* thing. I'd do six or seven at the same time!" one woman said.[39] Nevertheless, feminist accounts of chronic fatigue tend to insist on viral or neurological explanations and express hostility toward psychological explanations. Self-help books about coping with chronic fatigue far outnumber feminist efforts to understand its psychological and social contexts.

Many CFS patients, too, feel hostile to psychiatric or social explanations. David Bell writes, "Perhaps the most bitter argument surrounding chronic fatigue/immune dysfunction syndrome concerns the role played by depression. . . . The argument has been bitter because of the conviction and insistence of patients that although emotional symptoms are present in the illness, a primary emotional disturbance is not its cause. . . . Patients are angry and frustrated, interpreting the debate over emotions as trivialization of their illness and as the explanation for why so little has been done to help them."[40]

Moreover, chronic fatigue hystories have always staged a conflict between patient and doctor, with the skeptical doctor as the enemy of the helpless patient. According to Simon Wessely, "the principal theme of most of the self-help literature is the absence of recognition accorded to patients by relatives, colleagues, and the medical professions. Sufferers refer to a 'long uphill struggle against ignorance and inertia' and claim that 'most . . . doctors . . . are still lamentably ignorant of even the most basic facts of the disease.'"[41] Edward Shorter notes that "the chronic fatigue subculture brims with folklore about choosing physicians thought to be sympathetic."[42]

Every year patients and advocates intensify their attacks on the medical establishment, and find new links in their theories of conspiracy. As early as 1989, the London *Sunday Correspondent* reported that psychiatrists like Simon Wessely were getting hate mail and abusive phone calls; researchers like Stephen Straus have also become the targets of vilification.[43] Hillary Johnson charges that Straus is "indifferent to the fate of scientists outside his institution who wish to be involved in the discovery process, and, at worst, hostile to any scientific inquiry not his own."[44]

In August 1996, the conflict came to a head with an uproar over a televised confrontation on the BBC between ME sufferers and a skeptical physician. On "The Rantzen Report," host Esther Rantzen, the mother of an eighteen-year-old daughter with ME, staged a shouting match between patients and Dr. Thomas Stuttaford, a former Tory member of parliament and *Times* medical columnist, who represented the 75 percent of British physicians who view ME as a psychological problem. Audience members, some in wheelchairs, but most looking surprisingly fit, hissed and booed when Stuttaford called ME a form of depression. "I was set up, no doubt about that," he later told reporters. "There I was in my red socks and dark blue suit, typifying the English Trad. I was like Daniel walking into the lion's den. I don't think I have ever met such aggression and stubborn refusal to listen to, let alone understand, any opinion that was contrary to their own."[45] Victor Lewis-Smith, the dreadlocked television critic for the *Evening Standard*, denounced the program as a travesty of investigative journalism: "There was no desire to seek the truth, merely to belittle and indoctrinate in an ill-considered, inconsiderate, manipulative, and unscrupulous manner."[46] Lewis-Smith was so outraged that he protested to the Broadcasting Complaints Commission.

Dr. Anne McIntyre, the medical adviser for the ME Association, responded that "the current battle going on is akin to the hostility people with multiple sclerosis experienced 40 or 50 years ago when they were described as hysterical because their symptoms came and went. No one would dare to describe their illness as imaginary now." But Stuttaford sees her assumption that psychologically-caused illness is "imaginary" as part of the problem. The audience was hostile, he said, "because there are people who have not yet learned to regard psychiatric disease as a proper illness. They are still seeing it as a moral weakness."[47] Spurning the idea that they can be helped by psychotherapy and antidepressants, chronic fatigue patients may go on for years, becoming more and more invested in the fruitless quest for a medical breakthrough. At some point, although the initial causes of the symptoms may have disappeared, the syndrome itself becomes a self-perpetuating reality.

Caught in a cultural impasse over the meaning of their symptoms, many sufferers are understandably grateful to find a Reverend Bill. Faith healing is a cheap price to pay for being rescued from a disorder that has baffled medical opinion. Although sources of the fatigue may have disappeared, patients cannot easily discard their symptoms without some kind of face-saving intervention.

Chronic Fatigue: The Doctors

Doctors and other health workers have always been peculiarly susceptible to neurasthenia and other chronic fatigue syndromes. In both England and the United States, doctors who have themselves been sufferers are advisers to the patient associations. Ten percent of George Beard's neurasthenic patients in the 1880s were doctors, and both Beard and S. Weir Mitchell had overcome the disorder. In the 1980s, Dr. Melvyn Ramsay, late president of the British Myalgic Encephalomyelitis Association asserted that "the incidence of ME among doctors is out of all proportion to their numbers in the general population."

Paul Cheney specifies personal experience as the difference between the physician who "believes" in CFS as an organic illness and those who see it as a psychological syndrome. "The only people who really believe in this disease are the few clinicians who have seen enough patients to have seen the pattern, and isolated clinicians who either have the disease themselves or who have someone close to them who has it," he told Johnson. "Once you believe this disease is real, your whole attitude changes. If you get a negative result or an ambiguous finding, you say, 'Well, it's a negative result or an ambiguous finding,' and you keep going, because you know the disease is real." Clearly, what is at stake is an unwillingness to accept a psychological disorder as "real," and a view of the disorders of psychiatry as unreal forms of malingering or deceit.

Nonetheless, the majority of doctors and researchers maintain that CFS is a psychological syndrome, *and* that its symptoms and effects are real. In the mid-1980s, Stephen E. Straus had encouraged researchers to pursue the connection to Epstein-Barr virus and other immune dysfunctions, but by 1988 he concluded that "it is impossible to completely dispel the notion that the chronic fatigue syndrome represents a psychoneurotic condition." In a 1995 address at the American College of Rheumatology, Straus reiterated his view that CFS was "not a [single] disease entity but a mixed bag of entities." He spoke of the CDC's inability to replicate experiments that showed the presence of retroviruses or brain damage. Straus's caveats have drawn angry rebuttals from Hillary Johnson, who accuses him of bias, "hostility towards his study subjects, a majority of whom were women," and "propaganda" about the patients' psychiatric condition.[48]

A state-of-the-art analysis of chronic fatigue syndrome emerged from a 1992 symposium at the Ciba Foundation in London, attended by an international group of outstanding physicians, psychiatrists, medical historians, anthropologists, virologists, and biologists. The conference set out to devise a coping plan for the treatment of chronic fatigue, a cognitive therapy that would direct itself to behaviors rather than causes. Professor Arthur Kleinman, from the departments of anthropology and social medicine at Harvard, set the stage from the patient's perspective: "Imagine being a chronic fatigue patient. . . . We go to see a doctor and are sent on to a psychiatrist. All of a sudden, the fundamental illness experience we have is no longer the grounds of our talk; we are being asked about our families, our intimate personal life, our fears, our worries. We sense a distortion or incongruity about where our experience is located: it's in the *fatigue*. And the psychiatrist, just by his or her position, challenges and even alienates us, and makes us feel that our experience, our primary grounding in our bodies, is unreal, imaginary."

Kleinman strongly believes that CFS should be treated by a physician, not by a psychiatrist, to maintain the patient's self-respect. "One can affirm the illness experience," he concludes, "without affirming the attribution for it; in other words, we can work within a 'somatic' language and do all the interventions that we heard earlier had been done from the psychosocial side, but in such a way as to spare patients the . . . delegitimization of their experience."[49]

David Mechanic, a distinguished sociologist of medicine at Rutgers University, adds: "In order to convince people who have a psychological and even monetary stake in believing in CFS as a viral condition, one has to provide a plausible alternative theory which they find credible. Much as my inclination is to believe that CFS is influenced by psychological needs, I am not convinced that there isn't an important viral trigger or a viral perpetuating factor. . . . I see no reason why the public should give up that belief, when you don't have anything particularly good to offer in return."[50]

But these kindly, tolerant, and temporizing views do not address the ways that psychogenic epidemics escalate. Doctors may protect the self-esteem of their patients in the short run by prescribing placebos like vitamins and avoiding public statements about the history of effort syndromes. But in the long run, such acquiescence only creates more hystories. Modern psychological epidemics feed endlessly on new disease theories, such as immunology. Studies published in the *British Medical Journal* have shown that patients who believed their conditions were viral or infectious, and who became inactive, were least likely to have recovered after three years. Furthermore, in Wessely's view, "Such uncritical diagnoses may reinforce maladaptive behavior, and may create more severe and persistent morbidity than the initial illness."[51]

In *Osler's Web*, Johnson laments that "well into the 1990s, the story of the American epidemic and the people whose lives it destroyed continued to play out in a kind of half-light, unseen and unfelt in most regions of the culture . . . as a group [sufferers] inhabited a domain utterly removed from the mainstream."[52] But despite her claims of the twilight of CFS, it has not faded from the headlines and is unlikely to disappear anytime soon. Studies of CFS regularly identify and alert new victims. In a typically uncritical London *Times* article, a journalist reports that "at least 24,000 children in Britain" are suffering from ME, and that this may be "only the tip of the iceberg."

The figures come from a study by Elizabeth Dowsett, a microbiologist who "firmly believes" that ME is caused by enteroviral infections, and Jane Colby, a schoolteacher who suffers from the syndrome. Although a pediatrician specializing in ME is quoted as saying the "wide range and varying severity of symptoms can make diagnosis difficult," Dowsett nonetheless recommends "total rest" for a child with any of the symptoms: "Forcing a child to participate in lessons, PE, and 'normal' day-to-day activities will only make things worse." In her blanket warnings to parents, one can easily see an invitation to create invalidism in children, a Munchhausen-by-proxy syndrome. Dowsett says, "If the child has a rapid pulse or heartbeat, overexertion can be very dangerous. . . . So can exercising muscles before they're fully recovered, which, in extreme cases, can lead to paralysis. Also the stress of leading a normal life and keeping up with their peers can exacerbate the condition."[53] With scare literature like this, we can be sure that the anxious parents of many more children will soon be talking to doctors about ME.

Johnson herself points to the next adult phase of expansion for CFS: Gulf War syndrome. Toward the end of her book, in 1994 the story moves to New Jersey, where Dr. Benjamin Natalson has a $2.5 million grant from the NIH to study the relationship between chronic fatigue syndrome and Gulf War syndrome. "We think there has been a mini-epidemic of CFS among Gulf War veterans," Natalson says.[54] The epidemic stage is set for act two.

9

Gulf War Syndrome

"We've kicked Vietnam syndrome!" exulted President Bush in 1991, referring to American malaise after the disaster of Vietnam. But although most of its symptoms emerged later, the Persian Gulf conflict clearly marked the beginning of an unexplained illness that has been named Gulf War syndrome. In the summer of 1991, Brian Martin returned from Iraq to his family in Niles, Michigan. He was happy to be home but had a mysterious rash that wouldn't go away. During the next months other symptoms followed—memory lapses, mood swings, and finally debilitating fatigue. He can't work and gets some disability pay from the VA. But even worse symptoms have afflicted Brian's family. His son Deven, conceived shortly after Brian's return, was born with acute respiratory problems and an umbilical cord five feet long. His twenty-five-year-old wife, Kim, has suffered from seemingly unrelated and unconfirmed complaints—rashes, headaches, breast lumps, ovarian cysts, a thinning skull, and unexplained cervical infections. Now the Martins no longer have sex; after intercourse, Kim experiences cramps and a burning sensation: when her husband's semen touches her skin, she told *Redbook*, it feels "like it was on fire."[1] Doctors have been unable to find organic causes for any of the Martins' problems.

In Barrington, Illinois, the Albuck family is also suffering. Gulf War veteran Troy has fatigue, muscle soreness, swollen joints, headaches, diarrhea, and bleeding gums. His wife, Kelli, has hearing problems, migraines, and attacks of pelvic inflammatory disease. She reports that her husband's semen is a toxic substance that "causes sores—blisters which actually open and bleed." Worst of all, their son Alex was born prematurely in 1993 with a rare blood infection and now has cerebral palsy. When he was born, he had a rash that looked like the ones Troy and Kelli have had. Journalist David France declares that "doctors have been unable to explain their cause, give a diagnosis, or prescribe a remedy."[2]

In Yorkshire, England, Robert Lake's marriage has broken up since he returned from the Persian Gulf, plagued by headaches, vomiting, and diarrhea. Lake had become an army apprentice at sixteen and trained in Cyprus and Germany, where he moved at nineteen. Serving as a radar technician in the Gulf, he was shocked and frightened. On return, he began to have violent mood swings and nightmares of running away from an enemy; he made two suicide attempts and spent two months in psychiatric hospitals, where he was treated for PTSD. He continued to have angry outbursts, his German wife left him, and the army discharged him in 1993. Lake has lost about seventy pounds and has been diagnosed with anorexia nervosa. But he believes that his symptoms come from anthrax inoculations and antinerve gas tablets he took in the Gulf. "I am angry and disappointed," he told *The Guardian*, "that the MOD [Ministry of Defence] are so pig ignorant and uncaring."[3]

The Martins, the Albucks, and Robert Lake are among the thousands of American and British victims of what is called Gulf War syndrome (GWS), Saudi flu, or desert fever. Of the 697,000 U.S. troops who served in the Gulf, 60,000 have reported ailments from memory loss to cancer. The numbers in England are much smaller: 567 veterans, out of 45,000 British personnel, are seeking compensation or disability payments. Veterans' complaints include chronic fatigue, diarrhea, aches and pains, headaches, hair loss, bleeding gums, irritability, insomnia, muscle spasms, and night sweats. Two veterans in Mississippi have claimed to be shrinking.[4] Among physicians, politicians, journalists, and veterans who believe that Gulf War syndrome is a new and unique illness, ideas about its cause vary. Many believe that it is contagious and can be passed through sex, sweat, or the air.

Like CFS patients, Gulf War veterans have organized self-help networks. In 1994 David France reported in *Redbook* that "many vets rely on an informal word-of-mouth network to track the illness, tally developments, or find solace."[5] Veterans and their families who live on military bases trade stories, and electronic networks of Gulf War vets are humming; the Internet has hugely expanded opportunities to communicate. Most veterans and their families react angrily to the idea that they are suffering from post-traumatic stress disorder. Willie Hicks, a black veteran from Alabama, told *Esquire* journalist Gregory Jaynes, "Shit, I don't sleep more than two, three hours a day. Anxiety. . . . Couldn't get along with nobody. . . . Couldn't even get out of the house. . . . Post-traumatic stress, my black ass."[6] Carole Hill, an English nurse who began to feel tired six months after her husband returned to Cheshire from the Gulf, insists: "This can't be psychological. I've spoken to too many veterans whose families are suffering similar symptoms."[7]

GWS patients in England and the U.S. are convinced that the cause of their medical problems lies in their exposure to chemicals and drugs in the Gulf, and that their governments are conspiring to deprive them of health benefits and disability pay. Hicks says angrily, "Some of us bleed from the penis. Bleed all over the sheets. Government won't even pay for the sheets."[8] "We believe there's a cover-up," British-born Texan Vic Silvester tells *The Guardian*[9]. "I was a volunteer, so I have to take whatever I get," one American veteran says. "But my boy and my wife? They did not volunteer, they did not take my oath. They've been drafted against their will and they've got wounds from battle."[10] A group of sick wives in Texas has started its own secret research initiative—"secret," according to one of them, "because they fear the military might try to block their study for reasons she can only guess at."[11]

In fact, American government reactions to Gulf War syndrome have been concerned and sympathetic. No elected politician wants to risk his constituents' anger. The Clinton administration, mindful of alienation over Vietnam and the Agent Orange fiasco, has moved very carefully. President Clinton authorized a scientific advisory panel to investigate the symptoms. Hillary Rodham Clinton has come out as a "friend of Gulf War syndrome sufferers." At the opening session of the Presidential Committee meeting, she said, "Just as we relied on our troops when they were sent to war, we must assure them that they can rely on us now."[12] Politicians agree that Persian Gulf veterans deserve respect, attention, and full support, and no decent citizen could object to the research efforts and investigations funded by the government. Since 1994, the government has authorized disability payments for veterans with GWS.

The respectful and cautious responses of the U.S. government, however, have reinforced the suspicion that Gulf War syndrome is a unique disease and fed anxieties and conspiracy rumors about it. Dissenting views have been silenced; when Dr. Edward Young, chief of staff at the Houston VA Medical Center, announced, "There's been mass hallucinations. There's been mass post-traumatic stress disorder" and attributed some of the epidemic to frustration and anger, he was suspended by his boss, Jesse Brown, secretary of the Department of Veterans' Affairs.[13] But more skeptical responses of the British Defence Ministry have not quelled protests from MPs or veterans either.

The extraordinary conditions of the Gulf War—and Iraq's admission that they had biological weapons they didn't use—have added to suspicions that GWS is caused by a toxic agent. These concerns and questions reappeared when the Pentagon announced in June 1996 that a weapons storage area exploded by American troops contained toxic gases. But there is no clinical evidence that GWS soldiers were exposed to the blast nor that the minute traces of sarin and mustard gas could have caused the enormous variety of symptoms being reported by thousands of veterans five years later. In a "Sixty Minutes" special on August 25, 1996, a group of soldiers from the 37th Engineers Batallion who participated in blowing up an Iraqi arsenal near Kamisayah in March 1991 described their fears at the time of the demolition, and a variety of symptoms since. But CBS did not interview any doctors, specialists in the effects of nerve gas, or Pentagon officials who could support the claim that this chemical exposure could lead to fatigue, gastrointestinal symptoms, and other problems. What has seemed likely all along is that no one incident, toxin, virus, or disease entity is responsible for all the complaints that have been collected under the heading of Gulf War syndrome.[14]

Meanwhile doctors are pursuing many other explanations. Dr. Edward Hyman of New Orleans, who believes the syndrome is an arterial infection passed through the air like tuberculosis, has been voted $1.2 million by Congress for research.[15] Ross Perot is among those funding a Mayo Clinic project. Dr. Boaz Milner in Allen Park, Michigan, has treated more than three hundred GWS patients. He has suggested at least five possible causes for Gulf War syndrome: radiation poisoning, effects of experimental medicines, environmental contaminants, chemical compounds, and Iraq's biological arsenal. Dr. Eula Bingham, a professor of environmental health at the University of Cincinnati, suspects leishmaniasis, a parasitic infection caused by sand fly bites; but the Armed Forces Epidemiological Board says no. Researchers at Duke have found that the experimental nerve gas pill pyrodostigmine bromide, used in combination with pesticides, caused neurological problems in chickens. When Dr. Stephen C.

Joseph, assistant secretary of defense for health affairs, responded that pyrodostigmine stays in the human body for only a few hours, the next suggestion was multiple chemical sensitivity. One entomologist reported that an insect repellent used by 40 percent of the soldiers in the Gulf becomes more toxic when mixed with pyrodostigmine.[16] Among the latest stories is that aspartame, an artificial sweetener used in Nutrasweet, is linked to GWS. Now that Hillary Johnson and others are pointing out correspondences with chronic fatigue syndrome, researchers are investigating retroviruses.

Yet government investigations have produced no evidence of an organic syndrome. Dr. Francis Murphy, acting director of the office of environmental medicine and public health at the VA says, "We have found nothing in our investigations that we consider transmissible. We've found no clear-cut evidence that this is being transmitted either casually or sexually."[17] A defense department study of more than a thousand ailing veterans indicated that 60 percent had organic ailments with known causes, which were not disproportionate to their random occurrence in the population. Another 25 percent had psychological disturbances, including depression and post-traumatic stress disorder. About 15 percent had unexplained ailments, including headache, memory loss, fatigue, sleep problems, and intestinal and respiratory complaints.[18] In January 1995, a panel affiliated with the National Academy of Sciences recommended a fuller and more coordinated study of the problem.[19] By April 1996, the results were announced: conducted at a cost of $80 million, the survey of 18,924 veterans found "no single cause or mystery ailment to support suspicions about the existence of a gulf war syndrome."[20]

In England, results were similar. "I have seen or heard nothing that makes me believe there is a specific syndrome directly attributable to the gulf war," says surgeon-general Tony Revell. A Ministry of Defence study indicated that about 52 percent of those surveyed had minor ailments like asthma. Fourteen percent had more serious disorders, including leukemia and kidney disease. Solicitor Hilary Meredith, whose law firm represents 567 veterans, say nine have died from cancer. Twenty-two percent had post-traumatic stress disorder, and 14 percent had other psychological symptoms, including depression and anxiety.[21] In July 1995, the Royal College of Physicians gave its official backing for further investigations, although a preliminary study had concluded that "there was no single cause for the variety of illnesses suffered by the servicemen and women who have been examined."[22]

Gulf War Syndrome and Shell Shock

Many of these symptoms sound like war neurosis, shell shock, or post-traumatic stress disorder. Despite the rapidity with which PTSD has entered the language, most people do not understand what it means or know about its long history: from the Civil War on, battle fatigue, shell shock, combat neurosis, or PTSD has been observed, studied, and documented, not only in American medicine and psychiatry but around the world.

Since the Gulf War, however, journalists, doctors, government offi-cials, and psychologists have been surprisingly silent about PTSD. Instead, the media have exacerbated fears of Gulf War symptoms. By the summer of 1995, more than two hundred newspaper stories about Gulf War syndrome had appeared in England.[23] Even *Doonesbury* picked up on the controversy, with B.D. complaining to Boopsie about his symptoms and denying that they could be caused by stress: "It does-n't explain why this thing is showing up in family members too! I'm terrified I might end up passing it on to you!"

In the United States, both conservative and liberal journalists have long promoted the idea that Gulf War syndrome is a contagious dis-ease being covered up by the government. In *Redbook* David France asks why the VA has not authorized semen tests on veterans. In the feminist *Women's Review of Books*, Laura Flanders writes, "Today many women who served in the Gulf are still in combat, only this time their fight is with the Department of Defense and the Veterans Administra-tion. . . . After months of struggle and increasing sickness, the tears are now of rage."[24] Flanders has also written about GWS for *The Nation*, where she declares that "fears are growing about just how contagious Gulf War Syndrome may be. Outgoing Senator Donald Riegel con-ducted a study of 1,200 sick male veterans last year and found that 78 percent of their wives had been affected. . . . Penny Larrissey, a veteran's wife who told me last year that during intercourse her husband's semen burns, has been in touch with military wives around the coun-try who report not just discomfort but terrible vaginal infections, cysts, blisters and even bleeding sores. Most military family members remain outside the national test samples. And some are invisible alto-gether. Thanks to the Pentagon's devotion to discrimination, gay men and lesbians whose partners are sick are too scared to ask for help and too intimidated to tell."[25]

This kind of journalism makes classic hystory: scare headlines, vague statistics, uncritical descriptions of "studies" and "reports," and the extension of anxieties to gays in the military. Perceptions are reported as facts; undifferentiated and unsubstantiated responses taken seriously as medical evidence. Senator Riegel's staff, for example, surveyed six hundred veterans, 77 percent of whom *said* that their spouses had some symptoms. On the page opposite Flanders's story, an ad claims, "The most skeptical people in America subscribe to *The Nation*." One has to wonder why.

Some of the most alarmist, upsetting, and irresponsible journalism has been about birth defects related to GWS. Immediately after the war, there were persistent rumors of birth defects among the families of returning veterans. Laura Flanders notes dramatically that "freakish births are being reported around the country and even internationally."[26] In November 1995, *Life* magazine published a special issue entitled "The Tiny Victims of Desert Storm: Has Our Country Abandoned Them?" On the cover was a color picture of Gulf War veteran Sgt. Paul Hanson and his three-year-old-son Jayce, born with hands and feet attached to stumps. In the story, heart-rending photos of Jayce, "the unofficial poster boy of the Gulf War babies," accompany text full of dire warning and no firm medical or statistical evidence. "During the past year," the story says, "*Life* has conducted its own inquiry into the plight of these children. We sought to learn whether U.S. policies put them at risk, and whether the nation ought to be doing more for them and their families."

The story describes the anguish of seven families whose children have birth defects, from spinal bifida to mitral heart valve disorder. But reporters Jimmie Briggs and Kenneth Miller do not provide numbers of complaints or controls, although they sneer at "Pentagon bureaucrats" who claim that "at least 3 percent of American babies are born with abnormalities." One activist group, the Association of Birth Defect Children, has gathered data on ailing babies born to 163 of the 970,000 who served in the Gulf War. According to *Life*, "No one . . . knows how many babies have been born to Gulf vets," and "many still question whether Defense Department scientists are really seeking the hard answers,"[27] despite more than thirty studies of Gulf vets by 1995.

Esquire reported in 1994 that "of fifty-five children born to four Guard Units in Mississippi thirty-seven are not normal."[28] According to the Mississippi Department of Public Health, however, two babies in these units were born with severe defects and three with minor defects. The VA maintained in May 1994 that the percentage of birth defects in the Mississippi units fell within the normal range—a conclusion that "enraged" one mother, who argued that birth defect statistics were not the point: "Our babies are sick all the time. Why didn't they study our children's immune systems?" Dr. Alan Penman, director of a study by the Centers for Disease Control and Prevention, responded: "We don't believe that there's an excessively high rate of common illnesses in this group."[29]

Angry parents like Ammie West, whose daughter Reed was born with a chronic respiratory infection, have condemned the Mississippi study, like other government statistics and responses that offer facts and reassurance, as part of a cover-up. A Pentagon survey of the army's six largest military installations showed that the rate of spontaneous abortion or miscarriage among veterans' wives was about half the rate of society as a whole. But, says David France, "This result has been denounced by vets as a partial finding at best."[30] Parents are understandably anxious and grief-stricken, but we have to question the usefulness of scare stories.

Journalists could be more helpful by reminding readers of the atmosphere leading up to the Gulf War and the many forces that contributed to stress and disorientation for participants. In a report on 10,020 Gulf War participants issued in August 1995, the defense department announced, "Physical and psychological stressors were major characteristics of the Persian Gulf. The effect of both acute and chronic stress is a major etiologic consideration when evaluating Persian Gulf veterans. U.S. troops entered a bleak, physically demanding desert environment, where they were crowded into warehouses, storage buildings, and tents with little personal privacy and few amenities. No one knew that coalition forces eventually would win a quick war with relatively few battle casualties. Consequently, most troops did not fight a 'four day war' but spent months isolated in the desert, under constant stress, concerned about their survival and their family's well-being at home, and uncertain about when they would return home."[31]

In an article for the London *Times*, Dr. Simon Wessely reminds us just how stressful service in the Persian Gulf was. Troops were afraid that Iraq might use devastating chemical and biological weapons, and "to be ever alert for a silent attack by nerve gas or invisible deadly microbes must have taken a constant toll. . . . The situation was made worse by the cumbersome protection suits, ill-adapted for the desert heat, that had to be worn as a consequence."[32]

Testimony from Gulf War veterans with GWS confirms these descriptions. Seventeen percent of Gulf War forces came from National Guard reserve units who had never expected to be on active duty, especially under such ominous conditions. They had heard about the ruthlessness of Saddam Hussein and his unbeatable "elite Republican Guard." That Saddam's troops proved to be ill-equipped and outnumbered did not undo the months of fearful anticipation. Iraqi Scud attacks on civilian populations intensified fears of a bestial enemy, while propaganda about biological and chemical warfare made every new experience potentially threatening. Soldiers also had to deal with frightening gossip about the preventive medications offered to them.

One Hingham, Massachusetts, soldier, Larry McGinnis, took eight of the anti–nerve gas pills—more than the recommended dose—and vomited for several hours. "Here we were," he told a reporter, "driving into Iraq with the 82nd Airborne and me puking over the side into the sand. . . . I thought I was going to die."[33] McGinnis had reason to fear death. In his testimony to the House Subcommittee of the Committee on Veterans' Affairs, he recalled crossing the DMI "with the thought of the body bags and coffins that were being delivered. . . . But the one thought that kept coming back was Gas Chemical Warfare."[34]

Women too had profoundly disturbing combat experiences. Sergeant Carol Picou, an army medical officer, drove a hospital truck into Iraq, where she saw charred and smoldering bodies of animals and humans beside the highway. Although Picou had seen burned bodies before, she was frightened: "These bodies were different. They weren't normal." For two weeks Picou and her unit lived near the battlefield, treating injured soldiers and Iraqi civilians from Basra. After she returned from the Gulf, Picou began to suffer from muscle pain, bladder problems, and memory loss. She is convinced that her symptoms were caused not by horror, anxiety, and disgust but by the drug pyrodostigmine.[35]

Gulf War syndrome is shaping up to be a tragic standoff of men and women suffering from the all-too-real aftereffects of war, doctors unable to combat the force of rumor and panic, and a government that feels the need to be supportive of veterans. As Representative Joseph Kennedy told the House Subcommittee, "They come back, were told when they begin to complain of various illnesses that these can be explained through PTSD or through stress. It's one thing for us to hear that. It's another thing, if you've got all these sicknesses . . . and you are being told by a doctor that you go in to see at the VA that, listen, there is nothing really wrong with you—all it is, you know, you've got some psychological problem that is getting in your way—which must be an enormous burden for these individuals to carry around.... Now if in the end the conclusion is that these are illnesses that are explained only through PTSD, that might be the conclusion but it seems to me that we are a long way from drawing that conclusion at the moment."[36]

That was in the fall of 1992. Years have gone by, but each time the government eliminates a chemical or bacterial cause, suspicion, resistance, and bitterness grows. As Paul Cotton commented in a 1994 report in the *Journal of the American Medical Association*, the Pentagon's effort to reassure Persian Gulf veterans seems to have "created a candy store for conspiracy buffs." Among the persistent rumors surrounding GWS are stories of 2,000 concealed deaths among Gulf veterans, mass burials of contaminated Iraqi bodies, the release of a Russian chemical called Novachok, mysterious deaths of camels and goats in the desert, exposure to depleted uranium, the use of soldiers as guinea pigs for unauthorized drugs or vaccines, and widespread burning of soldiers' medical records.[37] Meanwhile, thousands of men and women who could be helped by psychotherapy are instead encouraged to pursue endless tests and medical exams; they tend not to see psychotherapists even when their stories make clear that anxiety, fear, and anger are among their symptoms.

Studies have shown that "very substantial proportions of Vietnam veterans with readjustment problems" have never sought help from mental health specialists. Ignorance of therapy, fear of stigma, ideas about masculine self-sufficiency, and lack of information were the main reasons veterans did not seek help. "By far the most frequently reported reason ... was the hope or belief that the individual could solve the problem on his own.... Other major reasons ... were feeling as though treatment would not help, not knowing where to get help, distrust of mental health professionals, the respondent's fear of what he might learn from consulting a mental health professional, and the time and cost involved in seeking treatment."[38] Education could have changed the way veterans perceived themselves and allowed them to seek care without feeling diminished as men. We do not want the same ignorance and misinformation to persist for Gulf War veterans.

We owe our war veterans a serious debt, but continuing to deny the validity of war neurosis is not the way to pay it. The suffering of Gulf War syndrome *is* real by any measure, and the symptoms caused by war neurosis are just as painful and incapacitating as those caused by chemicals, parasites, or smoke. But until we can acknowledge that even strong and heroic men and women, fighting in a just cause, can be affected by the conversion of strong emotions into physical symptoms, no double-blind tests or expensive studies will change the likelihood that veterans of even the greatest military victories will continue to become sick. As charges of sinister conspiracy and high-level government cover-up move in to displace and supplant the medical debate, Gulf War Syndrome becomes an epidemic of suspicion, a plague of paranoia that threatens a greater malaise than even Vietnam.

IO | Recovered Memory

In her influential book *Trauma and Recovery* (1992), Harvard Medical School professor Dr. Judith Lewis Herman compared the traumas of male veterans to those of female civilians. "Not until the women's liberation movement of the 1970s," wrote Herman, "was it recognized that the most common post-traumatic disorders are those not of men in war but of women in civilian life." In her view, "the psychological syndrome seen in survivors of rape, domestic battery, and incest" is "essentially the same as the syndrome seen in survivors of war." The implications of this analogy are horrifying, and Herman does not deny them: "There is war between the sexes. Rape victims, battered women, and sexually abused children are its casualties. Hysteria is the combat neurosis of the sex war."[1] These views make the petite, dark-haired Herman a compelling speaker to female audiences. When I heard her at Scripps College in California, she mesmerized an undergraduate audience with her slide talk of "survivors" such as Anna O. and Anita Hill.

Along with her Harvard Medical School colleague Bessel A. Van der Kolk, Herman reintroduced Pierre Janet's dissociation theories and Freud's seduction theory into the interpretation of trauma: hysterical symptoms were post-traumatic symptoms and could be caused by repressed experiences of sexual abuse, often incestuous, that the patient might be able to remember during intensive therapy. In his work on traumatic stress disorder, Van der Kolk concluded: "Actual experiences can be so overwhelming that they cannot be integrated into existing mental frameworks and instead are dissociated, later to return intrusively as fragmented sensory or motoric experiences." These traumatic memories "need to be integrated into existing mental schemes, and be transformed into narrative language," in order to be relived and relieved.[2]

Herman believes that unlike the traumas of war and crime, however, traumas of childhood abuse are deeply disguised. Survivors of childhood trauma, according to Herman, come to the therapist because of their "bewildering array of symptoms" or "because of difficulties with relationships. . . . All too commonly, neither patient nor therapist recognizes the link between the presenting problem and the history of chronic trauma," even though "many or even most psychiatric patients are survivors of childhood abuse." Herman writes that "50–60 percent of psychiatric inpatients and 40–60 percent of outpatients report childhood histories of physical or sexual abuse or both." She adds that treating sexual abuse patients is difficult because "the patient may not have full recall of the traumatic history and may initially deny such a history, even with careful, direct questioning."[3]

Herman writes that a cure can be achieved if the therapist and the patient together construct a memory story. In her view, an unspoken, untreated memory of trauma is wordless, imagistic, and incoherent, a "prenarrative" or an "unstory" that lacks cathartic power. Transforming the traumatic memory into a therapeutic story involves a process of articulation and revision, carried out in friendly collaboration between patient and therapist, who produce "a fully detailed, written trauma narrative" told in the first person. The therapist plays the role of ghost writer or editor in eliciting and shaping the patient's story. Furthermore, this narrative is not private. Herman believes the survivor transcends her trauma completely when she can make it public as testimony.[4]

The therapist and the patient can construct the trauma narrative through dialogue. Herman specifies, however, that occasionally "major amnesiac gaps in the story remain even after careful and painstaking exploration." In these cases, she writes, hypnotherapy, group therapy, psychodrama, or sodium amytal may be effective.[5] Chronic fatigue syndrome patients are angry with unsympathetic physicians, Gulf War syndrome patients suspect political coverups, recovered memory patients accuse family members—a father or mother, grandfather or grandmother, uncle or brother—of abusing them. Many therapists believe that the full circle of healing is incomplete until the patient has confronted her abuser. In most cases these confrontations are symbolic or ritualistic, but in the United States and England direct confrontations have become common in the 1990s. Patients send letters to their alleged abusers. They make announcements on talk shows, at conferences and meetings, or in sensational autobiographies.

Louise Armstrong, an elegant American journalist now living in London, and herself a survivor of childhood incest she never forgot, is disgusted by the media circus that has exploited sexual abuse, and by women's collusion in the process: "By the late 1980s," she writes in *Rocking the Cradle of Sexual Politics: What Happened When Women Said Incest* (1996), "the networks had discovered the idea of women's pain and pathology as a daily event.... By 1993, in the northeast, you could choose from seventeen talk shows between nine in the morning and six in the evening. It was now a rare day when incest was not on the menu."[6] Armstrong remonstrates against the way "Celebrity Incest" drowned out feminist activism and the way personal narratives of abuse have substituted for a collective political analysis.

By 1994 over three hundred cases involving repressed memory had been filed in American courts. George Franklin was convicted of murder in 1990 and sentenced to life imprisonment when his daughter Eileen "remembered" seeing him kill a child in 1969—a conviction overturned five years later, when U.S. District Judge D. Lowell Jensen cited improprieties in the trial and the scientific problems of recovered memory evidence. Gary Ramona, a former California winery executive, received half a million dollars in damages after his daughter Holly charged that she remembered incestuous sexual abuse; Ramona lost his job and his family because of the charges. In 1989, Holly, then a student at UC Irvine, went to a therapist for treatment of bulimia. The therapist told her that 70 percent to 80 percent of bulimics had been sexually abused. Subsequently, Holly was given sodium amytal by Dr. Richard Rose, and over a period months recalled rapes and incidents when her father forced her to have oral sex with the family dog. Holly now plans to become a therapist who works with abused children.[7]

In a relatively short time, Frederick Crews writes, "A single diagnosis for miscellaneous complaints—that of unconsciously repressed sexual abuse in childhood—has grown from virtual nonexistence to epidemic frequency."[8] Richard Webster adds, "One of the obstacles which stands in the way of any realistic appraisal of the recovered memory movement is the difficulty most people have in imaginatively grasping the sheer scale of the extraordinary speed with which it has come to dominate the mental health debate in North America, and to move rapidly up mental health agendas in other countries."[9]

Louise Armstrong asks how incest and child sexual abuse, once issues for feminist politics and action, have in fifteen years become an opportunity for therapy and healing: "Somewhere along the way, rather than feminism politicizing the issue of incest, incest-as-illness had overwhelmed and swallowed feminism. The result was the mass infantilization of women."[10]

Therapists and patients in the recovered memory movement often ask why anyone would want to come up with memories of childhood sexual abuse if it were not the truth. Why, they inquire rhetorically, would anyone choose to take on the pain and turmoil of being a survivor? There are many plausible answers to this question. Some of them come from the structure of the therapy itself, from a combination of suggestibility and social coercion. Some of them come from the availability of this explanation for a variety of anxieties and discontents in women's lives. Claudette Wassil-Grimm offers sixteen reasons behind recovered memory, concluding that a woman may search for them "because she has become isolated and depressed due to current life problems, and an honored authority told her repressed memories of incest are a common cause of deep unhappiness."[11] I have come to doubt the validity of therapeutically recovered memories of sexual abuse, but I do not wish to belittle those who believe in their memories. People do not generate these confabulations out of an intention to deceive. They may need to define an identity, to work out anger toward the accused, or to respond to cultural pressures.

Recovered memory therapists often describe human memory as a computer in which information is stored; even if there is a trauma, a mental computer crash, the images are retained in the memory, waiting to be recovered. But scientists have countered that the computer is an inaccurate metaphor for memory. They describe memory as a plastic image subject to change and transformation. It is a process involving sensation, organization, storage, and retrieval. Elizabeth Loftus, a professor of psychology at the University of Washington, writes that memory decays over time and can easily be distorted by suggestion.[12] And confabulations—the technical word for narratives or memories constructed dialogically between client and therapist— cannot be distinguished from truth on the basis of internal evidence alone. Lie detectors measure not truth but confidence: does the speaker sincerely believe his images?

In *Suggestions of Abuse: True and False Memories of Childhood Sexual Trauma* (1994), Michael Yapko, a clinical psychologist who has written books on depression and a textbook on clinical hypnosis, clearly distinguishes between abuse remembered all along, abuse spontaneously remembered, abuse recovered in therapy, and abuse suggested in therapy. He reminds us that suggestion in therapy can come from the context of the dialogue as well as from the therapist's directives. If a patient comes to a doctor with microscopic traces of blood in the urine, the doctor may recommend, even prescribe, X-rays and sonograms to investigate the symptoms. Such laboratory procedures will not affect internal lesions or cysts. However, if a patient comes to a therapist with an eating disorder, work dissatisfactions, or sexual problems, and the therapist prescribes hypnosis to explore memories, memories can be summoned through the process and the assumptions behind it.[13]

Empirical evidence for the truth of recovered memories rests on a few often-cited studies, but critics of the movement have contested the validity of this research. In their appendix to *Making Monsters: False Memories, Psychotherapy, and Sexual Hysteria* (1994), Richard Ofshe and Ethan Watters take up three of the best-known papers and find them seriously flawed. In 1994 Linda Meyer Williams published a study of 129 women who had been seen at a hospital between the ages of ten months and twelve years for various kinds of sexual abuse, from fondling to rape. Seventeen years later, forty-nine of the women did not remember the occasion, although thirty-three remembered other incidents of molestation. Williams concludes from her research that "therapists should be open to the possibility of child sexual abuse among patients who report no memory of such abuse." Ofshe and Watters object that the study does not discriminate between kinds of abuse, ages of occurrence, or simple forgetting versus traumatic repression. Williams herself concedes that her study shows that children sometimes forget traumatic events, but does not address the validity of recovered memories or their association with adult symptomatology. Nonetheless, Williams's paper is still discussed in books from distinguished university presses as evidence of the truth of repressed memory; psychology professor Sharon Lamb, for example, cites it in *The Trouble With Blame* (Harvard University Press, 1996).

Ofshe and Watters also critique "Recovery and Verification of Memories of Childhood Sexual Trauma" by Judith Lewis Herman and Emily Schatzow, which they call the "most-often quoted paper in the recovered memory movement." Published in the *Journal of Psychoanalytic Psychology*, the study surveyed fifty-three women who had been in incest therapy groups and concludes that three out of four were able to obtain corroborating evidence for their memories of sexual abuse. But this "evidence" consists of the women's reports back to the group; Herman and Schatzow neither set guidelines for valid evidence nor confirmed it independently by checking with other sources. Ofshe and Watters point out that only fifteen of the women had not remembered sexual abuse before they joined the group, and they wonder why women who had no memories of sexual abuse signed up for "incest survivors" therapy.[14]

Incest Camp: Selling the Courage to Heal

Recovered memory is big business in the United States, with self-help tapes, T-shirts, recovery groups, and even a mass-market best-seller. Judith Lewis Herman's testimony to "the power of survivors" appears on the cover of *The Courage to Heal*, by Ellen Bass and Laura Davis, a popular guidebook for "women survivors of sexual abuse." Published in 1988 and now in its third revised edition, *The Courage to Heal* has sold more than 800,000 copies.

The two women who produced this book are dedicated feminist activists. Ellen Bass is a poet and creative writing teacher who has worked as a counselor and group facilitator since 1970. In 1983 Bass published *I Never Told Anyone*, a collection of essays by victims of abuse who had consciously suppressed their memories or hid them from others, but not forgotten their experiences. Bass traveled around the country, giving "I Never Told Anyone" workshops that offered sisterly support and a sense of community. She recalls that on one occasion, participants "nicknamed the workshop 'Incest Camp,' and one member sent everyone T-shirts with 'I.C. Survivors' printed across the front."[15] Laura Davis is a survivor who started to have flashbacks of abuse by her grandfather six months before she began her collaboration with Ellen Bass. Bass and Davis have become the most visible and influential women in the recovered memory movement, and they bring warmth, gentleness, and undeniable sincerity to their cause.

Bass and Davis believe sexual abuse is so widespread in the U.S. that it's almost routine: "One out of three girls and one out of seven boys are sexually abused by the time they reach the age of eighteen."[16] But apparent "statistics" like these are really only estimates that blend all degrees of "abuse," from rape to dirty jokes. Louise Armstrong, whose 1978 book *Kiss Daddy Goodnight* initiated the feminist investigation of incest, comments that in the 1980s, "statistics shot wildly all over the place! From 1 in 100 to 1 in 10 and even 1 in 4." In a 1986 study, Diane E. Russell found that 16 percent of all women had been sexually abused in some way by age eighteen, 4.5 percent by their fathers. Theresa Reed, executive director of the American Professional Society on the Abuse of Children, wrote to the *New York Review of Books* on January 12, 1995, that the most conservative data estimated that 1.3 percent of American women were victims of incest. At the opposite extreme, David Finkelhor, a therapist who writes on child-hood sexual abuse, sets the estimate for American female victims of abuse at 62 percent. These "statistics" do not give consistent definitions of sexual abuse.[17]

The Courage to Heal invites readers to identify with a checklist of seventy-eight effects of sexual abuse. The questions Bass and Davis list are sadly applicable to an enormous cross section of women: "Do you have a hard time nurturing and taking care of yourself? Do you have a sense of your own interests, talents, or goals? Can you accomplish things you set out to do? Do you feel you have to be perfect? Do you have trouble expressing your feelings? Are you prone to depression? Do you feel alienated or lonely? Do you find yourself clinging to the people you care about? Can you say no? Do you try to use sex to meet needs that aren't sexual? Are you satisfied with your family relation-ships? Are you overprotective of your children?"

"Are you turned on by violent, sadistic, or incestuous fantasies?" they also ask. The assumption that sexual fantasies are improper, incor-rect, sick, is at the heart of the recovered memory phenomenon. Many women feel they must disown these fantasies, and blame them on something or someone else. The title of Bass and Davis's book plays not only on the vocabulary of the twelve-step therapies but also on the rhetoric of feminist inspirational literature of the 1970s, particularly Adrienne Rich's powerful collection *The Will to Change* (1978). Yet Rich's poems, like the original Alcoholics Anonymous philosophy, were about self-determination, action, and responsibility. *The Courage to Heal* is about victimization and accusation. Ofshe and Watters com-ment on the element of absolution in the recovered memory move-ment: "For those plagued by anything from serious mental disorders that cannot presently be effectively treated to those haunted by the simple feeling that their lives are not as fulfilling as those of the peo-ple around them, the message that they are controlled by subterranean forces carries a type of absolution: the patient is forgiven the sins she appears to have committed against herself."[18]

Race and Recovered Memory

Recovered memory is primarily a white woman's phenomenon, although *The Courage to Heal* includes four testimonies of childhood sexual abuse from black, Chicana, and Native American women. Three of these women always knew they had been abused. The exception is Lorraine Williams, a blind albino African-American woman—burdened with an appalling set of disabilities—who was abused by her brother, cousin, and grandfather. She confronted her grandfather when she was twenty, after apparently recovering a memory in therapy.

Rape and incest, however, are powerful themes in African-American women's writing. Probably the most famous autobiography is Maya Angelou's *I Know Why the Caged Bird Sings*, a best-seller in England and the United States since its publication in 1969. Angelou movingly describes being sexually molested at the age of eight by her mother's boyfriend, Mr. Freeman. The family discovers that she has been raped, and she has to be treated in a hospital for injuries. When Mr. Freeman is tried for the rape, Maya is terrified to tell the court what happened. He's nonetheless convicted but never serves time. While he's out on appeal, anonymous members of the community beat him to death. Maya feels responsible for his death and decides that her penance must be to stop talking. For about five years, she speaks only to her brother. Finally a compassionate teacher breaks her silence. Toni Morrison's tragic novel *The Bluest Eye* (1970), Alice Walker's Pulitzer Prize–winning *The Color Purple* (1982), and Sapphire's *Push* (1996) also deal with the anguish of black girls who are raped by their fathers. Far from being forgotten, these experiences result in pregnancies, madness, and despair.

How much does this fiction reflect social reality? Oprah Winfrey is one of the most famous African-American women who has come forward as a survivor of childhood sexual abuse. Her television documentary about abuse, *Scared Silent*, ran on PBS, CBS, and NBC on September 4, 1992. Studies like Melba Wilson's *Crossing the Boundary: Black Women Survive Incest* (1993) describe incest and child sexual abuse as major problems for black women, but present the problem as one of deliberate secrecy and shame rather than repression.

Class and Recovered Memory

What about the role of class in the recovered memory movement? In 1994 on a visit to Cambridge, Massachusetts, I read a story in the

Harvard alumni magazine entitled "The Career Price of Sexual Abuse." It recounted the experience of Marion, a Radcliffe College alumna in her forties who had worked for twenty years as an occupational therapist in a large veterans' facility.[19] For some time, Marion had been feeling depressed and bored with her job. Finally, "too many sleepless nights got to her"; she sought psychotherapy and "uncovered an increasingly familiar trauma"—a memory of sexual abuse as a preschooler by "an older male authority figure," not a family member. When she began to think of herself as a survivor, Marion could explain many of the disappointments and failures in her professional life, including her decision to go into occupational therapy rather than medicine and her difficulties with male colleagues. Talking about her experience at the office, she found "twelve other people right around me" who had also suffered sexual abuse. When she mentioned her history to a male boss, he surprised her by being sympathetic. Encouraged by these responses, she was organizing a meeting of "childhood abuse survivors attending the Harvard-Radcliffe reunions." Marion reported that she was doing better on the job and that her health benefits allowed her not only to continue therapy but even to take sick leave "at the most painful moment in her recovery."

Clinical social worker Ann Dart, the assistant director of Radcliffe Career Services, thinks these benefits should be increased. "When all is raw," she says, "when women survivors are really fragile, they may require the safety of a hospital for a few weeks." Phyllis Stein, the director of Radcliffe Career Services, has seen many cases like Marion's. Stein and Dart have begun to explore analogies between abuse in the family and performance in the workplace. Surmising that people with a history of abuse "may work absurdly long hours," "may be unable to control their rage," or "may underachieve," they conclude that childhood abuse is a trauma that "pervades every aspect of your working life." Stein and Dart perceive themselves as catalysts and pioneers entering "uncharted" and "unexplored territory." They have already organized two conferences for other health care professionals, and are planning a third.

This hystory in a magazine with the imprimatur of a prestigious university illustrates how attitudes and beliefs about recovered memory have been written into American middle-class culture's symptom pool. In the slippage between hypothesis and dogmatic claim, Stein and Dart escalate recovered memory to cover a new set of work-related symptoms and recommend that workers recovering memories in therapy receive insurance benefits and even hospitalization. Marion recovers a memory of abuse by an unnamed male authority figure, not dad or uncle, so that the memory does not incur additional risks or discomfort for her. Under its umbrella, however, she redefines all the vocational disappointments of her life, from her original choice of a career to her uneasiness with male colleagues.

The experience of recovered memory seems to have been a good one for Marion both socially and professionally. She tells a male boss and unexpectedly gets sympathy. She confides in co-workers and, astonishingly, finds twelve right in the same office with similar problems. Cheered by these happenings, she becomes more assertive and secure at work, widens her social networks, and even decides to start a Harvard-Radcliffe organization of abuse survivors. Whether or not she actually was abused as a child, she has used the survivor's narrative to change her own behavior, and inevitably her co-workers respond to her new confidence. I am certain that many professional women besides Marion have found comfort and community through the process of recovered memory, but perhaps being bored with work cannot be cured by hospitalization.

Recovering Men's Memories of Sexual Abuse

In their preface to the third edition of *The Courage to Heal,* Bass and Davis note that if they were writing the book today, they would make one major change: "We wouldn't write the book just for women. It has become clear that boys are also sexually abused in large numbers." They have added a section on resources and books for men, which includes some controversial cases. Richard Berendzen, for example, was a college dean at American University convicted of making obscene phone calls with pedophile content. He then remembered sexual abuse by his mother fifty years earlier. Berendzen's book, *Come Here: A Man Overcomes the Tragic Aftermath of Childhood Sexual Abuse* (1993), is cited without mention of his crimes or conviction. Richard Rhodes, a scientist who has written about the making of the A-bomb but also about his sexual adventures, explains that he was abused in a book called *A Hole in the World: An American Boyhood* (1990). The Menendez brothers, Erik and Lyle, on trial in California for the murder of their parents, defended themselves by arguing that they had been sexually abused by their father. (They were convicted in March 1996.) Recently, other men have attributed adult problems to childhood sexual abuse. In *Secret Life* (1995), the poet Michael Ryan blames his lifelong "sex addiction" on being molested by a neighbor at the age of five.

Ellen Bass wrote the introduction to Mike Lew's *Victims No Longer* (1988), the major book for men who were abused or those seeking recovered memories. In most respects, the book follows the model of *The Courage to Heal*, with advice, personal testimonies, and checklists of symptoms. Lew, however, must deal with issues specifically, although not exclusively, relevant to men: the taboo against male emotion, questions about whether the abused become abusers, and problematic attitudes toward homosexuality. Lew suggests that in his experience "abuse is probably not the cause of sexual orientation, but it almost always leads the survivor to have *confused feelings* about his sexuality. . . . At its worst, internalized homophobia can cause gay men to wrongly blame themselves (or their gayness) for their being abused."[20]

Lew seems like a thoughtful and devoted therapist, but his book repeatedly indicates his expectations that abuse exists whenever a patient has forgotten large chunks of childhood experience. While he is careful to warn patients about the pitfalls of hypnosis, he doesn't seem aware of how much he himself is implanting suggestions. "When clients tell me that they have no recollection of whole pieces of their childhood," he states, "I assume the likelihood of some sort of abuse." He further believes that incest survivors have cultivated "slow, measured, soothing, lulling tones" of voice and when he hears such a voice, Lew suspects he has found another incest survivor. "When I find myself feeling as though I'm being soothed by a person who is talking to me . . . I assume that the speaker may have a history of abuse." Lew advises repeating the story, telling everyone who will listen, becoming the barroom bore of incest: "Each time the story of abuse is told, another piece of healing takes place. As the story is repeated, more details are recovered." He doesn't seem to realize that telling the story fixes it ever more firmly in the teller's belief system and encourages the fictional construction of a hystory in which plausible elaborations make sense of gaps and contradictions. What he calls details are more likely to be plot developments.[21]

The men's testimonies seem more extreme and bizarre than those in *The Courage to Heal*. Gerald John attempted suicide at age four and was an obese adolescent who had affairs with older men. He's an alcoholic, unhappy, and in therapy; at a meeting of Adult Children of Alcoholics, he hears a man tell about being sexually molested by his father. Weeping, John rushes to his therapist, who tells him that he "must be ready to face his own past incest." Unfortunately, John cannot remember a single detail. Three years of therapy have not produced any memories, but Gerald John is certain that his father molested him when he was three. Frank, brought into the recovery movement by his girlfriend, begins to have vague memories of abuse and decides to go to an incest survivors' group for help. He now has stopped working full-time and attends meetings of several therapy groups—Incest Survivors' Anonymous, Debtors' Anonymous, Sex and Love Addicts Anonymous—as well as individual therapy. Lew suggests that patients dealing with remembered abuse also try to heal themselves through New Age body work, including massage, cranio-sacral therapy, reflexology, Polarity Therapy, Rolfing, Soman, Feldenkrais, acupuncture, dance, aerobics, prayer, and meditation. *Victims No More* is now in its second paperback printing; Lew's preface announces his availability for workshops and provides the telephone number of his lecture agent.

The Memory Wars

We are well into the third act of the drama of recovered memory. These days the media concentrate less on recovered memories than on what Frederick Crews calls "the memory wars." As of the mid-1990s, the adversaries of recovered memory had established their own institutions, including the False Memory Syndrome Foundation in the U.S. and the False Memory Syndrome Society in the U.K. The cycle turns again: women who accused their parents of sexual abuse now blame their therapists, accusing *them* in a newsletter called *The Retractor*. The False Memory Syndrome Foundation, which publishes the newsletter, and the British False Memory Society contest a particular genre of trauma narrative that's often obtained while the patient is under hypnosis. The False Memory Syndrome Foundation wants to regulate the practice of psychotherapy through a Mental Health Consumer Protection Act, which would require the patient's informed consent, prohibit insurance funding for questionable or unproved treatments, criminalize false accusations of abuse, ban memory recovery and enhancement as courtroom evidence, and create a Model Licensing Act. They believe the law should require psychotherapists to keep records, carry malpractice insurance, and be liable for several years after the treatment.

Recovered memory therapists have of course fought back, in what they describe as a battle for abused children and adult victims. But it's also a fight for their own survival. The metaphors of their movement have become real on another level; many therapists feel abused, molested, and harassed. In the third edition of *The Courage to Heal*, for example, Bass and Davis respond to what they see as the backlash against recovered memory and offer reassurance and strategies for coping. They remind the reader that debate deters healing and protest that they've been quoted out of context: "Most of the coverage has been extremely adversarial, belittling survivors, depicting them as gullible victims, vengeful children, or simply crazy."[22] Bass and Davis accuse their opponents of being abusers or supporting abusers and charge that pedophiles and rapists stand to benefit from "false memory syndrome." They also claim that false memories of sexual abuse are uncommon: "Even if all five thousand families who've contacted the FMS Foundation were indeed falsely accused, that amounts to only .01%— or one-hundredth of a percent of the estimated number of adult survivors of child abuse in this country." Ultimately, Bass and Davis return to the authenticity of personal feeling: "We must reaffirm that survivors of child sexual abuse are the true experts on their experience. Many professionals have spoken out eloquently on behalf of survivors—and many others have insulted, pathologized, or dismissed them. Yet in the midst of all this debate *about* survivors, we need to remember that our greatest understanding comes not in listening to professionals, but to the survivors themselves."[23]

How can one accept or respect such reasoning? Five thousand real protesting families are compared to questionable *estimates* of the total number of abuses, whether or not they are reported. I am particularly disturbed by the ethical and moral relativism of the argument. If 5000 people—or five people, or one—are unjustly accused, that is important. It cannot be factored in as an allowable margin of error. We must remember that we are not talking about children forced to continue living with possibly abusive parents but about adults recalling past experiences. In a situation where the alleged abuse is well in the past, there is all the more reason for caution and consideration. Surely confronting outraged parents cannot be easy or helpful for patients either.

Feminism and Recovered Memory

Some think the heyday of recovered memory has already passed; at the *New York Times Book Review*, editors ask skeptically, "Wasn't the debate on false memory put to rest by the slew of books that came out last year?"[24] The answer, alas, is no, and feminism is involved in the wars over memory. Judith Lewis Herman is one of many feminist therapists who link their practice to the moral imperatives and political energies of the women's movement; Herman also connects her research on recovered memory with a feminist agenda and genealogy. The daughter of the pioneering feminist psychologist Helen Block Lewis, Herman dedicates *Trauma and Recovery* to her mother's memory and to her "compassion for the afflicted and oppressed." Gloria Steinem calls Herman's book a "landmark." Phyllis Chesler describes it as "one of the most important psychiatric works to be published since Freud."

Herman and Steinem are among the leading feminist figures who warn that a critique of therapies, of incest recovery and recovered memory movements, and of women's stories could undermine the credibility of all women's protest. "Historically," writes Herman, "every time a subordinate group begins to make serious progress, a backlash occurs. This is what happened one hundred years ago when Freud created the myth that hysterical women fantasize about sexual abuse."[25] They fear that if we challenge the current dogmas about hysteria and abuse, women will once more be prevented "from speaking—and being believed—about very real abuse."[26]

But the women being silenced today are other feminists who have criticized the ideas and methods of the recovered memory movement. Elizabeth Loftus, who has written and lectured about the myth of repressed memory, has been booed, hissed, denounced, and accused of disloyalty to women. Carol Tavris, a psychologist who published a critical assessment of movement literature in the *New York Times Book Review* in 1993, was bombarded with hostile mail; the editors ran three full pages of letters condemning her, including one from *Secret Survivors* author E. Sue Blume that placed Tavris "on the side of the molesters, rapists, pedophiles and other misogynists."[27]

I had a firsthand taste of this hostility when I gave a talk about recovered memory at the Dartmouth School of Criticism and Theory in the summer of 1994. Some of the women in the audience were so outraged by my remarks that they organized lunches and workshops; I was invited to defend myself against their anger and distress. They asked me how, as a feminist, I could wash our dirty linen, so to speak, in front of men, including Dartmouth undergraduates who might use my words against any women complaining of any kind of abuse. How could I live with myself, knowing I was making it harder for women to be believed? How did I dare challenge the authority of therapists and psychologists? A few of the women asked me to take the chapter out of my book. They looked stunned when I said that, on the contrary, I planned to expand it.

Of course, the sexual, physical, and emotional abuse of children is a terrible reality. My quarrel in this book is not with the realities of child abuse, or the vigorous investigation of *children*'s complaints, but with the ideologies of recovered memory and the process of accusation based on adult therapy. Feminism has a strong enlightenment, rationalist tradition of debate and skepticism, whose memory I attempt to recover and reassert. We betray our tradition if we succumb to easy answers. Our primary obligation must always be to the truth.

Meanwhile, novels and movies continue to reproduce recovered-memory plots. Jane Smiley's Pulitzer Prize–winning novel, *A Thousand Acres* (1991), uses recovered memory to update and explain *King Lear*. Iowa farmer Larry Cook divides his property between his two eldest daughters, Ginny and Rose, cutting out his favorite child, Caroline. Ginny narrates the novel, so we tend to side with her; but in the Shakespearian parallel, she is Goneril, one of the evil sisters. Smiley follows the *King Lear* plot with one major exception. When Ginny has an affair, quarrels with her father, and gets into a murderous rivalry with her sister, she recovers the memory of incestuous childhood rape. The malicious sister, Rose, first suggests the idea to Ginny, who resists and denies it; but returning to the room she lived in as a child, Ginny is abruptly flooded with horrible images: "Lying here, I knew that he had been in there to me, that my father had lain with me in that bed, that I had looked at the top of his head, at his balding spot in the brown grizzled hair, while feeling him suck my breasts. That was the only memory I could endure before I jumped out of the bed with a cry." Eventually she reconstructs a partial memory of her past: "I never remembered penetration or pain, or even his hands on my body, and I never worked out how many times there were. I remembered my strategy, which had been desperate limp inertia."

Is this memory or the after-effect of powerful suggestion? Should we reread *King Lear* as a play about child abuse? *A Thousand Acres* has been received as the account of a reliable narrator. As far as I can tell, none of the critics who so much admired Smiley's impressive novel questioned the reliability of Ginny's narrative, asked about the circumstances in which the partial memories were recovered, or pointed to the devastating effects on Ginny and her family. In the ongoing cycle of recovered memory, *A Thousand Acres* itself seems like a confirmation of trauma theory. Even in literary criticism, there are memory wars to be fought.

Multiple Personality Syndrome

On the TV Monday night movie, Heather Locklear plays a dowdy wife who is also a biker chick, a high school dropout with a secret gift for computers. Guess what—it's another case of multiple personality. Along with recovered memory, the diagnosis of multiple personality syndrome has become epidemic in the U.S. since the 1980s. Multiple personality disorder emerged in part as an answer to one of the most vexing questions for recovered memory advocates: how exactly did the child forget the experience of sexual abuse? After each episode? After the entire experience? Doctors and therapists maintained that children dealt with the pain, fear, and shock of sexual abuse through splitting or dissociation. The memory of abuse was always there but contained in another personality or many personality fragments— "alters" who sprang into being to contend with the trauma. Therapists could contact these alters through hypnosis, using the Inner Self-Helper, an alter who mediates between the various fragments. Then they could reach a child alter, who might testify to sexual abuse as well as to other suppressed or repressed aspects of the host personality. When theories of childhood sexual abuse, dissociation, and repression coincided in the early 1980s, the contemporary epidemic of multiple personality syndrome began. Between 1980 and 1984, the official diagnosis was Multiple Personality Disorder or MPD. In *DSM-IV* (1994), the official heading is "Dissociative Identity Disorder (*formerly* Multiple Personality Disorder)." Under either name, multiple personality has become a familiar hystory, and has developed its own styles of advocacy.

"If ever there was a movement," writes Ian Hacking, a rumpled professor of philosophy at the University of Toronto who has spent years studying multiple personality and the sciences of memory, and whose book, *Rewriting the Soul* (1995), is the most thoughtful recent study, "it is the multiple personality movement. It has a rather fresh, American quality to it. It appeals to down-home folks, who are much more at ease with the bizarre than city slickers are." Hacking says the movement has an "egalitarian look": patients and doctors share platforms, and both gay liberation and fundamentalist revival meetings contribute to the atmosphere of coming out. Both patients and doctors have become well-known, and have entered popular mythology.

Hacking believes that "the multiple movement germinated in the sixties, emerged in the seventies, matured in the eighties, and is adapting itself to new environments in the nineties."[1] Split or "multiplex" personalities have been described in medical literature for over a century under such names as "double consciousness" and "alternating personality," but between 1922 and 1972 fewer than fifty cases had been reported in the medical literature. Traditionally, multiple personality was linked with spiritualism and reincarnation, and with mediums like Madame Blavatsky.

But in 1973, *Sybil* appeared. Dr. Cornelia Wilbur, a New York psychotherapist, had for a very long period—2,534 office hours—treated a woman she called "Sybil Dorsett," a multiple personality with sixteen alters; Sybil's story, told by journalist and English professor Flora Rheta Schreiber, became a best-selling book and later a movie. Schreiber describes this as an example of "grande hystérie" and one of the psychiatrists who saw Sybil called her "a brilliant hysteric." According to journalist Mark Pendergrast, her case has provided "the template for the modern epidemic of MPD diagnoses."[2] Strikingly in Sybil's case, the mother rather than the father was the abusive parent who had sexually tormented her daughter. A new enemy had been identified: the abusive woman.

Wilbur chaired the first organized panel on MPD at the annual meeting of the American Psychiatric Association in 1977. By 1982 MPD had its own national organization, and *Time* magazine ran a cover story on the phenomenon. Newsletters, seminars, workshops, and regional study groups moved multiple personality from the margins of psychotherapy to the center. "According to movement folklore," writes

Hacking, "the die was cast on Saturday, 30 April 1983, at a historic dinner at Mamma Leone's restaurant in New York," when a group of MPD therapists decided to found the International Society for the Study of Multiple Personality and Dissociation.[3]

In 1984, therapist Richard Kluft, one of the society's founders, proposed a four-part model of MPD: it begins when "1) a child able to dissociate is exposed to overwhelming stimuli 2) these cannot be managed by less drastic defenses 3) dissociated contents become linked to underlying substrates for personality organization and 4) there are no restorative influences, or there are too many 'double-binds.'"[4] *DSM-III-R*, the diagnostic handbook of the American Psychiatric Association published in 1987, included streamlined criteria for MPD among its official diagnoses, making health and insurance coverage easier to obtain. "I love victory," George Greaves, then president of the ISSMPD, crowed in the *Newsletter*.[5] In 1988, the professional journal *Dissociation*, owned by Richard Kluft, began publication. By 1990, more than 20,000 cases had been diagnosed in the United States.[6] Dr. Colin Ross, an influential proponent of MPD, claims that one percent of the population—over two million Americans—"fit the criteria for being a multiple personality."[7]

But many specialists in dissociation maintain that MPD is actually an iatrogenic disorder created in therapy. In their view, MPD offers a paradigmatic case study of the ways institutions and charismatic physicians can spread a disorder. British psychologist Ray Aldridge-Morris calls MPD "an exercise in delusion"; Canadian psychiatrist Harold Merskey thinks it "never occurs as a spontaneous natural event in adults," and that "suggestion, social encouragement, preparation by expectation, and the reward of attention can produce and sustain a second personality."[8] Dr. Paul McHugh, director of the Department of Psychiatry and Behavioral Science at Johns Hopkins University, believes that "MPD is an iatrogenic behavior syndrome, promoted by suggestion and maintained by clinical attention, social consequences, and group loyalties."[9]

Even the most recent diagnostic manual of mental disorders, *DSM-IV*, is cautious about what it now terms "dissociative identity disorder": "Individuals with Dissociative Identity Disorder frequently report having experienced severe physical and sexual abuse, especially during childhood. Controversy surrounds the accuracy of such reports, because childhood memories may be subject to distortion and individuals with this disorder tend to be highly hypnotizable and especially vulnerable to suggestive influences."[10]

MPD and Gender: The Patients

Like chronic fatigue syndrome and recovered memory, multiple personality is primarily a female disorder; nine out of ten patients are women. In addition, according to *DSM-IV*, "Females tend to have more identities than do males, averaging 15 or more whereas males average approximately 8 identities." Hacking describes a prototypical case in the 1980s: "a middle-class woman with the values and expectations of her social group. She is in her thirties, and she has quite a large number of distinct alters—sixteen, say. She spent a large part of her life denying the existence of these alters. The alters include children, persecutors, and helpers, and at least one male alter. She was sexually abused on many occasions by a trusted man in her family when she was very young. She has suffered many other indignities from people from whom she needs love. The needs are, among other things, part of her class values, which may be abetted or taken advantage of by her abuser. She has previously been through parts of the mental health system and has been diagnosed with many complaints, but her treatments have not helped her in the long run until she came to a clinician sensitive to multiple personality. She has had amnesia for parts of her past. She has the experience of 'coming to' in a strange situation with no idea of how she got there. She is severely depressed and has quite often thought about suicide."[11]

"Molly," for example, is a forty-two-year-old divorced mother from the Midwest with a horde of alters she calls "little people": Little Girl, Girl, Mute, Elizabeth, Abbie, Lizzie, Maggie, Jane, and Clear. A patient at Baltimore's Sheppard-Pratt Institute, Molly mutilates herself and relives in therapy her recovered memories of repeated childhood sexual abuse. She is described by James M. Glass in *Shattered Selves: Multiple Personality in a Postmodern World*: "When Molly tells how her father forced her to watch chickens being slaughtered, when he insisted she disembowel them, then raped her repeatedly in the shed behind the chicken coop, she speaks of experiences that created a series of identities. . . . Molly's many identities derive from a brutality, exercised by paternal will and power, which had literally no regard for her body or her being."[12]

In the 1990s, multiple personality patients were also reporting abuse by other women, and some feminist activists had begun to assert that abuse by mothers was a hidden, underestimated problem. This assumption seemed to come from popular narratives like *Sybil* and *The Flock*, where abusive mothers are villains with the will and power to hurt their daughters. In a study of these best-sellers, the literary critic Rosaria Champagne has noticed that the therapists are surrogate mothers who seem to use the same power: "Daughters who suffer from MPD find wholeness only when they shift loyalty from the evil mother to the good one, a shift often accomplished with bribes and solicitations from the mother-therapist. These mother-therapists are indeed better mothers than the sadistic mothers who precede them, but their cure comes with a price: entrapment, always, in some mother's narrative."[13]

Louise Armstrong sees the shift from the abusive father to the abusive mother as a move away from feminist action to psychiatric intervention: "Not seeing a high incidence of abuse on the part of mothers meant it was there, but so much *worse* that no one could speak out. And if that were so—then there was no need to challenge *male* privilege; we could simply focus on human pathology."[14] The British anthropologist Jean La Fontaine concurs: "The insistence that there is much sexual abuse perpetrated by women which is never revealed may be the product of discomfort with the idea that this sexual problem is solely a masculine one."[15]

Why do women predominate in the world of multiple personality? Hacking reminds us that in the nineteenth century, these patients were often diagnosed as hysterics, and that the label of hysteria was much more commonly assigned to women than to men. He presents a four-part hypothesis: first, men act out the latent anger that produces dissociation in violence and crime; women direct it against themselves, often in acts of self-mutilation. Various forms of self-mutilating behavior, such as hair-pulling, slashing, and head-banging, appear in many MPD cases, and Dr. Richard Ofshe observes that the reported incidence of self-mutilation among female patients has doubled since multiple personality was heralded a decade or so ago, while psychologist Dusty Miller, in *Women Who Hurt Themselves*, also cites MPD as a factor.[16] Second, Hacking suggests, dissociation is a culturally reinforced way for women to express inadmissible emotions; "dissociative behavior is a language of distress . . ."The increasing number of female personalities or alters seems related to the increased number and complexity of social roles women are expected to fill. Third, more girls than boys are subjected to childhood sexual abuse. Fourth, women are socialized to accept therapeutic suggestion, and men are socialized to resist it.[17]

Meanwhile, multiple personality is a popular defense for male serial killers. The Hillside Strangler, a California serial killer, used an MPD defense in his trial; in Florida, journalist Sondra London fell in love with serial killer Danny Rolling, called "the Gainesville Slasher," and maintained that multiple personalities accounted for his crimes. "I have a different relationship with each of the Dannys," she claimed. His evil "Gemini" personality did the rapes and murders.[18] Hacking argues that "the deep-felt need on the part of some clinicians to find more multiple males virtually guarantees that in the short run an increasing proportion of males will be diagnosed with dissociative identity disorder, and that they will come from convict populations in prison, from Vietnam and Gulf War vets, and from juvenile delinquents."[19]

Another specialist, Jim Schnabel, writes that discussions of multiple personality are culture-bound, and that analyzing non-Western forms is revealing: "Many spirit-possession syndromes in the Third World have aspects and dynamics remarkably similar to those found in the modern multiple personality movement." Many anthropologists believe women predominate in these cults because they need to voice "forbidden desires in male-dominated societies."[20] Sherrill Mulhern points out that many analysts see spirit possession "as a theater for voicing frustrations and grievances in male-dominated societies, or as a coercive tool used by women to secure retribution or revenge against men." In circumstances where "women have been subjected to starvation, beating, mutilation, and divorces under social and legal systems that deprive many of them of any means of recourse, . . . the idiom of spirit possession may be the only culturally available refuge."[21]

How should we interpret women's vulnerability to MPD? Ian Hacking points out that "if there was ever a field that needed some caustic feminist analysis, it is multiple personality."[22] Margo Rivera, a feminist clinical psychologist who has worked with multiples, has noticed that women often have vulnerable, weak child alters who are female, and tough, strong, protective alters who are male. She hypothesizes that "the experience of these alter personalities as they fight with each other for status, power, and influence over the individual is powerfully illustrative of the social construction of masculinity and femininity in our society."[23]

Looking at literary and social history suggests that for over a century, multiplicity has offered women a way to express forbidden aspects of the self. At the turn of the century, Dr. Norton Prince in Boston treated two famous cases, whom he called Miss Beauchamp and B.C.A. As in the celebrated *Three Faces of Eve* (1957), which set the style for female multiplicity before child abuse entered the picture as a cause, these women had developed three personalities to accommodate elements of sexuality, independence, and daring that were unacceptable in their decorous milieu. In treatment, however, Prince insisted that the wilder, more rebellious personalities had to be suppressed. Even in the 1990s, we should not be surprised that women find it difficult or impossible to acknowledge erotic, antisocial, unfaithful aspects of their own psyches. Confessional narratives and popular fiction establish a conventional MPD plot for women, in which the other selves and the "memories" of abuse emerge when an adult woman is doing something that makes her feel ashamed. Self-mutilation seems like a drastic way of punishing the body that commits these acts, while multiplicity both punishes and absolves the mind.

Narratives of Trauma

Fictional narratives inevitably interact with the hystories of MPD circulating in our culture. In women's novels and autobiography, remembering a childhood sexual trauma often leads to discovery of multiple selves, and ultimately to self-knowledge. One of the most frequently cited texts is Sylvia Fraser's *My Father's House: A Memoir of Incest and Healing* (1984), which describes a split personality created by Fraser's sexual relationship with her father, an experience she had forgotten until adulthood, when she consulted a therapist in Toronto. Under hypnosis with a sympathetic therapist Fraser recovered memories of abuse, which explain to her satisfaction why she has never been completely happy and why she had an affair that ended her marriage to a decent, loving man. Since her therapist believed that child abuse often leads to multiple personality syndrome, he encouraged Fraser to locate her other self. "When the conflict caused by my sexual relationship with my father became too acute to bear," she writes, "I created a secret accomplice for my daddy by splitting my personality in two."

It is the other self, Fraser tells us, who is writing the book: "My other self has learned to type. She presses my keys, throwing up masses of defiant memories." "Imagine this," she concludes, "imagine you discover that for many years another person intimately shared your life without you knowing it." Fraser does not have dramatic or even visible symptoms of either *grande* or *petite hystérie*. But she cannot accept responsibility for the affair that destroyed her marriage; she blames the affair on her other self. "It wasn't so much passion that tempted me,"

Fraser writes, "but compulsion that drove her. Like a sleepwalker I watched askance while someone who looked like me cast aside everything I valued to recreate an infantile world in which no will or desire existed outside of the illicit affair." In order to account for the adulterous affair, Fraser must posit an incestuous relationship with Daddy. Actually she never quite remembers the incest, but she knows it happened. It must have, for otherwise why wouldn't she be happy? Why wouldn't she be faithful? Seeing herself as a victim allows Fraser to forgive herself for the infidelity, for the damage to her husband, who died soon after the divorce, and even for writing books.[24]

Herman describes *My Father's House* as a paradigmatic survivor's narrative, a good hystory. "In Freud's time," she asserts, Fraser would "have been diagnosed as a classic hysteric. Today she would be diagnosed with multiple personality disorder. . . . With her remarkable creative gifts, she is able to reconstruct the story of a self formed under the burden of repeated, inescapable abuse."[25] But Fraser's narrative raises questions about its authenticity as a reconstruction. By her own account, Fraser feels terrible guilt for a sexual indiscretion that does not fit her standards of respectable behavior. She feels guilty about her husband's death. The abuse memory "returns" at a moment when Fraser is desperately trying to retain her self-image and self-esteem. Her artful use of literary conventions, including different typefaces, suggests that her story is shaped by the fiction of multiple personalities as well. In the decade before she remembered her sexual abuse experience, Fraser wrote four novels, "each rife with sexual violence that offended some critics and puzzled me. Where did this harsh impulse come from?" She studied psychology and "learned how to interpret dreams as messages from my unconscious."[26] Her memoir is a crafted and very literary work.

Roseanne is another much-publicized survivor of sexual abuse; her story has been cited even in the usually skeptical pages of the *New Yorker*. In *My Lives* (1994), Roseanne attributes her eating disorders, alcoholism, self-mutilation, teenage pregnancy, and bouts of delinquency and prostitution to childhood molestation by her father—an experience she says she repressed until her forties. Roseanne writes that sexual abuse led to a split personality as well: "The parts of me that knew everything . . . had each split off, become its own being, its own story, its own country." These other beings do all the things Roseanne regrets. In writing the book, she encourages other women to tell their stories: "How many of us are there? Shall we choose to march, to make ourselves and our numbers visible? How many times would we ring the world? I wish I could take away your pain and mine."[27]

Trauma theory also shapes the plots of several respected feminist novels, such as Margaret Atwood's *The Robber Bride* (1994), in which one of her three heroines has a split personality because of forgotten childhood sexual abuse. In a flashback scene to the childhood of Karen/Charis, Atwood describes this fragmentation or division taking place instantly when she is raped by an uncle:

> Then he falls on top of Karen and puts his slabby hand over her mouth, and splits her in two. He splits her right up the middle, and her skin comes open like the dry skin of a cocoon, and Charis flies out. Her new body is light as a feather, light as air.

Years later, Karen reemerges and attempts to murder the woman who has stolen Charis's lover.

The parallels between MPD case histories and novels are not coincidental. Many researchers who have written about multiple personality have commented on the overlap between confessional studies, pulp fiction, and serious novels. Hacking says that "in no other field of mental illness do fact, fiction, and fear play so relentlessly to each other. . . . If real child abuse is the major key for the popular acceptance of the theme of multiple personality, then fantasy crime is its minor."[28] Most gory paperback thrillers depict serial killers as multiple personalities who were sexually abused in childhood, but there are also a great many Sister Hydes in made-for-TV movies like "Shattered Mind," which aired on NBC in May 1996 with Heather Locklear playing shy Suzy, violent Ginger, little girl Bonnie, and math whiz Victoria. Three faces are no longer sufficient for the modern multiple heroine; as women's roles and options increase, so do their alters.

MPD: The Therapists

Since its inception, the MPD movement has been led by an unusually controversial group of doctors and therapists: Cornelia Wilbur, Richard Kluft, Ralph Allison, who came up with the idea of the inner self helper, Eugene Bliss, Frank Putnam, Bennett Braun, Richard Loewenstein, and Colin Ross. As in other epidemic hysterias, the disorders follow the doctors. Sheppard-Pratt Hospital in Baltimore, for example, has had a large increase in MPD patients since Dr. Richard Loewenstein arrived there in 1987, and at least one of his colleagues, psychiatrist Donald Ross, is troubled by the situation: "A group knowledge of MPD begins to circulate among the patients and, like a contagion of sorts, it multiplies. We see dissociative phenomena more readily.... The therapeutic techniques used—hypnosis, regression, and abreaction—give us a sense that we are doing something and that therapy is moving in an understandable direction."[29] Bennett Braun's dissociative behaviors unit at Rush Presbyterian in Chicago has been another environment in which MPD has spread. Shadows Glen Hospital in Houston, where Dr. Judith Peterson headed the dissociative disorders unit in the early 1990s, was a third center for MPD cases, seven of whom have now filed suit.

Furthermore, as disputes developed over their theories and practice, MPD therapists became increasingly conspiratorial in their beliefs. "By the early 1980s," Sherrill Mulhern contends, "conspiracy theory had become the lynchpin of multiple personality disorder."[30] I met Mulhern in London, and visited her in Paris at her office, where she showed me videotapes of TV talk shows about multiplicity from the 1980s that provided viewers with a visual and dramatic template of the disorder. A charismatic American expatriate with a husky voice and a ready laugh, Mulhern has attended many conferences around the world on MPD, and has watched tapes of private therapeutic sessions. Her notes and articles on MPD and satanic ritual abuse, written from the perspective of an anthropologist specializing in ritual cults, have been widely cited.

In an article for *The International Journal of Clinical and Experimental Hypnosis* in 1994, Mulhern analyzed the way multiple personality therapy grew enamored of conspiracy theory. First of all, some specialists assumed that the number and complexity of multiple personalities a patient revealed under hypnosis was an indicator of the degree of childhood sexual trauma. The more alters, the more abuse. So multiples witnessed to the "powerful social conspiracy of silence which surrounds child sexual abuse." Second, therapists developed a theory of the internal conspiracies of alters themselves. Over 80% of the MPD patients were unaware of their other selves before therapy. Doctors described the alter personalities as warring factions within the mind, independent covert actors who struggle for dominance, often with evil intent. Thus therapists saw themselves as agents in "the unconscious conspiracy of potentially unlimited numbers of personalities who must be identified, organized, contained, and coaxed into revealing their terrible secrets." Mulhern concludes that "although there is convincing evidence that during abreactive psychotherapy many multiples are not remembering experienced trauma but instead are confabulating traumatic narratives, this is not what either they or their clinicians think they are doing."[31] Instead, they believe that they are on a mutual quest to expose conspiracy and relieve suffering.

When their views are challenged, some therapists revise and expand their conspiracy model to include external enemies who are trying to silence them. Canadian Colin Ross, for example, the president of the International Society for the Study of Multiple Personality Disorder, is among the leading medical advocates of MPD. But Ross also believes that many of his patients are multiples because the CIA has trained them to be secret agents, "Manchurian candidates," who are "being used by the intelligence community on an ongoing basis for espionage and surveillance purposes and possibly for assassinations." He believes that Sirhan Sirhan and possible Lee Harvey Oswald were among their number. In a 1993 proposal for a book on satanic ritual abuse widely circulated in the therapeutic community, Ross charges that the CIA has been brainwashing children in secret laboratories. On Canadian television, he implied that attacks on MPD may be funded by the CIA: "If the dissociative field was starting to uncover mind-control programming that was hidden in the alters, naturally they wouldn't be enthusiastic about that happening. It would be necessary to have some sort of political strategy in place to counter that." In the United States, Dr. Bennett Braun, a former president of the ISSMPD, has said that the FBI is trying to assassinate him because he has implicated it in satanic conspiracies involving multiples.[32]

MPD As Epidemic: The American Connection

What will happen next to multiple personality? As of the mid-1990s, Hacking saw signs that the movement might split into a professional clinical group dominated by psychiatrists and a "populist alliance" of patients and therapists "who welcome a culture of multiples." These groups will be competing for clients and health insurance funding. Among the clinical group, "the message is, get rid of the personalities altogether. Dissociation has become the name of the game, of the disorder, of the journal, and of the organization." Among the populists, personalities are recognized, named, and spoken to; multiple personality has become a lifestyle with its own activities, even trips to amusement parks like Six Flags Over Georgia. Ironically, what may keep these two contending factions together is the appearance of the False Memory Foundation. Hacking writes, "There is nothing like a common enemy to heal splits."[33]

Following the pattern of other hysterical epidemics, multiple personality has turned up in many countries besides the U.S. In 1989, according to one standard medical guidebook, *Multiple Personality*, MPD was a syndrome frequent in the United States and virtually absent "elsewhere in the world."[34] In 1994, *DSM-IV* stated that "the relatively high rates of the disorder reported in the United States might indicate that this is a culture-specific syndrome."[35] But only a year later, the situation had dramatically changed, and multiple personality flourished wherever missionaries of American MPD had been received. Ebola virus or Lassa fever may be escaping from the rain forest, but multiple personality is being exported from the United States, through the testimony and diligence of therapists trained by American experts.

In the *International Society for the Study of Dissociation News*, for example, Ondra Williams, a therapist from New Zealand, writes that in 1989, when she had her first client with MPD, she was told "Oh, that's an American thing! We don't have that here!" But "interest continues to grow." Three therapists in Istanbul, "after reading the North American literature," diagnosed a case of multiple personality; now "weekly seminars, case presentations, and supervision meetings about dissociative disorders are held in our clinical psychotherapy unit." In Norway there have been seminars since 1993. In Germany therapist Michaela Huber reports, "We have been spreading the news to our colleagues. There are now several hundred German professionals trained by American, Dutch, and German experts in the field of dissociation." Many European training institutes require their students to take classes in dissociative disorders, and now New Zealand therapists have also introduced the concepts of satanic ritual abuse.[36] As courses, seminars, and workshops proliferate, we can be sure that cases of MPD will proliferate too. Multiple personality, in Hacking's words, has provided "a new way to be an unhappy person,"[37] and unhappiness is not just an American problem.

12 | Satanic Ritual Abuse

In 1986, therapists gathered in Chicago at the International Conference on Multiple Personality/Dissociation noticed a surprising development: about 25 percent of their MPD patients were describing memories of torture and abuse in secret satanic cults. Rather than feeling disturbed by these stories and the lack of evidence to support them, large numbers of therapists incorporated satanic ritual abuse (SRA) into their theoretical and psychological repertoire. The 1986 conference had one paper on satanic ritual abuse; a year later, there were eleven. By 1989, George Ganaway, director of the Center for Dissociative Studies at the University of Georgia, disclosed that almost half the patients in his clinic and elsewhere were "reporting vividly detailed memories of cannibalistic revels and extensive experiences such as being used by cults during adolescence as serial baby breeders for ritual sacrifices." Therapists kept up with patients by organizing seminars and publishing articles and books to circulate information and educate other mental health professionals about the problem. In *Out of Darkness: Exploring Satanism and Ritual Abuse* (1992), editors David Sakheim and Susan E. Devine described their field as "in its infancy."[1] But many psychiatrists in the field were skeptical, and the multiple movement is still divided over the truth of satanic ritual abuse.

The media soon got involved. "All over the country," wrote reporter Leslie Bennetts in 1993, "what seems to be an astonishing number of women are coming forward with similar tales of satanic cults and ritual abuse. The reports are being made by all kinds of women—

different socioeconomic backgrounds, different ethnicities, different religions, even different races.... Over and over again, women told me about being forced to kill and eat babies at satanic ceremonies, about seeing children dismembered and boiled and burned, about being drugged, tortured with cattle prods, branded with branding irons, raped with crucifixes and animal carcasses. They told me about being buried in coffins with live snakes and dead bodies, about being tied to crosses and hung upside down for days, about being photographed for child pornographers and caged by satanic child-prostitution rings that farmed out their tiny victims for further abuse."[2]

After the 1983 McMartin preschool case in California—finally dismissed seven years and $15 million later for lack of evidence—other women charged that their children had been ritually abused in day care centers or nursery schools. Then came sensational investigations by well-meaning but overzealous police, doctors, and social workers who performed rectal and genital examinations on the children, invited them to demonstrate what had happened with anatomically correct dolls, and asked leading questions. The first edition of *The Courage to Heal*, in 1988, quoted San Francisco policewoman Sandi Gallant: "People say children invent these stories after watching TV, but before there was any media coverage of these cases, the allegations these kids made were extremely consistent with the allegations other kids were making in other parts of the country. ... Children don't make up stories like these."[3]

Satanic ritual abuse stories also caught on in Britain. In Rochdale, near Manchester, twenty children were taken out of their homes in 1990 by social workers after a six-year-old boy told teachers that he had seen babies murdered, children drugged and caged, and people digging up graves. The claims were dismissed after a ten-week hearing in the High Court. In the remote Orkney Islands in 1991, nine children were removed from their homes after a villager reported peculiar practices by families that included Jews and Quakers. Children told investigators about participating in satanic rites with people dressed as Ninja Turtles. After an inquiry that cost six million pounds, charges against the adults were dismissed and social workers were criticized for their suggestive questions. In some cases, the pressures of evangelical Christians, along with the influence of horror films, evidently supplied the imagery and plot for imaginary narratives.[4]

From accusations of devil worshipers molesting children in day care centers, to agitation over rumors about the kidnaping and sacrifice of a blond, blue-eyed virgin, to talk of animal mutilation and ritual sexual abuse, the United States was rocked with stories of satanism and witchcraft in the late 1980s. Exacerbated by sensational TV programs and by fundamentalist "experts" on satanism, the hysteria moved from small town to small town, leaving frightened children and parents in its wake. Two kinds of stories combined in the epidemic: charges by children, and recovered memories of adults who had remembered nothing prior to therapy.

As witch-hunters' accusations become wilder and wilder, as courts reject lawsuit after lawsuit for lack of evidence, many therapists have become uneasy. Years of lawsuits and intensive investigations have unearthed no proof that these satanic cults even exist. Kenneth V. Lanning, special agent at the FBI Behavioral Science Unit in Quantico, Virginia, has studied over 300 SRA allegations since 1983, and has found no evidence to corroborate them. In 1994, the British government released a report based on a three-year inquiry into eighty-four cases of alleged SRA. The study—chaired by Dr. Jean La Fontaine, author of a respected book on child abuse and professor emeritus of social anthropology at the London School of Economics—found no evidence to support any of the charges. "It's a national scandal," says American psychiatric social worker Jan Larsen. "With all the satanic ritual-abuse cases, there's not a shred of evidence. I don't think it exists. I think it's hysterical contamination, but it's making people sick, making money, and hurting families."[5] Therapist George Ganaway warns, "Unless scientifically documented proof is forthcoming, patients and therapists who validate and publicly defend the unsubstantiated veracity of these reports may find themselves developing into a cult of their own, validating each others' beliefs while ignoring (and being ignored by) the scientific and psychotherapeutic community at large."[6]

What is the hystory of satanic ritual abuse? According to John Briere's widely used textbook *Therapy for Adults Molested as Children* (1989), patients describe "black magic or satanic rites, where the child victim is part of a ceremony involving desecration and sexual debasement. Examples of such activities include the child being forced to publicly masturbate with a crucifix; ceremonial gang rape by all (or a privileged few) of the male members of the cult; sexual contact with or dismemberment of a family pet; demands that the child drink blood or urine or eat vile substances; and ritualistic ceremonies where the child is stripped of clothing, tied to a crucifix or platform, sexually molested, and led to believe that she is about to be sacrificed."[7] Satanic

cult stories also may refer to brainwashing, programming, and hypnotic or post-hypnotic suggestion.

With their thematic emphasis on incest, infanticide, forced breeding, cannibalism, and conspiracy, these narratives touch on the deepest
and most frightening taboos and fantasies of our culture.[8] Alleged victims of satanic cults describe conspiracies by huge, intergenerational,
secretive criminal organizations that maintain total control over their
members and victims; leaders avoid detection by living in disguise as
normal members of the community. Fears of punishment and revenge
by the cult for betraying its secrets become so vivid in clinical settings
that hospital workers themselves begin to develop hypervigilant panics. In *Shattered Selves*, University of Maryland professor James Glass
describes the atmosphere of Sheppard-Pratt Hospital while an SRA
patient was being treated: "Suddenly books, police reports, compendia
of newspaper articles on cults materialized; staff whispered in the hall-
ways. . . . Many wondered if they should change their phone numbers
or find dummy addresses or even take secret vacations from work, to
throw off any would-be pursuers. People were careful whom they
spoke with, and a few staff members refused to talk with me about
anything to do with cults because they suspected that they and I were
being 'watched.' " Finally even Glass succumbs: he starts to believe that
his car is being followed, that the cult is breaking into his office, that a
suspicious stranger at his undergraduate lecture is "a cult plant."[9] In
Glass's view, it doesn't matter whether the terrors of SRA are real; but
he overlooks his own evidence of the suggestibility of perfectly normal people to the paranoid hystories of satanic ritual abuse.

Benjamin, Bunny, and Scarlet: A Prototype

Who are the patients claiming satanic ritual abuse? In *Diagnosis for
Disaster* (1995) Claudette Wassil-Grimm summarizes the prototype of
an SRA patient. A woman goes to a therapist because of problems such
as depression or bulimia. The therapist tells her she has symptoms that
resemble those of childhood sexual abuse. She is "exhorted to read
self-help books on incest, attend incest survivors' groups, and maybe
attend an intensive weekend-long group therapy session." She begins
to have vague memories of abuse. The memories grow. She sees many
family neighbors involved—it must be satanic ritual abuse. "When she
reports that she had a flashback of killing a baby and drinking the
blood," the process of remembering is over. She can begin to recover,

or "heal."[10] In a recent case that resembles the prototype, Connie Sievek started to see a psychotherapist for depression and remembered that she had seen her father and another man murder, disembowel, and bury a woman.[11] In another, "Tiffany Spencer" was branded, and her twin sister was sacrificed and dismembered.[12]

The third edition of *The Courage to Heal* (1994) adds a first-person narrative about MPD and ritual satanic abuse, which includes specifically Jewish imagery—significant, because many researchers have noted the link between SRA and the infamous "blood libel" of anti-Semitism, which goes back at least to the twelfth century.[13] It baffles researchers like Benjamin Beit-Hallahmi at the University of Haifa in Israel and Sherrill Mulhern in Paris that believers, many of whom are Jewish, ignore the connection between satanic narratives and traditional anti-Semitic lore. As Jeffrey S. Victor reminds us in *Satanic Panic: The Creation of a Contemporary Legend*, accusations of ritual child murder leveled at Jews reinforced beliefs "that Jews (like heretics) were in league with the Devil, that the Jews were agents of Satan on earth. . . . In the evolving Western demonology, the Devil was ultimately to blame for personal misfortune and social disaster. Therefore, the Jews, as the Devil's agents, could justly be punished for the pains of good and decent people."[14]

"S. R. Benjamin" is a Jewish biochemist in her forties with a Ph.D. from Yale. Her parents, she writes, belonged to a ring of child pornographers that also included a pediatrician, a psychologist, and an engineer. They used "pseudo-religious rituals with satanic overtones" to terrorize children, especially their own little daughter. Benjamin asserts she was auctioned into prostitution, witnessed the death of at least one child, and participated in the murder of a baby. She graphically describes being tortured with electricity and drugs, repeatedly raped by her father, and forced to sodomize her pet rabbit with a roofing nail. As a seventh grader, after her mother's death, she became pregnant and was compelled by her father and grandmother to undergo an abortion.

Benjamin was a prize-winning student who did not recall these horrifying experiences until 1986, when she was nearly through graduate school at Yale, married to a patient and supportive man, and having an extramarital affair. A veteran of many years of phobias and unsuccessful therapies, Benjamin attended a workshop for survivors of child abuse, and with dramatic suddenness the memories rose up. At Yale and then at Harvard, where she went for postdoctoral study, she remembered torture and began to present in therapy the three personalities she had developed to cope with it: "Benjamin—ageless, spiritual and protective; Bunny—little and worried; and Scarlet, the only female and the one who dealt with the sexual abuse." Benjamin's co-workers at Harvard were unsympathetic to her pain, tears, panics, and general dysfunction. She is still shocked by the "cruelty and scape-goating that most of the other postdoctoral fellows directed towards me," but she has forgiven them: they too may have been injured.

Despite her psychological difficulties, Benjamin finished her post-doctoral work and was hired as an assistant professor in a university research lab. There she began to recover memories of pornography and satanic rituals. She feels that she is finally coming to terms with her experience: "My history no longer defines me. It's something I've gone through, not who I am."

Like many of the names in *The Courage to Heal*, "S. R. Benjamin" is a pseudonym, but Bass and Davis tell us that her father, who belongs to the False Memory Syndrome Foundation, "vehemently denies that he ever abused his daughter in any way and has attributed his daughter's view of events to an irreversible psychosis."[15] Benjamin admits she is a phobic, self-mutilating, suicidal person who has panic attacks and carries around a lot of guilt. She relates this guilt to the possibility that she harmed other children through satanic rituals. She comforts herself with the thought that she was forced to commit these acts and that the crimes were possibly tricks, staged by the cult to keep her under control.

How has Benjamin managed to cope so well over the years? Can we believe that rape, abortion, child prostitution, even murder could have flourished undetected? Even Benjamin confesses to doubts about the truth of her account. But when a physical therapist explains away pains in her knees, she finds a more compliant physical therapist who validates her story. Benjamin says she reads about political torture, the Holocaust, Amnesty International, and satanic abuse. Watching an episode of *Star Trek* in which Commander Spock is tortured and broken yet retains his "competence and integrity" particularly inspires her.

Reading Benjamin's story as a hystory suggests that she is revealing her own sexual guilt and the puritanical values of her community, especially in relation to women. Nice Jewish girls are not supposed to be sexually titillated by the Holocaust or to betray decent husbands. Justifying such behavior to herself leads Benjamin to come up with a gigantic evil conspiracy. Having sexual feelings makes this otherwise docile intellectual feel so ashamed that she punishes herself—burns herself with cigarettes, feels suicidal. To exonerate and forgive herself, she imagines, imagines very vividly, that the sexuality comes from out-side herself, from those stronger than she. Benjamin's family might have conveyed with unusual strength their disapproval of sexual behaviors. Could she have become pregnant in the seventh grade, when her mother died? Was there really an abortion, which left her feeling like a child murderer? Is this adolescent trauma the memory she cannot bear to face?

Jean La Fontaine has suggested that the common "motif of infant sacrifice in satanic rituals derives from anxiety and guilt about abor-tion."[16] But no warning bells go off for Bass and Davis. They consider satanic, or what they call sadistic, ritual abuse in the final section of *The Courage to Heal* and insist that the stories are not implausible. Readers who raise questions, they say, are in "collective denial." Implausibilities or inconsistencies in the narratives exist because the satanists deliber-ately confused things, "to lessen a survivor's credibility should she or he seek help." Bass and Davis invoke the Talmud in asking people to confront these horrors.[17] English therapist Valerie Sinason also com-pares SRA denial with Holocaust denial.[18]

SRA and Gender

It should come as no surprise that most adults recovering memories of SRA are women. Leslie Bennetts writes that psychiatrists explain that "traumatized women tend to turn up in the mental-health system while men with similar histories act out, often in violent ways, and end up in jail."[19]

Women also dominate the SRA subculture—that is, the people who have been most upset by allegations of satanic ritual abuse. Journalist Debbie Nathan and lawyer Michael Snedeker, who co-authored *Satan's Silence: Ritual Abuse and the Making of a Modern American Witch Hunt* (1995), suggest that "being a ritual-abuse victim's parent is a fem-inine role. 'Believing the children,' in other words, is women's work." They add that "mothers become far more involved in the cases, doing everything from shuttling their children to therapy, to attending sup-port groups, to trekking day after day to court." Nathan and Snedeker hypothesize that outrage about alleged SRA allows women a sanctioned outlet for frustrations and angers otherwise ignored. More mothers of children in SRA cases sought counseling than fathers did, and these women used the therapy "to consider matters that had troubled them for years, but which they were only able to deal with now because they linked them to their children's victimization." They often complained about indifferent or demanding husbands; some said they withdrew sexually from their husbands after the children's alleged abuse. Many couples separated or divorced. "Ritual abuse," Nathan and Snedeker conclude, "thus helped women disengage from unsatisfactory marriages without feeling guilty about being bad wives or mothers. After all, the reason they weren't getting along with their husbands was because they cared so much about their children."[20]

SRA and Feminism

Feminist therapists, activists, and academics have been entangled in the SRA dispute, as they have in other areas of the recovered memory movement—especially in England, where they have played a leading role as theorists. According to Nathan and Snedeker, "Feminists were particularly susceptible to sex-abuse conspiracy theories."[21] In the feminist journal *SIGNS* in 1993, Linda Alcoff and Laura Gray, two Syracuse University professors, compare the testimony of ritual abuse with testimony of rape victims who may not be believed: "Survivors of especially heinous ritualized sexual abuse are not believed. The pattern that emerges from these disparate responses is that if survivor speech is not silenced before it is uttered, it is categorized within the mad, the untrue, or the incredible."[22]

Ironically, the SRA panic derives in large part from religious fundamentalists and political conservatives who are antagonistic to feminist goals. By the late 1980s, Nathan and Snedeker declare, "opponents of state involvement in family life were using ritual-abuse accusations as a warning about the dangers of child protection and therapy, and issuing across-the-board condemnations of feminism and feminists as predatory wreckers of happy homes. Ritual-abuse proponents responded by dismissing every criticism as antifeminist and antichild backlash, all the while ignoring their own complicity in discrediting child protection and the women's movement."[23]

Nathan and Snedeker deplore the alliance between such feminists as Gloria Steinem and "a moral crusade engaged in dangerous flirtation with antiabortionists, homophobes, racists, and proponents of the principle that a woman's place is in the home. . . . Indeed, during the past decade, belief in ritual abuse has become so ensconced in this wing of feminism that the arrest, trial by ordeal, and lifelong incarcer-

ation of accused women have occasioned hardly a blink from its proponents. They have remained silent as convicted mothers and teachers
are sent to prison."[24]

Telling Satanic Stories

Why do so many intelligent, educated, concerned people believe these
bizarre stories? The term *satanic ritual abuse* is a large and messy one
that can be stretched to cover several phenomena; its vagueness and
inclusiveness make it seem plausible to many reasonable people who
recall having read or heard something that may relate to it. Although
advocates frequently compare SRA with the Manson murders or the
Jim Jones mass suicides in Guyana, followers of Manson or Jones were
not masked as ordinary upstanding citizens. Child molesters, pornographers, and child sex rings exemplify real abuse that has no documented connection to satanism. Marginalized teenagers playing heavy
metal music and tattooing themselves with skulls may alarm adults, but
they are not the transgenerational secret satanists of rumor.

Language plays a role as well. Therapists speak of "satanic ritual
abuse" rather than "alleged satanic ritual abuse which has never been
proven or corroborated." "The result," writes Sherrill Mulhern, "is
that by the magic of language, ritual abuse suddenly appears. We are
talking about it as if it had some objective meaning outside of the subjective meanings that each individual ... attributes to the terms. This
confers an aura of reality on phenomena which may or may not have
ever occurred."[25]

Finally, SRA is a way of dealing with horrifying human pathologies.
Jean La Fontaine writes that "a belief in evil cults is convincing
because it draws on powerful cultural axioms. People are reluctant to
accept that parents, even those classed as social failures, will harm their
own children, and even invite others to do so, but involvement with
the devil explains it. The notion that unknown, powerful leaders control the cult revives an old myth of dangerous strangers. Demonising
the marginal poor and linking them to unknown satanists turns
intractable cases of abuse into manifestations of evil."

Hystories of SRA are flexible and creative. When basic practical
questions are asked, details of the satanic narrative shift. If a patient
claims to have seen babies murdered and buried but the police can find
no bodies, the therapist explains that the patient had been hypnotically
programmed to conceal the site, or that she was afraid to expose the

real perpetrators, or that the cult had duped her into believing a crime had been committed so that she would not be believed in the future.[26] If bodies cannot be found, patients sometimes allege that the satanists ate or burned them. If police explain that ordinary fire is not hot enough to totally destroy a body, patients tell stories of special industrial furnaces.

SRA advocates defend the consistency of the narratives but seem not to understand the power of literary conventions, the morphology of folk tales, the repetition of rumors, and above all the way that suggestion works to produce confabulation. At conferences and seminars therapists are exhorted to believe. They hear emotional testimony from "survivors," followed by standing ovations. All the sensational theater that worked so well at the Salpêtrière is put to use on the SRA conference circuit. Patients learn to tell their stories too. Sherrill Mulhern, who has looked at transcripts, says that "initially, patients were not saying the same things but came to say similar things over time." Memories of satanic rituals develop slowly after a patient has spent a lot of time in therapy: "They begin as isolated images and/or affects—distributed over a number of different personalities—which must be gradually identified and pieced together." The "satanism" of the satanic ritual abuse narratives, Mulhern concludes, is "essentially a rehashing of the satanic confabulations of a variety of individuals, which have been homogenized into a single Satanism through hours of networking between therapists, Satan investigators, and survivors."[27] Therapists elicit memories by asking patients questions about a long list of items, by focusing on vague feelings, by giving shape and meaning to fragments.

Even when they describe the cultural source of satanic images, however, many therapists seem not to recognize its influence. They quote Tolkein, or describe a movie called *The Witches* (1966), in which Joan Fontaine plays a school teacher who stumbles upon a secret coven, or draw attention to the popularity of movies about devils, witchcraft, and possession. Others quote medieval studies of witchcraft as if they were finding historical evidence rather than plot motifs in folk lore and popular religion. Yet, says George Greaves, "no single book or movie contains the material of even a single patient."[28]

Ira Levin's best-selling novel *Rosemary's Baby* (1967), made into a hit film starring Mia Farrow in 1968, remains a significant source for the details and decor of much SRA narrative. The movie had unusual cultural power because the wife of director Roman Polanski was herself murdered by the Charles Manson cult—an event that drew worldwide publicity. The diabolist of the novel, also named Roman, leads a satanic cult that makes a deal with Guy, a struggling young actor; he will find success and fame if he helps them trick his wife, Rosemary, into bearing Satan's child. Rosemary begins to have suspicions of her neighbors and does research on witchcraft: "They use *blood* in their rituals, because blood has *power*, and the blood that has the *most* power is a *baby's* blood, a baby that hasn't been baptized, and they use *more* than the blood, they use the *flesh* too!" Despite her struggles, Rosemary has the baby, which she beholds in a black bassinet, wrapped in a black blanket, surrounded by black candles and black-wrapped presents. She decides to cooperate with the cult, and to raise her child.

Rosemary's Doctors

Novels and movies create popular imagery, but satanic ritual abuse stories can't flourish unless therapists are willing to stake their reputations on the cases. In the United States, distinguished therapists who have taken SRA seriously respond to the call for clear-headed investigation of the evidence with passionate claims that they are healers, not law enforcement officers. "I'm a psychology person," Dan Sexton of the National Child Abuse Hot Line said in 1989, "so I don't need the evidence."[29]

SRA therapists have themselves been at the center of lawsuits and exposés. Judith Peterson, a therapist at Spring Shadows Glen in Houston, has been sued by seven patients. Another controversial therapist, Bennett Braun, hospitalized Mary Shanley, a thirty-nine-year-old primary school teacher. Although she disliked Braun, Shanley was impressed by his colleague Roberta Sachs. Medicated with Inderal, Xanax, Prozac, Klonopin, and Halcion, among other tranquilizers, SSRIs, beta blockers, and sedatives, Shanley believed she had been trained by her mother to be the high priestess of a satanic cult: "I remembered going to rituals and witnessing sacrifices. I had a baby at age 13, supposedly, and that child was sacrificed." After a workshop with Cory Hammond, Shanley and her husband were persuaded that her nine-year-old son should also be treated or the cult would kill him. Shanley was sent to Spring Shadows Glen under the care of Judith Peterson.[30]

In a "Frontline" TV documentary called "The Search for Satan," produced by Ofra Bike and Rachel Dretzin, Shanley, called "Mary S.," told her story. The program suggested a financial motive behind the cases: MPD and SRA patients are often covered by "very rich benefit plans." Mary S.'s insurance company paid more than $2.5 million for her treatment, and a nurse testified that the unit at Spring Shadows Glen Hospital was "very profitable."[31] Peterson, now in private practice, has hired lawyers to defend her against patients' allegations and file counter-suits. She sees herself, Mark Pendergrast reports, as "an altruistic, idealistic person trying to help the world. She started her career working with migrant workers and Head Start children and parents." In Peterson's view, *she* is the victim of her patients: "The shame and guilt were then transferred to me, the therapist. Kill the messenger. Lie. This client relieved the trauma by victimizing me. Suddenly, the therapist is the victim."[32]

Professor Cory Hammond of the University of Utah Medical School has long maintained that satanic cults are part of a Nazi conspiracy led by a renegade Jew. Hammond, a psychologist and specialist in hypnosis, has been teaching and lecturing about satanic abuse for many years, despite his stated fears that the cults will assassinate him for betraying their secrets. At a meeting of the Fourth Annual Regional Conference on Abuse and Multiple Personality Disorder in 1992, he declared that satanic cults in the United States are masterminded by a Jewish doctor named Green, originally Greenbaum. As a teenager in Germany, Green collaborated with satanic Nazi scientists, helped by his knowledge of the Kabala. Once in the United States, he joined forces with the CIA to work on brainwashing and mind control. Hammond believes that Green's satanic cults intend to create "tens of thousands of mental robots who will do pornography, prostitution, smuggle drugs, and engage in international arms smuggling. Eventually, those at the top of the satanic cult want to create a satanic order that will rule the world."[33]

Hammond describes how the programming of children begins when they are two or three. They are strapped down, hooked up to an intravenous supply of Demoral, and connected to electrodes; the programmers use electric shocks to reinforce their message. Hammond's description of alter personalities sounds like Huxley's *Brave New World*:

> Alpha represents general programming. Beta appears to be sexual programs, such as how to perform oral sex in a certain way or how to produce and direct child pornography films or run child prostitution rings. Delta are killers. Delta-alters are trained

to kill in ceremonies and also do some self-harm stuff. Theta are psychic killers. This comes from their belief in psychic abilities including their belief that they can make someone develop a brain tumor and die. Omega are self-destruct programs which can make the patient self-mutilate or kill themselves. Gamma systems are protection and deception programs which provide misinformation to try and misdirect you. There are also other Greek letter programs. Zeta has to do with the production of snuff films. Omicron has to do with their association with the Mafia, big business, and government leaders.[34]

In Hammond's view, cult members control these robots with laptop computers and activate them with hand signals. He believes that the program can also be activated by reciting an erasure code to the patient. "When you give the code and ask what the patient is experiencing, they will describe computers whirring, things erasing and things exploding and vaporizing." In his communication with patients under hypnosis, Hammond uses finger signals to elicit agreement. Patients have virtually no verbal input; all is appropriated and incorporated into Hammond's hystory—a singularly detailed, anti-Semitic, and scary one. When asked about the absence of evidence, Hammond responds, "The things that therapists hear all over this country are that morticians are involved in many cases, physicians who can sign phony death certificates."[35]

England too has therapist-advocates who believe in horrific conspiracies, such as Joan Coleman, associate specialist in Psychiatry at Healthlands Mental Health Services in Surrey. In 1989 Dr. Coleman, an "expert" on the structure of satanic cults, organized RAINS, the Ritual Abuse Information Network and Support. Coleman's first SRA patient described witnessing the ritual abuse and murder of three Vietnamese children in 1967. In her story, the ritual involved classic paraphernalia of the witches sabbath—candles, inverted crosses, robes, and masks. Satanists drank blood from a chalice and practiced cannibalism: "Much of the children's flesh was eaten prior to the remains being burnt." Coleman expresses her horror at the story, but apparently didn't ask her patient how these children, described as "among the first contingent of 'boat people' brought to Southampton from the USA," could have traveled such an odd and circuitous route to England and then disappeared without any publicity. Coleman's second SRA patient recounted stories of feral, retarded, or traumatized children hanging in cages in the basement of a house, "brought out only for abuse or experimental operations performed by the cult leader, who, she thought, was a doctor."[36] Coleman offers no evidence of the truth of this appalling story.

Coleman calls SRA "a way of life," with children indoctrinated at home by their mothers. She provides an elaborate outline of the hierarchical structure of cults, which include prominent and distinguished members of the community—doctors, lawyers, politicians, clergy, and ambassadors, as well as members of the upper class. The basic unit is the thirteen-person Coven, which gathers into larger groups of circles or lodges headed by high priests or priestesses. In their religious rituals, the Covens worship Satan through weekly or holiday festivals, using clothing and ceremonies that parody Christian ritual, and practice human sacrifice. Children in the cults must submit to intense brainwashing and mind control. They are given talismanic objects or poppets; some also remember operations in which a surveillance device was implanted, to punish them if they betrayed the cult. (Among Valerie Sinason's patients, Jane had to kill and eat her pet budgie; Rita found her slaughtered dog in her bed; Malcolm had to lie on a female corpse.)[37] Children are regularly sexually abused by parents and priests or priestesses. Some of the abuse involves electric shocks, and Christian symbols are often part of the ritual.

Coleman mentions "poppets" as if she never heard of *The Crucible*, in which the poppet planted in the home of one of the accused is such an important plot device. The range, detail, and credulity of Coleman's list—all of it without the least scrap of evidence—is shocking. Like other therapists, she has worked out an elaborate system to explain the absence of substantiating evidence. The big stuff, like altars, is concealed in members' garages. Ritual objects, like the goats' heads and daggers, are kept in "shops selling military memorabilia or antiques." The evil books are locked up in safes. Tarpaulins cover traces of blood. Corpses are buried, sunk in rivers, burned in furnaces or crematoria, dissolved in acid baths, minced in machines, fed to dogs and pigs, or eaten by the coven. Victims come from anonymous populations: runaways from deprived families who have not reported them missing, aborted fetuses, children of cult members, vagrants, and renegades.

Cult members apparently have to keep up with their busy public careers as well as running around to coven meetings, doing their share of molesting, and getting rid of bodies through time-consuming and elaborate methods. Why do they put up with such a life? Coleman responds that those at the top of the heap make vast sums from extortion and child pornography and prostitution rings, maybe even a little arms dealing. Those on the bottom are bribed with money to pay off their mortgages, take holidays, or buy new cars and "string-pulling to further their careers, sometimes with the aid of Masonic connections."[38]

Joan Coleman was predictably unhappy with the La Fontaine report. In a letter to the *London Review of Books*, she pointed to the internal consistency in stories from unrelated sources and to the inexplicable weirdness of male professional behavior: "Personally, I, too, have difficulty with the concept of satanic worship and I am no nearer to believing in black or any other sort of magic than I ever was, but it's almost equally hard to understand how grown men, mostly from the professional classes, can go along with the extraordinary initiation rites involved in Freemasonry."[39]

The most distinguished advocate of SRA in England is Valerie Sinason, consultant child psychotherapist at the Tavistock Clinic, who has edited an influential book called *Treating Survivors of Satanist Sexual Abuse*. Many of my friends in the London psychiatric community urged me to meet Sinason (I did not) and assured me that I would like and respect her. Her peers regard her as a skilled clinician who has done exemplary work with mentally handicapped patients, including adults who have a mental age of less than eight (and therefore have no legal rights to testify in English courts). Sinason regards herself as the advocate of severely handicapped patients—patients few therapists are willing to treat. Like the clinicians who developed automatic writing with Ouija boards for autistic patients but did not consciously know that they themselves were transmitting messages, guiding the planquettes, Sinason denies projecting abuse and satanism onto her patients. Leslie Wilson, who interviewed Sinason for the *London Review of Books*, says that she "has the intensity of the embattled campaigner rather than the obsessional quality of a zealot."

Sinason has staked her professional reputation on belief in satanic ritual abuse. It would be more than awkward for her to back down. When the English government's report found no evidence to support claims of devil worship in eighty-four cases, Sinason stuck to her guns, telling the press that although some people might have satanist fantasies, abuse really existed.[40] "If you see people you care about not getting justice," she told Leslie Wilson, "it is your duty to bring that to the attention of the proper structure."[41]

Sinason's introduction to the English edition of Lawrence Wright's *Remembering Satan* is a vivid instance of her skill in negotiating the borders between scientific objectivity and her own convictions about SRA. Wright is a journalist whose investigation of the Ingram family case in Olympia, Washington, had a huge impact in 1993 when it appeared in the *New Yorker*. In 1988 Paul Ingram's two teenage daughters accused him of abuse and implicated the whole family of conservative fundamentalists, as well as many other people, in satanic ritualism. Ingram, a devout churchman, went along with the accusations. He recanted too late and was sentenced to twenty years in prison. Lawrence Wright's thoughtful, thorough, and compassionate study of the case alerted Americans to the dangers of recovered memory and religious fundamentalism. Persuading Wright to accept an introduction written by Valerie Sinason and persuading Sinason to write a respectful introduction to a book that, if taken seriously, discredits everything she has been doing was no mean task for the editors at Serpent's Tail, a small radical press based in London.

But the introduction is a small masterpiece of evasion. Sinason appears at first to acknowledge the justice of Wright's argument, calling *Remembering Satan* a "highly significant, intelligent book which raises serious concerns."[42] But this superficial flexibility soon disappears in a thicket of conditional "if" clauses and passive impersonal constructions. On the rhetorical level, Sinason tries to eat her cake and have it too—"if" Wright is correct, *then* a "serious injustice has been unwittingly perpetrated on one family." The identity of the perpetrators? Unnamed. Did they have any control over their acts? No, they behaved "unwittingly." The phrase "one family" is important too. Sinason concedes, perhaps, a single mistake but insists that cases of mistaken accusations are rare and unimportant compared to the enormity of abuse. There are more "real incidents" than complaints of false accusation. She cites a colleague's "cautious estimate" that 15 to 30 percent of all sixteen-year-old girls have suffered some kind of sexual abuse, much of it incestuous.

In defending her position, Sinason tries to present the issue as one of different opinions or different perspectives or different interests or different interpretations or different conclusions. She pleads for tolerance of others' opinions, for "different ways of seeing," and asserts that the absence of hard evidence matters less than the concern expressed by clinicians who have heard the stories of abuse. These trained clinicians, Sinason writes, "were far more likely to accurately perceive behaviour linked to abuse," but she offers no real evidence of this assumption, nor a definition of what "accurate" means.

Out of Darkness: The Dangers of SRA

Is satanic ritual abuse a fad diagnosis or a sign of social danger? Mulhern calls the satanism scare "a rumor in search of an inquisition."[43] Newspaper accounts see the rumor as a clear sequence of events and epidemic contagion. Like stories of the genesis of AIDS, the narratives often point to a single source or mediating figure, a Satanist Patient X. Journalists also seek to pin blame for the epidemic on an external source. The London *Times*, for example, blames Americans: "Influence by American Christian fundamentalists led to allegations of satanic abuse surfacing in Britain in the late 1980s. The term originated in America after the publication in 1980 of *Michelle Remembers* by Lawrence Pazder, a psychiatrist, which told the story of a girl being ritually abused by satanists, one of whom was her mother." According to the newspaper, the term "caught on in Britain when Pamela Klein, who worked at a rape crisis center at Southern Illinois University, moved here in 1985." Mrs. Klein "organized a conference on child abuse at Reading University in 1989, and theories of satanic abuse spread among social workers."[44] Under the headline "Beast that runs wild in US imagination," another *Times* journalist wrote, "The mythical beast known as satanic sex abuse was born in America, where it has all the hallmarks of a panic craze fed by films, television and books, nurtured by fantasy, maintained by a plethora of accusations and bolstered by the credulity of psychotherapists and the public."[45] English journalists have denounced satanic ritual abuse as a kind of "American social disease."

But the reality is more complicated. Michelle was actually Canadian, and English satanist theories come from several independent sources. Indeed, as Bryan Appleyard recognized in a 1994 essay, "Who the Devil Shall We Blame?" in *The Independent*, "Satan was always a metaphor for what is inside, not what is outside." Despite the human tendency to locate evil fantasies outside the self, they reflect impulses within all individuals and cultures. English or American, until we can accept that truth, we have not outlived Satan's dark legacy.

In the courts, satanic abuse accusations are now facing more skeptical juries. In December 1995, Robert and Constance Roberson, a lay pastor and his wife from Wenatchee, Washington, were acquitted of

charges that they led a sex ring in which children were raped and ritually abused. "There was nothing to this case," a juror told the *New York
Times*. "Why did they bring this to trial? Here were all these people
who had attended every church service for the past three or four years,
who had never seen anything like what the prosecution was describing, and their prosecutors had never even talked to them."[46] More than
a dozen verdicts have been overturned since 1990, and Linda Fairstein,
chief of the Manhattan District Attorney's sex crimes unit, calls mass-
molestation cases "the most flawed class of prosecutions ever."[47]

Yet many others who have been accused remain imprisoned.
Rather than accept the lack of evidence for their claims, many patients, therapists, and believers have expanded their definitions of
abuse, as Debbie Nathan and Michael Snedeker observe, "replacing the
term *satanic* with *sadistic* and lengthening the list of possible conspira-
tors to include more traditional social devils such as the KKK, the neo-
Nazis, the survivalists, marginal religious cults, and the brainwashing
enthusiasts of the CIA."[48] Their fascination with conspiracy bodes ill for
the prospect that we will soon emerge from this darkness. Kenneth
Lanning cautions "overzealous intervenors" that relentless publicity
can exacerbate the problem: "Are we encouraging needy or traumatized individuals to tell more and more outrageous tales of their victimization? Are we now making up for centuries of denial by blindly
accepting any allegation of child abuse no matter how absurd or
unlikely?"[49] The answers to these questions over the next few years
will determine whether SRA rumors become hysterical inquisition or
just historical curiosities.

13 | *Alien Abduction*

E ven for those who accept satanic ritual abuse, alien abduction seems a little over the top. It's one thing to fear the Devil, and another to believe in visits from small gray ETs. Yet an inverse relation of logic pertains, which I'll call Showalter's Law: As the hystories get more bizarre, the experts get more impressive. Among those defending alien abduction are Pulitzer Prize–winning Professor John Mack of Harvard Medical School, Professor David Jacobs, a historian at Temple University in Philadelphia, distinguished journalist C. D. B. Bryan, and successful novelist Whitley Strieber.

Some of these experts call themselves ufologists. Language and terminology are as crucial in the world of alien abduction as they are among believers in MPD and repressed memory. The lowest status ufologists are "contactees," people who peddle sensational stories about being contacted by extraterrestrials and taken to remote planets or whatever. Most of these folks popped up before the heyday of alien abduction, claiming to have special messages from extraterrestrials; ufologists regard them, with barely concealed amusement, as cranks, religious fanatics, "Space Brothers," or frauds. "Abductees," who say they've been abducted by aliens, occupy the next level of the hierarchy: most of them have been in touch with therapists, hypnotists, and ufologists, and their stories follow a fairly consistent pattern. The preferred term in the mid-1990s is *experiencers*, perhaps because it avoids the question of abduction and moves the whole issue to a higher, more spiritual plane. Bryan calls these episodes "close encounters of the fourth kind," evoking the enormously popular Steven Spielberg movie.

Abduction narratives have changed considerably since the first scattered reports of flying saucers fifty years ago. In late June 1947, a pilot named Kenneth Arnold described seeing nine bright saucerlike craft in the sky over Washington state. A week later, after a flurry of saucer sightings around the United States, newspapers alleged that a flying saucer had crashed in the desert near Roswell, New Mexico, and that the government had covered up the incident for reasons unknown. Over the years, contactees began to tell stories about extensive meetings with beings from other planets. Keith Thompson explains, "The contactee experience typically takes the form of a savior story. The contactee is cast as a modern prophet, an intermediary between recalcitrant mortals and extraterrestrial helpers intervening to save mankind from its reckless ways. Many contactees report early life experiences with strange aerial phenomena and meetings with strange beings who offer esoteric teachings, and overall life guidance at key points in their lives. Some contactees seek contact with superior beings; others have premonitions of impending contact; still others say they are chosen."[1] Although the aliens were from several planets—Venus, Jupiter, Mars—early contactees said they looked like human beings. By the 1950s, these stories had been embellished: UFO witnesses reported that men in black had showed up at their homes, often driving black cars. Ufologist John Keel thought he was being followed by black Cadillacs on back roads.

Those who regarded themselves as serious ufologists debunked and scorned these contactee hystories, but the stories clearly tied in with the folklore of satanism and conspiracy. In 1959, Carl Gustav Jung published a symbolic interpretation of the UFO phenomenon called *Flying Saucers: A Modern Myth of Things Seen in the Sky*. In this brief book, Jung suggested that UFO narratives reflected religious myths and archetypes in the collective human unconscious, and were an early symptom of the coming millennium.

Second-wave abductee stories began in 1966, when an interracial couple named Barney and Betty Hill told of being abducted while driving in the White Mountains of New Hampshire. Under hypnosis by Boston psychiatrist Benjamin Simon, they said that, once aboard the UFO, the aliens separated them: they gave Betty a pregnancy test and took a sperm sample from Barney. On returning, the Hills forgot the episode until bad dreams made them seek psychological help. Simon maintained that the story was a folie à deux or shared fantasy, possibly having to do with the repressed tensions of maintaining an interracial marriage. Other researchers have since speculated that the Hills incorporated imagery from a movie, *Invaders From Mars* (1953), and TV programs about space aliens. Nevertheless, Betty and Barney Hill have become renowned as the founding parents of the alien abduction movement.[2]

In the 1970s, alien abduction stories were so common that abductees organized conventions. But the stories, David Jacobs explains, were "so different from one another that it was almost impossible to tell what, if anything, had actually happened."[3] In other words, inconsistent or dissimilar stories were discounted. Only when abductees talked with ufologists who knew the metanarratives did patterns emerge. All the abductees had lost their memories and had to be treated with hypnosis—an obstacle, or perhaps an advantage, for researchers.

The shaping of the narrative began in the 1970s as various ufologists, reporting their work in magazines and journals, speculated that Beings from other planets were visiting earth to investigate human sexual functioning. Rereading the details of the Betty Hill story, they suggested that laparoscopy was being performed. At the same time, some channelers switched their contacts from dead spirits to aliens. In 1981, Budd Hopkins's *Missing Time* gave a published record of the abduction experience, a metatext for others to imitate.

The contemporary abduction hystory is extremely conventionalized, an aspect credulous journalists as well as professionally invested ufologists take as the strongest evidence for its reality and legitimacy. The basic elements in this plot were first outlined by David Jacobs, the Charcot of alien abduction, who has worked hard to establish a system and structure in the narratives; his book *Alien Encounters* even provides a diagram of the abduction experience from start to finish, which he calls the "common abduction scenario matrix."

According to Jacobs, alien abduction scenarios have three major motifs: physical, mental, and reproductive. The aliens are conducting "an ongoing genetic study" whose "focus is the production of children." The majority of abductions "begin at night when the victim is alone, either awake or asleep. No abductions have surfaced that took place in the middle of a very large group of people, in full view at a public event."[4] The Beings appear, bathed in mysterious light, descending in a spaceship or coming through walls and windows. They transport their victim back through closed windows, a phenomenon never witnessed because they are rendered invisible. Anyone else in the vicinity is rendered unconscious.

In the first phase of the abduction scenario, the victim is taken into the space ship's examining room by Small Beings, usually called Small Grays. These creatures study the victim's body, palpating, minutely scrutinizing skin from toes to head, and conducting gynecological examinations on female abductees. Sometimes they take scraping and tissue samples from the genitals and other parts of the body. This part of the examination concludes when the aliens implant "a small, round, seemingly metallic object in the abductee's ear, nose, or sinus cavity, or remove such an object."[5] The implant usually goes into the nose, and ufologists see nosebleeds as a sign of having been abducted by aliens. Occasionally the implant goes into the genitals, including the penile shaft.

While they perform these tasks, the Small Grays stare intensely at their victim with black pupilless eyes. When they finish, they are replaced by a Tall Gray Being many female abductees intuitively feel is male, a doctor, and an authority figure. He first performs what Jacobs calls Mindscan—bending over the victim, gazing deep into her eyes like an extraterrestrial Heathcliff or Fabio, filling her with love and eagerness to give herself completely. (When the abductee is a child, sometimes this Tall Being is a motherly female, but this is a rare exception.)

For Jacobs, the climactic moment is what he calls egg harvesting, embryo implantation, or embryo extraction. A Taller Being may insert a very long, slender needle into the woman's body to take an egg or even an embryo. Sometimes a fertilized egg is inserted into the woman's body, and she then feels pregnant; "her breasts swell and retain water, [and] she may have 'morning sickness.' . . . She may take a home pregnancy test that shows positive, and she may go to a physician for a blood test that confirms her suspicions—she is pregnant. But about six to twelve weeks later her period mysteriously begins again. She is inexplicably not pregnant. She has no miscarriage, no expulsion of fetal material, no indication that something was 'wrong.' She goes to her physician, who confirms that the fetus has suddenly disappeared."[6]

Meanwhile, back at the spaceship, an attractive female alien extracts sperm from male abductees. According to Jacobs, "All males after puberty experience the sperm–collection process," done with a pump–like machine. These procedures, he writes, "help aliens reproduce other Beings. . . . They are not here to help us. They have their own agenda and we are not allowed to know its full parameters." He ominously concludes, "We have been invaded."[7]

If David Jacobs is the Charcot of alien abduction, the one who attempts to provide systems, rules, and laws, Professor John E. Mack is the Freud, the thinker, philosopher, and theorist. Mack received a Pulitzer Prize in 1977 for his psychoanalytic biography of Lawrence of Arabia. He has been an important presence at the Harvard Medical School, founded the psychiatry department at Cambridge Hospital, and directs the nonprofit Center for Psychology and Social Change, which receives about two-thirds of its annual budget, some $250,000 a year, from Laurence S. Rockefeller. In 1994, Mack published *Abduction: Human Encounters With Aliens*, in which he argued that alien abduction was beyond the ken of Western empirical methodologies and required us to develop a new worldview. These stories were merely one sign that "we participate in a universe or universes that are filled with intelligences from which we have cut ourselves off, having lost the senses by which we might know them." Mack drew connections between this restricted, positivist worldview and other global problems, including corporate greed, ethnic violence, and ecological destruction.[8]

Some researchers suggest that alien abduction narratives might be cover-ups for sexual abuse, satanic ritual, or multiple personality, but Mack speculates that those recovered memories might actually screen episodes of alien abduction. (Some of his patients also remembered previous lives.) He agreed with Hopkins and Jacobs that "the abduction phenomenon is in some central way involved in a breeding program that results in the creation of alien/human hybrid offspring." But he felt certain that the purpose of these experiments was benign, that "the abduction process is not evil, and that the intelligences at work do not wish us ill. Rather, I have the sense—might I say faith—that the abduction phenomenon is, at its core, about the preservation of life on Earth at a time when the planet's life is profoundly threatened."[9]

C. D. B. Bryan is a reporter whose previous work includes *Friendly Fire*, a classic piece of investigative journalism about Vietnam. *Close Encounters of the Fourth Kind* (1995) takes a sympathetic look at ufologists and their patients. In it, Bryan meticulously describes the proceedings of an Abduction Study Conference held at (but not sponsored by) MIT in 1992. He doesn't have his own theory about alien abductions, but takes the narratives seriously and feels that "something very mysterious is going on." James Wolcott, a *New Yorker* writer who researched some of the same events and phenomena Bryan writes about, came away with his cynicism untouched. The abductees struck Wolcott as "a quasi cult of deluded cranks ... [who had] browsed the

entire New Age boutique of reincarnation, channeling, auras, and healing crystals. They seemed to be testing how far they could take their
personal narratives."[10]

Alien Abduction Narratives

The books by Hopkins, Jacobs, Mack, and Bryan consist largely of
interviews with abductees, often question-and-answer dialogues. The
"investigator" attests frequently to the extreme emotion and sincerity
displayed by the abductees as they recount their experiences under
hypnosis or after hypnosis. The writers present these emotions as primary evidence of the narratives' authenticity. Symptoms of possible
abduction echo the usual list of past hysterias as well as fear of the
dark, of being alone at night, of hospitals, flying, elevators, animals, and
flying insects. Rashes, scars called "scoop marks," nosebleeds, sinus
pain, and gastrointestinal symptoms are also seen as possible indicators
of abduction.

Ufologists insist that abductees represent a normal cross-section of
the population. Mack says he first thought they were more likely to be
working-class but now believes that professionals are merely more
reluctant to come forward. Doctors and lawyers seem to be unpopu-
lar targets for aliens.

How many people are involved? The actual numbers of those
claiming to have been abducted is quite small, and compared to
chronic fatigue or repressed memory, alien abduction is in its infancy.
John Mack has studied about fifty cases that meet his criteria. David
Jacobs based his book on sixty cases and says he has studied 350. Budd
Hopkins, sometimes called the father of the field, claims about fifteen
hundred. Predictably, all sorts of pseudostatistics and projections get
tossed about. Mack thinks more than a million Americans may be
experiencers.[11] Journalists sometimes cite a poll indicating that more
than 500,000 Americans have had alien abduction experiences, but
this is a fake statistic, based on extrapolation from a percentage in a
small sample, that's passed from one harried feature writer to the next.
Undoubtedly these polls and projections will to some degree become
self-fulfilling, as people adapt their symptoms and memories to the
new cultural model.

Many abduction narratives are embellished with details about conspiracies and especially surveillance. Linda, Budd Hopkins's "Queen
Bee abductee," tells a story of CIA safe houses, United Nations limou-

sines, and harassment by government agents. Carol and Alice, Bryan's star patients, describe seeing black helicopters over Alice's farm after they had been abducted. Black helicopters feature in UFO periodicals, and believers contend that they are UFOs disguising themselves as helicopters, or military surveillance vehicles conspiring to cover up evidence of UFOs.[12] Like the men in black driving their black Cadillacs, black helicopters appear in the literature of right-wing militias and paramilitary groups; they link abduction narratives and other forms of paranoid conspiracy. Implants and microchips also turn up in the thinking of people like Timothy McVeigh.

From a narrative point of view, we might first notice how conveniently these plot elements avoid questions of evidence, objective confirmation, and proof. Abductions do not occur in front of witnesses, ufologists argue, because aliens want secrecy. They take place at night because the abductee's absence is likely to go undetected and they can be disguised as dreams. Apart from the medical equipment, abductees recall little about the spaceships—which do not, for example, seem to have bathrooms or kitchens.

Details inconsistent with material reality are dismissed by ufologists as "mysteries," things we do not know and cannot understand because they exist on a higher spiritual and cognitive plane. Working with abductees, Mack writes, "has led me to challenge the prevailing worldview or consensus reality."[13] How Beings use light to "transform and transport matter," says Jacobs, is unknown, but not impossible.[14]

An Alien Made Me Do It

Most abductees are female; most aliens are male. Of the seventy-six cases studied by Mack, forty-seven were women, and in some ways their narratives resemble those of childhood sexual abuse or satanic ritual abuse. Alien perpetrators, however, do not belong to this world. Moreover, they are benignly motivated; abductees often see themselves as the chosen heralds of a superior intergalactic race.

A *New Yorker* cartoon recently commented on the folklore of alien seduction: a haughty matron accepts a bouquet from her alien visitor but complains, "I understood there were going to be bizarre sexual experiments." Tall Beings are usually hypermasculine, commanding, and erotic. Jacobs notes that they can "induce rapid, intense, sexual arousal and even orgasm in women as part of their Mindscan program."[15] Alice, an abductee Bryan found particularly impressive, tells him that she had erotic dreams for two months after her abduction experience. "I don't know what's causing it. Something's going on."[16]

Abduction scenarios closely resemble women's pornography, from the soft-core rape fantasies of bodice busters to the masturbation fantasies recounted by writers like Shere Hite or Nancy Friday. Many of Nancy Friday's stories from the 1970s even have similar imagery of gynecological examinations with faintly masochistic overtones, often with occult or medical details. Although some women who tell Jacobs and Bryan their stories belong to puritanical religious groups or are celibate, this imagery is a normal part of women's sexual fantasies. The abductees, however, seem particularly uneasy about sex. "He's making me feel things," one young woman reported. "He's making me feel things in my body that I don't feel. He's making me feel feelings, sexual feelings. . . . I wouldn't feel them. He's making me feel them."[17] These desires for touch, gazing, penetration have to come from very very far away, even outer space.

Some male abductees report bizarre and disturbing sexual "visions" that imply revulsion from female sexuality. John Mack's patient Joe, for example, sees a "giant vaginal hairball" that is "gross, slimy, and dirty."[18] Men also fear implants. An abductee named Richard Price produced an amber-colored item he described as an implant that had been in his penis, but lab tests at the Wellman Laboratories at Massachusetts General Hospital established conclusively that the "implant" was cotton fiber, perhaps from his underwear.[19]

Communion

Whitley Strieber's 1987 book *Communion* created a great stir in the UFO community and led to numerous subsequent stories. Just as *Rosemary's Baby* provided much of the imagery and style of satanic abuse narratives, *Communion* provides the narrative model for alien abduction. Subtitled "A True Story of Encounters With the Unknown," it was a number one best-seller as nonfiction in both England and the United States. Strieber writes about his dreams and memories of being abducted by extraterrestrial visitors and subjected to cerebral needle examinations and rectal probes during several months in the mid-1980s. He later tried to recover memories of his experience through hypnosis, discussions with Budd Hopkins and other ufologists, extensive reading in UFO literature, and meetings with fellow abductees.

Whitley Strieber is a remarkably appropriate author for this book.

A man of powerful, almost obsessive imagination, a dabbler in New Age theologies and mysticism, he had a successful career writing supernatural best-sellers like *Wolfen* and *The Hunger*, along with several other published and unpublished books. In an interview, Strieber once described a Texas childhood filled with violence and mysticism. An uncle had been murdered, his grandfather had "died in front of my eyes in abject agony," his house had burned down. In 1966, Strieber was almost killed when Charles Whitman went on his shooting spree at the University of Texas in Austin: Whitman "shot two girls right behind me. And they were lying there in the grass, screaming, begging, pleading for help. . . . One was vomiting pieces of herself out of her mouth. And I could smell the blood and the odor of stomachs."[20]

In *Communion*, Strieber denies the recollection: "For years I have told of being present at the University of Texas when Charles Whitman went on his shooting spree from the tower in 1966. But I wasn't there."[21] Indeed, what Strieber describes in *Communion* is a life history of false memories, invented tales, and bizarre behavior. As a student at the University of Texas in the late 1960s, he had longer and longer experiences of what appear to be fugue states, ranging from a few hours to six weeks. Strieber tells us that he invented a number of narratives to account for his whereabouts during these times and to explain his anxiety and need to escape. In January 1968, he got a loan to study film at the London School of Film Technique. After a frightening incident in which he found himself inexplicably on the roof of a friend's flat, Strieber felt an urgent need to flee.

He set out for Europe on a six-week odyssey but says he remembers virtually nothing about it. He thinks he was in Florence, Strasbourg, and Barcelona, where he "holed up in back room in a hotel on the Ramblas. . . . like a fugitive, never wanting to be alone, haunting the Ramblas, grateful for the unceasing crowds. The rest of the memory is a jumbled mess." For eighteen years after the trip—that is, until writing the book—he told people that he had spent six weeks in Florence. For a while, then, he told a story that he actually went to Russia and then to France for the uprisings of May 1968, although he knew full well that "they ended two months before I crossed France." "Why do I need these absurd stories?" Strieber asks himself. "They are not lies; when I tell them, I myself believe them. I don't lie. Perhaps I tell them to myself when I tell them to others, so that I can hide from myself whatever has made me a refugee in my own life."[22]

Strieber married in 1970, and has clearly benefited from his happy marriage and the love of his wife, Anne. He published *Wolfen* and sold it to Hollywood; apart from scattered episodes of panic and foreboding, his life was more stable. But after the birth of his son in 1979, some of the old terrors returned. One night, Strieber recalls, he was "awakened by the bizarre impression that there were people pouring in through the windows of our rather isolated house." By the early 1980s things were getting worse, and in March 1983 he had another fugue episode. Strieber felt panicky and obsessed with moving, with running. He and his wife bought a cabin in a isolated part of upstate New York. During the two years that preceded his "abduction" experience, Strieber had a number of puzzling experiences. In spring 1985, while reading in bed, he felt that he was flying around the room. When he told his wife, "she just laughed and continued to act as if everything were totally normal." In October 1995, the couple went through a crisis because of his "demands and accusatory behavior."[23]

The "abduction" experience took place the day after Christmas, but Strieber didn't remember it until he was hypnotized several months later. Instead, he went into a deep depression and wrote a short story called "Pain," with imagery much like that of his novels: "It is about a man who encounters an enigmatic woman named Janet, who proves to be some sort of superhuman being, perhaps an angel or a demon. She draws this man into a strange experience of capture and incarceration in a tiny, magical cabinet. From the agony that ensues, he gains immense insight and new spiritual strength."[24]

Strieber describes himself as a "contentious, rebellious Catholic, sometimes an Episcopalian." He says, "I have been a witch. I have experimented with worshipping the earth as a goddess/mother." He has a long-standing interest in religious mysticism, from the works of Meister Eckhart to Zen Buddhism and the Gurdjieff Institute.[25] Before his own abduction in December 1985, Strieber says, he'd read a *Look* magazine story about the Hills and "a book or two" about UFOs, including *Science and the UFOs*, a present from his brother. Even Budd Hopkins had suspicions about Strieber's reliability when he heard stories that Strieber later denied, acknowledged he had made up, or maintained despite opposing evidence. He announced that right-wing terrorists had threatened to kidnap his son and that the CIA was conspiring to prevent publication of *Communion*. He told another abductee, Kathy Davis, that during one of his own abductions he had seen her decapitated head on a shelf—a statement he afterward disclaimed.[26]

With witnesses as unreliable as Whitley Strieber, and without evidence to support them, alien abduction narratives have nonetheless won adherents. Their slogans have a familiar ring: "If what these abductees are saying is happening to them *isn't* happening, what *is*?" Mack demands.[27]

Perhaps women are seeking external explanations for their own sexual dreams, unconscious fantasies, and sensations, in a culture that still makes it difficult for women to accept their sexuality. Or maybe we're witnessing the birth of a folk religion, with aliens functioning much like the angels who have sprouted all over the country as the millennium approaches. According to English journalist Tom Hodgkinson, UFO stories have a strong spiritual component: "The UFO offers a satisfying blend of techno-futurism, religion, and a spiritual quest which is personally motivated and does not require a commitment to an externally imposed set of social rules. In a reason-based society, it is almost easier to believe in aliens, poised to descend and save the earth at any moment, than it is to believe in God. The UFO myth is also satisfying for those who distrust governments and authorities; talk among ufologists is inevitably peppered with references to cover-ups, to notions of us and them. The alien is co-opted as an ally against hostile leaders."[28]

Whatever the explanation, we can be sure that alien abduction myths will not be wiped out by the accumulation of negative evidence. To Mack, looking for material evidence is a logical error, typical of the material bias of Western scientists, who operate at a lower level of consciousness than the aliens. In May 1995, a Harvard faculty committee convened by Dean Daniel Tosteson submitted a report sharply critical of Mack's research. Mack's lawyers, Roderick MacLeish and Daniel Sheehan, countered that academic freedom was being challenged. "When you do something that breaks with the reality of your culture," Mack protested, "you are going to draw some flak. The subject is difficult for the Western worldview, because it says several things. Not only that we are not the top of the intelligence pyramid, but that we don't have control of our fates."[29] In August 1995, Harvard backed down.[30]

According to ufologist Jacques Vallee, the phenomenon feeds on itself in a continuous loop: "Conventional science appears more and more perplexed, befuddled, at a loss to explain. Pro-ET ufologists become more dogmatic in their propositions. More people become fascinated with space and with new frontiers of consciousness. More books and articles appear, changing our culture in the direction of a new image of man."[31] It's disturbing that the myths do not stay static and circular—they escalate, incorporating previous hystories of childhood sexual abuse, multiple personality, and satanic ritual. The current stage—hystories that include details of reproductive experiment, surveillance, mind control, and government conspiracy—leads to the right-wing militias of the American fin de siècle. We cannot afford to ignore or indulge space-age fantasies as harmless science fiction.

For the moment alien abduction is largely an American phenomenon. According to Mack, the United States leads all other countries in reports, with "England and Brazil following behind, chiefly because of the availability of practicing hypnotists and therapists working with abductees in these countries." However, abduction narratives from other countries do not follow the American pattern of contact with gray Beings of various sizes. Europeans apparently extend their traditional cosmopolitanism to the alien world: as Mack puts it, they "have contact with a greater variety of entities." In the Netherlands, for instance, aliens come tiny and green, orange, or purple. The French have observed aliens in silver suits. British abductees tend to see a "Robert Redford/Scandinavian type" buffs call a Tall Blond, Nordic, or Guardian Angel alien. Always male, he is "six to seven feet tall, handsome, with blond shoulder-length hair. His blue ayes are kind and loving. He is paternal, watchful, smiling, affectionate, youthful, all-knowing, and wears a form-fitting uniform."[32] He smells like cinnamon. This is the kind of alien *I* want to be abducted by, but as an American, my chances are pretty slim.

When a video of an alleged autopsy of female aliens was shown simultaneously on British, American, and French television on August 28, 1995, the French scientists assembled to discuss it in a television symposium the next evening could hardly keep straight faces and went through the Gallic repertoire of scornful body language and mocking mouth noises. The program began with another tape: a confiscated Russian documentary of a space ship crash and alien autopsy, with odd black shapes and meaty slices in a pan. The panelists then revealed this tape to be a hoax, a parody assembled by a French filmmaker. They dismissed alien abduction as ridiculous and expressed irritation that national television would so abuse the intelligence of its viewers. After a TV show about abductions, two German therapists offered their services free to anyone wishing to come forward; disappointingly, only twenty people responded.[33] An Irish commentator, Anne Enright, had a field day with the "American aliens." In Ireland, Enright explained, "we don't need aliens; we already have a race of higher beings who gaze deep into our eyes and force us to have babies against our will. We call them priests."[34]

But American ufologists are optimistic. They're thinking about ways to export methodologies to other countries and traveling to conferences around the world. "It is likely that with the publicizing of therapeutic and hypnosis techniques currently being pioneered in the United States," Mack writes confidently, "much more information about abduction experiences overseas will be available in coming years."[35]

14 | The Crucible

In Nathaniel Hawthorne's classic story "Young Goodman Brown," a man leaves his bride of three months for a secret tryst with the devil. He is understandably anxious about his journey into the forest, but the devil, who bears "a considerable resemblance" to Goodman Brown and indeed might be taken for his father, reassures him: "I helped your grandfather, the constable, when he lashed the Quaker woman so smartly through the streets of Salem; and it was I that brought your father a pitch-pine knot, kindled at my own hearth, to set fire to an Indian village, in King Philip's war. They were my good friends, both; and many a pleasant walk have we had along this path, and returned merrily after midnight." Indeed, when they get to the center of the forest, Goodman Brown is shocked to see the most upright folk of the community gathered to worship Satan. Alongside the pious, chaste, and reputable are "men of dissolute lives and women of spotted fame." All of them seem to be on very good terms. And standing at the altar is another new convert: his own wife, Faith.

In this celebrated fable, Hawthorne is not, of course, saying that the good folk of Salem were all secretly worshiping the devil. Rather, he suggests that behind the stern facade of American puritanism fanaticism expressed itself in acts of persecution and violence that culminated in the Salem witch trials. Looking eagerly for sexual and religious sin, the Puritans ignored their own eagerness to punish and condemn. As Arthur Miller argues in *The Crucible*, witch-hunts began when individualism challenged the rigid ideologies of Salem.

Hawthorne suggests another interpretation of the story. "Had Goodman Brown fallen asleep in the forest and only dreamed a wild dream of a witch-meeting?" If we follow this line of thought, the story is also about a husband's faithlessness—his repressed desire to betray his bride, which becomes a projected fantasy that she is betraying him. Stories about witchcraft always function on at least these two levels, as indictments of the intolerance and paranoia lurking behind religious fundamentalism and as psychological projections of anxiety and sexual guilt.

How does "Young Goodman Brown" illuminate the hystories of the 1990s? Like the witch-hunts of the 1690s, the mesmerism craze of the 1790s, or the hypnotic cures of the 1890s, the hysterical syndromes of the 1990s clearly speak to the hidden needs and fears of a culture. We are still dealing with the projection of sexual fantasy and real or imagined guilt, with malice and with genuine confusion. No one has been hung or burned, but scores of innocent people have had their lives destroyed by false accusations, and hundreds of thousands are wasting their lives pursuing costly therapies without relief or cure.

Hawthorne understood the force of sexuality denied. In his overture to *The Crucible*, Arthur Miller observed that "our opposites are always robed in sexual sin, and it is from this unconscious conviction that demonology gains both its attractive sensuality and its capacity to infuriate and frighten." Many contemporary syndromes have strong sexual content, a content disavowed and projected onto some external source—a father, a cult, a chemical, an alien being. Patients often express intense guilt and shame about this sexual content and about their fears of being bad because they experience it as both pleasurable and painful. There is still much cultural work to be done, especially for women, in relieving sexual guilt.

Hawthorne saw demonology as the other side of religion. Many writers have wondered whether a spiritual void and an unconscious quest for religious certainty lie behind the hysterical syndromes of the 1990s. Ian Hacking sees similarities between recollection of trauma and Protestant conversion experience: recovered memory "begins with the watchword 'denial.' . . . Then comes therapy as conversion, confession, and the restructuring of remembrances of one's past. But informing this familiar pattern there is an almighty twist. Accusation. Your confession is not to *your* sins, but to your father's sins."[1]

Mark Pendergrast believes that recovered memory is a substitute faith that has won many converts during a time of spiritual crisis. "We are dealing with a religious phenomenon," he writes, "which is why so many Christian therapists and pastoral counselors are among the most zealous memory retrieval advocates." The professionals and therapists may be the priests of the movement, but "the Survivors are the movement's acolytes, its martyrs, its devotees, and often its prophets. For many of the women I interviewed, the hunt for memories has become an exciting spiritual adventure."[2] Richard Webster compares the doctrines of recovered memory to "Puritan revivalism," which has "swept through Puritan North America not *against* the tide of Christian fundamentalism but in alliance with it."[3] The myths and symbols of satanic ritual abuse obviously mimic religious rituals, and alien abduction stories often have an explicit religious component. Even chronic fatigue syndrome can sometimes be cured by a faith healer. In anxious times, good men and good women can be susceptible to the answers provided by narratives of sin and blame, and by the comforting role of the Survivor.

In Hawthorne's fable Young Goodman Brown does not return to Salem, confront and accuse his neighbors, and ruin their lives. Many today have less restraint: contemporary hystories blur the line between therapeutic narrative and public testimony. Psychoanalysis and religion have traditionally offered private forms of confession and solace. Psychotherapists and clergymen have not found it necessary to play the role of detective, investigating what their clients say. In August 1992, for example, at the American Psychiatric Association conference in Washington, Dr. Michael Nash described a distressed patient who said he'd been abducted by aliens. Nash successfully treated this "highly hypnotizable" man with therapy and hypnosis; after three months the patient was able to resume his normal habits. Talking about his alleged abduction and integrating it into his overall identity did him a great deal of good. Yet he walked out of Nash's office "as utterly convinced that he had been abducted as when he walked in." Nash concluded that "in terms of clinical utility, it may not really matter whether the event actually happened. . . . In the end, we [as clinicians] cannot tell the difference between believed-in fantasy about the past and viable memory. . . . Indeed there may be no structural difference between the two."[4]

But rituals of narrative have become rituals of testimony. Testimony, as Judith Herman acknowledges, "has both a private dimension which is confessional and spiritual, and a public aspect, which is political and judicial."[5] Literary critics especially know that narrative can be healing, and that the act of telling one's story may be therapeutic even when it is fictional. The writing cure, the acting cure, the dancing cure, all forms of creativity and art, are effective, meaningful forms of self-help. What psychologist Roy Schafer calls "retelling a life" is an important part of psychological growth, responsibility, and self-acceptance. Whether the details of these narratives are demonstrably true may not be as important as their imaginative and spiritual resonance for the individual. But extending private psychoanalytic or artistic testimonies to the media and the courts is risky. We must exercise caution as a society when hystories take on that political, judicial form, when they stop being therapeutic and cross the line into accusation and prosecution.

The problems and realities behind modern hystories are all too real. War does make people ill. Men suffering aftereffects of the Gulf War have had to deal with conflicting social mythologies: on one hand, the mythology that psychological illness is unmanly and illegitimate; on the other, the mythology of the warrior hero, Rambo or wildman, gangbanger or paramilitary leader, living out what James William Gibson calls the "warrior dreams" of Post-Vietnam America.[6] Gulf War syndrome provides an external solution to conflicts that go very deep into our culture's definitions of masculinity and its glorification of war.

The conflicts women try to resolve with hystories are equally complex. Recovered memories of sexual abuse are unreliable, but child abuse, rape, and violence against women is an everyday reality that affects every woman's sense of security and autonomy. Women have traditionally used hysterical disorders to compensate for the absence of adventure and challenge in their lives and to deal with real sorrows, dissatisfactions, and disappointments. Feminism is problematic for women in the 1990s in part because it has raised our expectations without having the power to fulfill them. In some respects, neither feminism—nor any other utopian philosophy or ideology—can ever fulfill all the hopes it raises. But feminism can help us accept the struggle and resist regression into victimization, infantilization, or revenge.

Historically, witch-hunts tended to be short. Communities decided that the trials were worse than the alleged crimes; they ran out of marginal victims and discovered malice or fraud in accusers. Resisters rose up, or governments stepped in. In his epilogue to The Crucible, Arthur Miller gives an elegiac summary of the end of the witch-hunts in Salem: "In solemn meeting, the congregation rescinded the excommunications—this in March 1712. . . . The jury . . . wrote a statement praying forgiveness of all who had suffered. Certain farms which had belonged to the victims were left to ruin, and for more than a century no one would buy them or live on them. To all intents and purposes, the power of theocracy in Massachusetts was broken." In Salem, Mackay says, "the revulsion was as sudden as the first frenzy. All at once, the colonists were convinced of their error. The judges put a stop to the prosecutions, even of those who had confessed their guilt. The latter were no sooner at liberty than they retracted all they had said. . . . The jurors on the different trials openly expressed their penitence in the churches; and those who had suffered were regarded as the victims, and not the accomplices of Satan."[7] The political witch-hunts of the 1950s also came to an end, although not without damage that could never be undone.

The hysterical witch-hunts of our own time may be waning as well. People accused of abuse on the basis of recovered memory are being acquitted. Convictions have been overturned. Retractors are taking back their accusations of satanic ritual or childhood abuse. Journalists in Britain and the United States have taken up the cause of those falsely accused. Books and TV documentaries have helped turn the tide of credibility, especially around recovered memory and satanic ritual abuse.

But the hysterical epidemics of the 1990s have already gone on too long, and they continue to do damage: in distracting us from the real problems and crises of modern society, in undermining a respect for evidence and truth, and in helping support an atmosphere of conspiracy and suspicion. They prevent us from claiming our full humanity as free and responsible beings. Although *The Crucible* has been produced more often than any of Miller's other plays, its message has still to be fully understood. It was not simply about Salem, nor yet about McCarthyism, but rather about the human propensity to paranoia.

Today, as one form of hystory is contested, another seems to spring up in its place. No sooner does the Pentagon release a study showing that Gulf War syndrome does not exist than a doctor writes to the *New York Times* claiming that the symptoms "are almost identical to chronic fatigue immune dysfunction."[8] As the hystory of satanic ritual abuse has been challenged, its underlying themes of infant sacrifice and government programming have been transferred to other targets. Fantasy TV series like *The X-Files* are not alone in exploring ideas of aliens, conspiracies, cover-ups, and cults; in April 1996, *Wall Street Journal* media critic Dorothy Rabinowitz complained that "the number of alleged governmental deceits and plots against the citizenry that are uncovered daily in, say, a single night's TV watching is dizzying to con-template."[9] Moreover, these television images shape belief. In an op-ed piece in the New York *Times* in August 1996, professor Wayne Anderson of Sacramento City College reported that half of the students in his astronomy class credited the idea of a government conspiracy to conceal UFOs, and cited television programs as evidence.[10]

Men and women, therapists and patients, will need courage to face the hidden fantasies, myths, and anxieties that make up the current hysterical crucible; we must look into our own psyches rather to invisible enemies, devils, and alien invaders for the answers. I don't expect many recanters to come forward because of this book. Yet I believe our human dignity demands that we face the truth. Hysteria is neither the sign of a higher consciousness nor the badge of a shameful weakness. Women still suffer from hysterical symptoms not because we are essentially irrational or because we're all victims of abuse but because, like men, we are human beings who will convert feelings into symptoms when we are unable to speak—when, for example, we feel over-whelmed by shame, guilt, or helplessness. Looking back on Salem, Miller wrote, "One can only pity them all, just as we shall be pitied someday. It is still impossible for man to organize his social life without repressions, and the balance has yet to be struck between order and freedom."[11] If we can begin to understand, accept, pity, and forgive ourselves for the psychological dynamics of hysteria, perhaps we can begin to work together to break the crucible and avert the coming hysterical plague.

Notes

1. The Hysterical Hot Zone

1. Laurie Garrett, *The Coming Plague: Newly Emerging Diseases in a World Out of Balance* (New York: Penguin, 1995), 32.

2. Ilza Veith, *Hysteria: The History of a Disease* (Chicago: University of Chicago Press, 1965), 273–74.

3. Roberta Satow, "Where Has All the Hysteria Gone?" *Psychoanalytic Review* 66 (1979–80): 463–77.

4. Etienne Trillat, *Histoire de l'hystérie* (Paris: Seghers, 1986), 274 (my translation).

5. Norman Cohn, *The Pursuit of the Millennium* (London: Secker & Warburg, 1957), 314.

6. Sigmund Freud, "The Etiology of Hysteria," trans. James Strachey, in Jeffrey Masson, *The Assault on Truth* (New York: Farrar Straus Giroux, 1984), 265.

7. Quoted in Hillary Johnson, *Osler's Web: Inside the Labyrinth of the Chronic Fatigue Syndrome Epidemic* (New York: Crown, 1996), 351.

8. David M. Jacobs, *Alien Encounters* (London: Virgin Books, 1994), 28. (Jacobs's book, called *Secret Life* in the United States, was published by Simon & Schuster in 1992.)

9. Roy Porter, "The Body and the Mind, the Doctor and the Patient: Negotiating Hysteria" in Sander Gilman, Helen King, Roy Porter, G. S. Rousseau, Elaine Showalter, *Hysteria Beyond Freud* (Berkeley: University of California Press, 1993), 235.

10. Mark S. Micale, *Approaching Hysteria* (Princeton: Princeton University Press, 1994), 182.

11. Robert M. Woolsey, "Hysteria: 1875 to 1975," *Diseases of the Nervous System*, 37 (July 1976): 379.

12. See David E. Sanger, "What Great Grief Has Made the Empress Mute?" *New York Times* (October 25, 1993): A4. The Empress recovered her voice in February 1994.

13. Micale, *Approaching Hysteria*, 288–91.

14. Nielltje Gedney, "The Backlash and Beyond," *Journal of Psychohistory*, 4 (Spring 1995): 436.

15. Mark J. Penn and Douglas E. Schoen, "A Tale of Four Cities," *New York* (August 21, 1995): 30.

16. Jacques Lacan, quoted in Elisabeth Roudinesco, *La bataille de cent ans: Histoire de la psychanalyse en France*, 2 vols. (Paris: Ramsay, 1982), 1:82–83 (my translation).

17. Jacobs, "A Note to the Reader," *Alien Encounters*, 15.

18. Lynne V. Cheney, *Telling the Truth* (New York: Simon & Schuster, 1995), 172.

19. Diane Price Herndl, "The Writing Cure," *NWSA Journal*, 1 (1988): 54.

20. Porter, "Body and Mind," in Gilman et al., *Hysteria Beyond Freud*, 242.

2. Defining Hysteria

1. Phillip R. Slavney, *Perspectives on "Hysteria"* (Baltimore: Johns Hopkins University Press, 1990), 1–2.

2. Charles Lasegue, "Des hystéries périphériques," *Archives générales de médecine*, 1 (June 1878): 655; quoted in Micale, *Approaching Hysteria*, 109n3.

3. Edward Shorter, "The Reinvention of Hysteria," *Times Literary Supplement*, June 17, 1994, 26.

4. Roy Porter, "Body and Mind," in Sander Gilman et al., *Hysteria Beyond Freud* (Berkeley: University of California Press), 226.

5. Edward Shorter, *From Paralysis to Fatigue* (New York: The Free Press, 1992), x.

6. Porter, "Body and Mind," in Gilman et al., *Hysteria Beyond Freud*, 229.

7. Henry Maudsley, *The Pathology of Mind* (London: Macmillan, 1879), 450.

8. Gregorio Kohon, "Reflections of Dora: The Case of Hysteria," *International Journal of Psychoanalysis*, 65 (1984): 73.

9. Janine Chasseguet-Smirgel, "The Femininity of the Analyst in Professional Practice," *International Journal of Psycho-Analysis* 65 (1994): 169–78.

10. Georges Guillain, *J.-M. Charcot, 1825–1893: His Life*, ed. and trans. Pearce Bailey (London: Pitman Medical Publishing, 1959), 135.

11. Richard Webster, *Why Freud Was Wrong* (New York: Basic Books, 1995), 544.

12. Porter, "Body and Mind," in Gilman et al., *Hysteria Beyond Freud*, 242.

13. Robert A. Aronowitz, "From Myalgic Encephalitis to Yuppie Flu: A

History of Chronic Fatigue Syndromes," in *Framing Disease*, ed. Charles E. Rosenberg and Janet Golden (New Brunswick, N.J.: Rutgers University Press, 1992), 155.

14. Ian Hacking, *Rewriting the Soul: Multiple Personality and the Sciences of Memory* (Princeton: Princeton University Press, 1995), 24, 33, 34, 35.

15. Edward Shorter, *From Paralysis to Fatigue* (New York: The Free Press, 1992), 8–9.

16. S. A. K. Wilson, "Some Modern French Conceptions of Hysteria," *Brain*, 33 (1901): 297.

17. See Joan Jacobs Brumberg, "From Psychiatric Syndrome to 'Communicable' Disease: The Case of Anorexia Nervosa," in *Framing Disease*, 134–54. My analysis is indebted to that of Professor Brumberg.

18. Henri F. Ellenberger, "Psychiatry and its Unknown History," in *Beyond the Unconscious: Essays of Henri F. Ellenberger in the History of Psychiatry*, ed. Mark S. Micale (Princeton: Princeton University Press, 1993), 239–53.

19. Hilde Bruch, *Eating Disorders: Obesity, Anorexia Nervosa, and the Person Within* (New York: Basic Books, 1973), 251.

20. Brumberg, "From Psychiatric Syndrome," 142.

21. Ibid., 143.

22. Brumberg, *Fasting Girls: The Emergence of Anorexia Nervosa as a Modern Disease* (Cambridge: Harvard University Press, 1988), 16, 17, 269.

23. Susan Gilbert, "More Men May Seek Eating-Disorder Help," *New York Times*, August 28, 1996, C9.

24. Simon Wessely, "Have You Heard? We Are Being Poisoned," *The Times* (London), July 4, 1995, 14.

25. "Doctor Faults State Report on Faintings," *New York Times*, September 4, 1994, 31.

26. Miraya Navarro, "A Monster on the Loose? Or Is It Fantasy?" *New York Times*, January 26, 1996, A10.

27. Richard Hofstadter, "The Paranoid Style in American Politics," in Hofstadter, *The Paranoid Style in American Politics and Other Essays* (New York: Knopf, 1965), 39.

28. Brian Levack, *The Witch-Hunt in Early Modern Europe*, 2d ed. (New York: Longman, 1995), 159.

29. Norman Cohn, *The Pursuit of the Millennium* (London: Secker & Warburg, 1957), 74.

30. Levack, *Witch-Hunt*, 173.

31. Ibid., 174, 177.

32. Arthur Miller, *The Crucible: Text and Criticism*, ed. Gerald Weaks (New York: Viking, 1971), 7, 20.

33. Katherine Dunn and Jim Redden, "Fear and Loathing," *Los Angeles Times Book Review*, June 4, 1995, 11.

34. Michael Kelly, "The Road to Paranoia," *New Yorker* (June 19, 1995): 62, 64.

35. Alex Wichel, "To Rise Again from a Life in Ruins," *New York Times*, January 4, 1996, C10.

36. Sherrill Mulhern, "Satanism, Ritual Abuse, and Multiple Personality Disorder," *International Journal of Clinical and Experimental Hypnosis*, 42 (October 1994): 266.

37. Miller, *The Crucible*, 34.

38. Thomas Stretch Dowse, *Lectures on Massage and Electricity in the Treatment of Disease* (London: Hamilton, Adams, 1889), 191.

39. Edwin Bramwell and John Tuke, quoted in Micale, "Hysteria Male/ Hysteria Female," in *Science and Sensibility*, ed. Marina Benjamin (London: Basil Blackwell, 1991), 23.

40. J. Mitchell Clark, *Hysteria and Neurasthenia* (London/New York: John Lane, 1904), 5.

41. Simon Jenkins, "Dumbing the Tories," *The Times*, July 1, 1995, 18.

42. David Bell, "Hysteria: A Contemporary Kleinian Perspective," paper delivered at "Hysteria Today: 100 Years Since Freud," Freud Museum Conference on Hysteria, February 1995.

43. Pierre Janet, *The Major Symptoms of Hysteria* (New York: Macmillan, 1920), 2–3, 5.

3. The History of Hysteria: The Great Doctors

1. Axel Munthe, *The Story of San Michele* [1929] (New York: Carrol & Graf, 1991), 206.

2. "Banquet offert à M. le professeur Charcot," *Progrès médical*, 11 (1883): 999.

3. A. Souques, "Charcot intime," *Presse médicale*, 42 (May 27, 1925): 17.

4. Pierre Janet, quoted in Georges Guillain, *J.-M. Charcot, 1825–1893: His Life* (London: Pitman Medical Publishing, 1959), 55.

5. Henri Ellenberger, "Charcot and the Salpêtrière School," in Mark S. Micale, ed. *Beyond the Unconscious: Essays of Henri F. Ellenberger in the History of Psychiatry* (Princeton: Princeton University Press, 1993), 139.

6. Martha Noel Evans, *Fits and Starts: A Genealogy of Hysteria in Modern France* (Ithaca: Cornell University Press, 1991), 34.

7. Mark S. Micale, *Approaching Hysteria* (Princeton: Princeton University Press, 1994), 269.

8. Ellenberger, "Charcot and the Salpêtrière School," 145.

9. See Edward Shorter, *From Paralysis to Fatigue*, 168–70.

10. Jan Goldstein, *Console and Classify: The French Psychiatric Profession in the Nineteenth Century* (New York: Cambridge University Press, 1987), 326.

11. Munthe, *The Story of San Michele*, 218.

12. Ibid., 231–32.

13. Charles Richet, "Les démoniaques d'aujourd'hui at d'autrefois," *La revue des deux mondes*, 37 (1880): 346.

14. Evans, *Fits and Starts*, 11.

15. George Frederick Drinka, *The Birth of Neurosis: Myth, Malady, and the Victorians* (New York: Simon & Schuster, 1983), 138.

16. Albert D. Vandam, "The Trail of 'Trilby,'" *The Forum* 20 (September 1895–February 1896): 434–35.

17. See Ulrich Baer, "Photography and Hysteria: Towards a Poetics of the Flash," *Yale Journal of Criticism*, 7 (1994): 66ff.

18. Goldstein, *Console and Classify*, 330.

19. Ellenberger, "Charcot and the Salpêtrière School," 150.

20. Evans, *Fits and Starts*, 41.

21. Mark S. Micale, "On the 'Disappearance' of Hysteria: A Study in the Clinical Deconstruction of a Diagnosis," *Isis*, 84 (1993): 525.

22. Paul Dubois, *The Psychic Treatment of Nervous Disorders*, Eng. trans., 6th ed. (New York, 1909), 15–16, quoted in Shorter, *From Paralysis to Fatigue*, 185.

23. Micale, "On the 'Disappearance' of Hysteria," 89.

24. A. Steyerthal, *Was ist Hysterie?*, quoted in Webster, *Why Freud Was Wrong* (New York: Basic Books, 1995), 138.

25. Micale, "On the 'Disappearance' of Hysteria," 500.

26. Ibid., 501.

27. Webster, *Why Freud Was Wrong*, 9.

28. John Forrester and Lisa Appignanesi, *Freud's Women* (New York: Basic Books, 1993), 71.

29. For a provocative discussion of the importance of this case, see Dianne Hunter, "Hysteria, Psychoanalysis, and Feminism: The Case of Anna O.," *Feminist Studies*, 9 (Fall 1983): 465–88.

30. Sigmund Freud, *An Autobiographical Study* [1925] (New York: Norton, 1952), 33.

31. *The Complete Letters of Sigmund Freud to Wilhelm Fliess*, ed. Jeffrey Moussaief Masson (Cambridge: Harvard University Press, 1985), 212.

32. Jeffrey Moussaief Masson, *The Assault on Truth: Freud's Suppression of the Seduction Theory* (New York: Farrar Straus Giroux, 1984), xv–xxiii.

33. Judith Lewis Herman, *Father-Daughter Incest* (Cambridge: Harvard University Press, 1981), 10.

34. Masson, *The Assault on Truth*, 144.

35. See Richard Webster, "The Seduction Theory," in *Why Freud Was Wrong*, 195–213.

36. Frederick Crews, *The Memory Wars: Freud's Legacy in Dispute* (New York: New York Review Books, 1995), 59.

37. Webster, *Why Freud Was Wrong*, 213.

38. Sigmund Freud, *Dora: An Analysis of a Case of Hysteria* (New York: Collins, 1964), 20. See also Charles Bernheimer and Claire Kahane, eds., *In Dora's Case: Freud-Hysteria-Feminism* (New York: Columbia University Press, 1985).

39. Jeffrey M. Masson, *Against Therapy* (London: Fontana, 1990), 101.

40. Kurt Eissler, "The Effect of the Structure of the Ego in Psychoanalytic Technique," *Journal of the American Psychoanalytic Association*, 1 (1953): 114.

41. Juliet Mitchell, "The Question of Femininity and the Theory of Psychoanalysis," in *The British School of Psychoanalysis*, ed. Gregorio Kohon (London: Free Association Books, 1986), 386.

42. Evans, *Fits and Starts*, 2.

43. Frederick Crews, "The Unknown Freud," *New York Review of Books*, November 18, 1993, 55.

44. Frederick Crews, letter to the editor, *New York Times*, December 13, 1995, A22.

45. Sebastian Faulks, "Freudian Snips," *The Guardian*, October 31, 1995, 6.

46. Sherry Turkle, *Psychoanalytic Politics: Jacques Lacan and Freud's French Revolution* (New York: Basic Books, 1978; London: Burnett Books, 1979), 14.

47. Elisabeth Roudinesco, *Jacques Lacan & Co.*, trans. Jeffrey Mehlman (Chicago: University of Chicago Press, 1990), 420.

48. Evans, *Fits and Starts*, 174.

49. André Breton and Louis Aragon, "Le cinquantenaire de l'hystérie, 1878–1928," in Breton, *Oeuvres complètes* (Paris: Gallimard, 1988), 1:948–50.

50. Catherine Clément, *The Lives and Legends of Jacques Lacan* (New York: Columbia University Press, 1983), 12, 55.

51. Mark S. Micale and Roy Porter, eds. *Discovering the History of Psychiatry* (New York/Oxford: Oxford University Press, 1994), 13.

52. See Stuart A. Kirk and Herb Kutchins, *The Selling of DSM: The Rhetoric of Science in Psychiatry* (New York: Aldine de Gruyter, 1992), 8.

4. Politics, Patients, and Feminism

1. Judith Lewis Herman, *Trauma and Recovery* (New York: Basic Books, 1992), 32.

2. William Barry, "The Strike of a Sex," *Quarterly Review*, 179 (1894): 312.

3. Lisa Tickner, *The Spectacle of Women* (Chicago: University of Chicago Press, 1988), 315n188.

4. Fritz Wittels, *Die Fackel*, May 1907, quoted in Hannah S. Decker, *Freud, Dora, and Vienna 1900* (New York, The Free Press, 1991), 201.

5. S. Weir Mitchell, *Doctor and Patient* (Philadelphia: Lippincott, 1888), 48.

6. John Forrester and Lisa Appignanesi, *Freud's Women* (New York: Basic Books, 1993), 68.

7. See Elizabeth Lunbeck, *The Psychiatric Persuasion* (Princeton: Princeton University Press, 1994), 209–28.

8. "Sof'ia Niron" (pseud.), in *Russkie vedemosti* 1 (November 1888), rpt S. V. Kovalevskaia, *Vospominaniia Povesti* (Moscow: Izdatel'stvo Nauka, 1974), 275–81. Thanks to Prof. Debora Silverman, History Department, UCLA, for this reference.

9. Georgette Déga, *Essai sur la cure préventive de l'hystérie féminine par l'éducation* (Paris: Alcan, 1898), 24, 26.

10. Martha Noel Evans, *Fits and Starts: A Genealogy of Hysteria in Modern France* (Ithaca: Cornell University Press, 1991), 73.

11. Nancy Chodorow, *Feminism and Psychoanalytic Theory* (New Haven: Yale University Press, 1989), 199–218.

12. Chodorow, *Feminism and Psychoanalytic Theory*, 208–10.

13. Forrester and Appignanesi, *Freud's Women*, 319.

14. Chodorow, *Feminism and Psychoanalytic Theory*, 213, 217.

15. Carroll Smith-Rosenberg, "The Hysterical Woman: Sex Roles and Role Conflict in Nineteenth-Century America," *Social Research*, 39 (1972): 652–78. Reprinted in Smith-Rosenberg, *Disorderly Conduct: Visions of Gender in Victorian America* (New York: Knopf, 1985), 197–216.

16. Mark Pendergrast, *Victims of Memory: Incest Accusations and Shattered Lives* (Hinesburg, Vt.: Upper Access, 1995), 429.

17. Nancy Tomes, "Feminist History of Psychiatry," in Mark S. Micale and Roy Porter, eds., *Discovering the History of Psychiatry* (New York/Oxford: Oxford University Press, 1994), 358.

18. Evans, *Fits and Starts*, 205

19. Ibid., 203–4.

20. Ibid., 215.

21. Hélène Cixous, "Sorties," in *The Newly Born Woman*, trans. Betsy Wing (Minneapolis: University of Minnesota Press, 1975), 99.

22. Evans, *Fits and Starts*, 210.

23. Claire Kahane, "Introduction: Part Two," *In Dora's Case: Freud-Hysteria-Feminism*, Charles Bernheimer and Claire Kahane, eds. (New York: Columbia University Press, 1985), 27.

24. Mandy Merck, "The Critical Cult of *Dora*," in Merck, *Perversions* (London: Virago, 1993), 33–44.

25. Mark S. Micale, *Approaching Hysteria* (Princeton: Princeton University Press, 1994), 84.

26. Janet Malcolm, "Reflections: J'appelle un chat un chat," *In Dora's Case*, 2d ed., 305.

27. Dianne Hunter, "Hysteria, Psychoanalysis, and Feminism: The Case of Anna O.," *Feminist Studies*, 9 (Fall 1983): 484.

28. Diane Price Herndl, "The Writing Cure," *NWSA Journal*, 1 (1988): 53.

29. See Ilene J. Philipson, *On the Shoulders of Women: The Feminization of Psychotherapy* (New York/London: Guilford Press, 1993), 54–55.

30. Ibid., 114, 116, 148.

31. Ellen Bass and Laura Davis, *The Courage to Heal*, 3d ed. (New York: Harper Perennial, 1994), 482.

32. Ian Hacking, *Rewriting the Soul: Multiple Personality and the Sciences of Memory* (Princeton: Princeton University Press, 1995), 62.

33. Judith Lewis Herman, *Father-Daughter Incest* (Cambridge: Harvard University Press, 1981), 29.

34. Laura S. Brown, "Not Outside the Range: One Feminist Perspective on Psychic Trauma," in *Trauma: Explorations in Memory*, ed. Cathy Carruth (Baltimore: Johns Hopkins University Press, 1995), 102–3.

35. Maria P. Root, "Reconstructing the Impact of Trauma on Personality," in *Personality and Psychopathology: Feminist Reappraisals*, ed. L. S. Brown and M. Baillou (New York: Guilford, 1992).

36. Carol Tavris, *The Mismeasure of Woman* (New York: Simon and Schuster, 1992), 321.

5. Hysterical Men

1. S. Weir Mitchell, "A Case of Uncomplicated Hysteria in the Male," unpublished manuscript in Philadelphia College of Medicine, 1904.

2. Mark S. Micale, "Hysteria Male/Hysteria Female," in *Science and Sensibility*, ed. Marina Benjamin (London: Basil Blackwell, 1991), 3.

3. Pierre Marie, "Eloge de J.-M. Charcot," *Bulletin de l'Académie de Médicine*, 93 (1925): 576–93, quoted in Georges Guillain, *J.-M. Charcot, 1825–1893: His Life*, trans. Pearce Bailey (London: Pitman Medical, 1959), 146.

4. See J.-M. Charcot, *Clinical Lectures on Diseases of the Nervous System*, Ruth Harris, ed. (New York/London: Tavistock, 1991). Charcot's major lectures on male hysteria were originally published in *Oeuvres completes de J-M Charcot*, 9 vols. (Paris: Bureau de Progrès Medical, Delahaye et Lecosnier, 1886–1893).

5. Robert Brudenell Carter, *On the Pathology and Treatment of Hysteria* (London: Churchill, 1853), 34.

6. Thomas Laycock, *A Treatise on the Nervous Diseases of Women* (1840), quoted by Janet Oppenheim, *Shattered Nerves: Doctors, Patients, and Depression in Victorian England* (New York: Oxford University Press, 1991), 143.

7. Ernst von Feuchtersleben, *The Principles of Medical Psychology* (1847), quoted in Ilza Veith, *Hysteria: The History of a Disease* (Chicago: University of Chicago Press, 1965), 169.

8. "Un mécanicien de locomotive hystérique! Un homme fort, solide, habitué aux intempéries des saisons, est-ce raisonnable? On peut s'imaginer une femmelette parfumée et pommadée souffrant de ce mal bizarre; mais qu'un ouvrier robuste ait ses nerfs et des vapeurs comme une dame de grand monde, c'est trop!" Emile Batault, *Contribution à l'étude de l'hystérie chez l'homme* (Paris, 1885), 48.

9. Jean-Martin Charcot, quoted in Jan Goldstein, *Console and Classify: The French Psychiatric Profession in the Nineteenth Century* (New York: Cambridge University Press, 1987), 336.

10. Brian Donkin, quoted in Oppenheim, *Shattered Nerves*, 144, 115.

11. F. S. Gosling, *Before Freud: Neurasthenia and the American Medical Community* (Urbana: Illinois University Press, 1987), 47.

12. Archibald Church, quoted in Gosling, *Before Freud*, 115, and Oppenheim, *Shattered Nerves*, 144.

13. See "The Railway God," in George Frederick Drinka, *The Birth of Neurosis: Myth, Malady, and the Victorians* (New York: Simon & Schuster, 1983), 108–22.

14. Jean-Martin Charcot, quoted in Mark S. Micale, "J.-M. Charcot and the Idea of Hysteria in the Male," *Medical History*, 34 (October 1990), 25.

15. Paul Fabre, "De l'hystérie chez l'homme," *Gazette médicale Paris*, 3 (December 3, 1881): 867.

16. Charcot, "Six Cases of Hysteria in the Male," in *Clinical Lectures on*

Diseases of the Nervous System, ed. Ruth Harris (London: Routledge, 1991), 236–42.

17. Charcot, "Des propensités hystéro-traumatiques chez l'homme," *Semaine médicale*, 7 (1887): 491.

18. Charcot, *Leçons du mardi*, 2:50

19. Jules Déjerine, quoted in Micale, "Charcot and the Idea of Hysteria in the Male," 36.

20. Charcot, "Six Cases," 236–42.

21. Ruth Harris, "Introduction," *Clinical Lectures*, xxxiii.

22. Charcot, "Six Cases," 236–42.

23. Emile Batault, *Contribution à l'étude de l'hystérie chez l'homme*, 110.

24. Charcot, "Six Cases," 239.

25. J.-M. Charcot, "Hystérie et dégénérescence chez l'homme," in' Etienne Trillat, ed., *L'hystérie* (Toulouse: Edouard Privat, 1971), 143–53 (my translation).

26. On the astonishing iconography of tattoos among *28 million* male prisoners and Soviet labor camps in the Soviet republics, see Arkady G. Bonnikov, "Body Language," *New York Times*, November 6, 1993, 23.

27. Michèle Ouerd, "Introduction," Charcot, *Leçons sur l'hystérie virile* (Paris: Le Sycamore, 1984), 27.

28. Goldstein, *Console and Classify*, 154.

29. Cyril Burt, *The Subnormal Mind* (Oxford: Oxford University Press, 1977), 5.

30. Philip Gibbs, in Eric Leed, *No Man's Land: Combat and Identity in World War I* (Cambridge: Cambridge University Press, 1979), 187.

31. Ibid., 185.

32. See Oswald Bumke and Hans Burger-Prinz, *Ein Psychiater berichter* (Hamburg: Hoffman und Campe, 1971), 102, trans. Edward Shorter in *From Paralysis to Fatigue* (New York: The Free Press, 1992), 271.

33. P. LeFebvre and S. Barbass, "L'hystérie de guerre: Etude comparative de ses manifestations au cours des derniers conflits mondiaux," *Annales médico-psychologiques*, 142 (1984): 262–66, quoted in Shorter, *Paralysis and Fatigue*, 265.

34. Martin Blumenson, *Patton: The Man Behind the Legend* (New York: Morrow, 1985), 210–11.

35. See Nathan G. Hale, Jr., *The Rise and Crisis of Psychoanalysis in the United States* (New York: Oxford University Press, 1995), 276–81.

36. Zahava Solomon, *Combat Stress Reaction: The Enduring Toll of War* (New York: Plenum Press, 1993), vii, 163.

37. See Richard A. Kuhl et al., *Trauma and the Vietnam War Generation* (New York: Brunner/Mazel, 1990).

38. See "Closer Look Strips Glory from Vietnam War 'Hero,'" *San Diego Evening Tribune*, October 10, 1989, cited in Michael Yapko, *Suggestions of Abuse* (New York: Simon & Schuster, 1994), 3.

39. Harriet E. Lerner, "The Hysterical Personality: A 'Woman's Disease'"

in *Women and Mental Health*, ed. Elizabeth Howell and Marjorie Bayes (New York: Basic Books, 1987), 205, 196.

40. Freud, "Extracts from the Fliess Papers," *Standard Edition of the Complete Works of Sigmund Freud*, 24 vols., trans. James Strachey (London: Hogarth Press, 1953–1974), 1:228. Hereafter abbreviated as *SE*.

41. Wilhelm Reich, *Character-Analysis*, 3d ed., trans. Theodore P. Wolfe (New York: Farrar Straus Giroux, 1949), 189.

42. Carroll Smith-Rosenberg, *Disorderly Conduct: Visions of Gender in Victorian America* (New York: Knopf, 1985), 331.

43. "The Storming of St. Pat's," *New York Times*, December 12, 1989, A24.

44. Jane Ussher, *Women's Madness: Misogyny or Mental Illness?* (New York and London: Harvester/Wheatsheaf, 1991), 169.

45. Lucien Israel, *L'hystérique, le sexe, et le médecin* (Paris: Masson, 1983), 60.

6. Hysterical Narratives

1. Libby Purves, "I Think I Was a Good and Faithful Wife," *The Times* (London), February 4, 1994, 15.

2. Charles Richet, "Les démoniaques d'aujourd'hui et d'aurefois," *La revue des deux mondes* 37 (1880), 348.

3. Francisque Sarcey, "Le mot et la chose," (1863), 261, quoted in Jacqueline Carroy-Thirard, "Hystérie, théâtre, littérature au dix-neuvième siècle," *Psychanalyse à l'université* (March 1982): 299 (my translation).

4. Jann Matlock, *Scenes of Seduction: Prostitution, Hysteria, and Reading Difference in Nineteenth-Century France* (New York: Columbia University Press, 1994), 126–27.

5. Claire Kahane, "Hysteria, Feminism, and the Case of *The Bostonians*," in *Feminism and Psychoanalysis*, ed. Richard Feldstein and Judith Roof (Ithaca: Cornell University Press, 1989), 286–88.

6. Pioneering work on this topic has been done by professor Michele Birnbaum, especially "Racial Hysteria," a paper presented at the MLA panel on Hysteria and Narrative, December 1992.

7. Max Nordau, *Degeneration*, ed. George L. Mossé (Lincoln: University of Nebraska Press, 1993), 15.

8. Sigmund Freud, *Studies in Hysteria*, SE 2:160–61.

9. Sigmund Freud, *Dora: An Analysis of a Case of Hysteria* (New York: Collier, 1963), 7, 10.

10. Steven Marcus, "Freud and Dora: Story, History, Case History," in Bernheimer and Kahane, eds., *In Dora's Case*, 79.

11. Peter Brooks, *Body Work: Objects of Desire in Modern Narrative* (Cambridge: Harvard University Press), 235.

12. John Forrester, *The Seductions of Psychoanalysis* (Cambridge: Cambridge University Press, 1990), 8.

13. Susan Katz, "Speaking Out Against the 'Talking Cure,'" *Women's Studies* 13 (1987): 297–324.

14. Hélène Cixous, "The Laugh of the Medusa," *New French Feminisms*, ed.

Elaine Marks and Isabelle de Courtivron (Amherst: University of Massachusetts Press, 1980), 257.

15. Elaine Hedges and Shelley Fisher Fishkin, *Listening to Silences: New Essays in Feminist Criticism* (New York: Oxford University Press, 1994), 3. My discussion of Tillie Olsen's work on feminist critical theory is indebted to Hedges and Fishkin, especially their introduction to the book.

16. Patricia Yeager, *Honey-Mad Women: Emancipating Strategies in Women's Writing* (New York: Columbia University Press, 1988), 153–54.

17. Janis Stout, quoted in Hedges and Fishkin, *Listening to Silences*, 5.

18. Toril Moi, *Feminist Theory and Simone de Beauvoir* (London: Basil Blackwell, 1990), 92.

19. Evans, *Fits and Starts*, 282.

20. Sandra M. Gilbert and Susan Gubar, *The Madwoman in the Attic* (New Haven: Yale University Press, 1979), 98, 99.

21. Alice Walker, *In Search of Our Mother's Gardens* (New York: Harcourt Brace Jovanovich, 1983), 232–33.

22. Jean O. Love, *Virginia Woolf* (Berkeley: University of California Press, 1977), 195.

23. Louise DeSalvo, *Virginia Woolf: The Impact of Childhood Sexual Abuse on Her Work* (London: The Woman's Press, 1989), 1, 13, 14, 234.

24. Jan Marsh, *Christina Rossetti: A Literary Biography* (London: Jonathan Cape, 1994), 258, 259.

25. Barbara White, "Neglected Areas: Wharton's Short Stories and Incest, Part II" *Edith Wharton Review*, 8 (Fall 1991): 6,7.

26. Maureen Freely, "Blowing Hot and Hotter," *The Observer Review*, July 16, 1995, 12.

27. Julia Kristeva, in Marks and de Courtivron, eds., *New French Feminisms*, 166.

28. Juliet Mitchell, "Psychoanalysis: Child Development and Femininity," in *Women: The Longest Revolution* (London: Virago, 1984), 289–90.

29. Mary Jacobus, *Reading Woman* (New York: Columbia University Press, 1986), 201.

30. Jill L. Matus, "St. Teresa, Hysteria, and *Middlemarch*," in *Journal of the History of Sexuality*, 1 (1990): 216.

31. Brooks, *Body Work*, 231–32.

32. Eve Kosofsky Sedgwick, "Preface," *The Coherence of Gothic Conventions* (New York: Methuen, 1986), vi.

33. Jacobus, *Reading Woman*, 197.

34. Diane Price Herndl, "The Writing Cure," *NWSA Journal*, 1 (1988): 68.

35. Jacobus, *Reading Woman*, 229.

36. Barbara Johnson, "Is Female to Male as Ground Is to Figure?" *Feminism and Psychoanalysis*, ed. Richard Feldstein and Judith Roof, (Ithaca: Cornell University Press, 1989), 255, 258.

37. Gillian Brown, "The Empire of Agoraphobia," *Representations*, 20 (Fall 1987): 152n3.

38. Michelle A. Massé, *In the Name of Love: Women, Masochism, and the Gothic* (Ithaca: Cornell University Press, 1992), 16.

39. Herndl, "The Writing Cure," 74.

40. Lisa Gornick, "Developing a New Narrative: The Woman Therapist and the Male Patient," in *Psychoanalysis and Women: Contemporary Reappraisals*, ed. Judith L. Alpert (Hillsdale, N.J.: The Analytic Press, 1986), 257–85.

41. See Casey Miller and Kate Swift, *Words and Women* (New York: Anchor Books, 1977), 60–61.

42. Sandra Gilbert and Susan Gubar, "The Man on the Dump versus the United Dames of America; or, What Does Frank Lentricchia Want?" *Critical Inquiry*, 14 (1988): 386–406.

43. Jan Goldstein, "The Uses of Male Hysteria: Medical and Literary Discourse in Nineteenth-Century France," *Representations*, 34 (Spring 1991): 143.

44. See Katz, "Speaking Out Against the 'Talking Cure.'"

45. "Interview with Pat Barker," in Donna Perry, *Backtalk: Women Writers Speak Out* (New Brunswick, N.J.: Rutgers University Press, 1993), 43–62.

46. Martin Amis, *The Sunday Times* (London), September 24, 1995.

7. Hysteria and the Histrionic

1. Jules Falret, *Etudes cliniques sur les maladies mentales et nerveuse* (Paris: Librairie Ballière et Fils, 1890), 502.

2. Jacqueline Carroy-Thirard, "Hystérie, théâtre, littérature au dix-neuvième siècle," *Psychanalyse à l'université*, 7 (March 1982): 302.

3. Georgette Déga, quoted in Martha Noel Evans, *Fits and Starts* (Ithaca: Cornell University Press, 1991), 72.

4. See the fascinating article by Rae Beth Gordon, "Le Caf'con et l'hystérie," *Romanticisme*, 64 (1989): 53–66.

5. Hélène Zimmern, "Eleanora Duse," *Fortnightly Review* (1900): 983, quoted in John Stokes, "The Legend of Duse," in *Decadence and the 1890s*, ed. Ian Fletcher (London: Edward Arnold, 1979), 162; and Michael Robinson, "Acting Women: The Performing Self and the Late Nineteenth Century," *Comparative Criticism*, 14 (1992): 3–24.

6. Elin Diamond, "Realism and Hysteria: Toward a Feminist Mimesis," *Discourse*, 13 (Fall-Winter 1990–91): 63.

7. Harry Campbell, *Differences in the Nervous Organization of Man and Woman: Physiological and Pathological* (London, H.K. Lewis, 1891), 169.

8. See also Felicia McCarren, "The 'Symptomatic Act' Circa 1900: Hysteria, Hypnosis, Electricity, Dance," *Critical Inquiry*, 21 (Summer 1995): 748–74.

9. Sigmund Freud and Josef Breuer, "Fraulein Anna O.," *Studies on Hysteria* (New York: Avon, 1966), 76.

10. Kay H. Blacker and Joe P. Tupin, "Hysteria and Hysterical Structures: Development and Social Theories," in Mardi J. Horowitz, ed., *Hysterical Personality* (New York: Jason Aronson, 1977), 130.

11. Gunnar Brandell, *Freud: A Man of His Century*, trans. Ian White, (Hassock: Harvester Press, 1979), 35, 38. See Lis Muller, "The Analytical Theatre: Freud and Ibsen," *Scandinavian Psychoanalytic Review*, 13 (1990): 113.

12. Max Nordau, *Degeneration*, ed. George L. Mosse (Lincoln: University of Nebraska Press, 1993), 414.

13. Ibsen, 166.

14. Charles Spencer, *Daily Telegraph*, May 9, 1991.

15. John Peter, *Sunday Times*, June 30, 1991.

16. Fiona Shaw, Celebritea discussion, Royal National Theatre, London, August 20, 1993.

17. Fiona Shaw, "The Post-Feminist Myth," *the sphinx* (London: Sadler's Wells, 1991), 53.

18. See reviews of *Hedda Gabler*, by Michael Billington, *The Guardian*, September 5, 1991; Maureen Paton, *Daily Express*, September 5, 1991; Rhoda Koenig, *Punch*, September 11, 1991; Milton Shulman, *Evening Standard*, September 4, 1991, and Christopher Edwards, *Spectator*, September 7, 1991.

19. Kerry Powell, *Wilde and the Theatre of the 1890s* (Cambridge: Cambridge University Press, 1990), 79.

20. Mann, *Richard Strauss: A Critical Study of the Operas* (London: Cassell, 1964), 50–51.

21. Sander L. Gilman, *Disease and Representation: Images of Illness From Madness to AIDS* (Ithaca: Cornell University Press, 1988), 168–69.

22. See Janet Walker, *Couching Resistance: Women, Film, and Psychoanalytic Theory* (Minneapolis: University of Minnesota Press, 1993), 52.

23. Don Black and Christopher Hampton, *Sunset Boulevard* (London and Boston: Faber and Faber, 1993), 26.

24. See McCarren, "The 'Symptomatic Act,'" 772–73.

25. Dianne Hunter, "Representing Mad Contradictoriness in *Dr. Charcot's Hysteria Shows*," *Themes in Drama*, ed. James Redmond (Columbia University Press, 1993), 101.

26. Mady Schutzman, "Dr. Charcot's Hysteria Shows," in *Women & Performance* 5 (1990): 183–89.

27. Evans, *Fits and Starts*, 216, 217.

28. Judith Roof, "Marguerite Duras and the Question of a Feminist Theater," in Feldstein and Roof, *Feminism and Psychoanalysis* (Ithaca: Cornell University Press, 1989), 327.

29. Kim Morrissey, *Dora: A Case of Hysteria* (London: Nick Hern Books, 1994), 30.

30. See Elaine Showalter, " 'Mrs. Klein': The Mother, the Daughter, the Thief, and Their Critics," *Woman: A Cultural Review* I (Summer 1990), 144–48.

31. Paul Taylor, "It's the Way We Tell 'em," *The Independent*, April 6, 1994, 25.

32. Lizzie Francke, "Funny Girls," *The Guardian*, April 12, 1994, 17.

33. Hélène Cixous and Catherine Clément, *The Newly Born Woman* (Minneapolis: University of Minnesota Press, 1975), trans. Betsy Wing, 13.

34. See Paul Smith, "Action Movie Hysteria, or Eastwood Bound," *Differences*, 1 (1989): 103, 105.

35. Barbara Creed, "Phallic Panic: Male Hysteria and *Dead Ringers*," *Screen*, 31 (Summer 1991): 133.

36. Lynne Kirby, "Male Hysteria and Early Cinema," *Camera Obscura* 17 (1991), 124, 128.

37. Ed Sikov, *Laughing Hysterically: American Screen Comedy of the 1950s* (New York: Columbia University Press, 1994), 190–91.

8. Chronic Fatigue Syndrome

1. Olivia Fane, "He Said: You Can Walk. And She Could," *The Independent*, April 4, 1994, 18.

2. Liz Hunt, "Despair in a Doll's House," *The Independent*, May 17, 1994, 19.

3. J. Seligmann, P. Abranson, P. Shapiro, D. Gosnell, and M. Hager, "The Malaise of the Eighties," *Newsweek*, October 7, 1986, 105–6.

4. Anthony K. Komaroff, "Clinical Presentation and Evaluation of Fatigue in CFS," in *Chronic Fatigue Syndrome*, ed. Stephen E. Straus (New York: Marcel Dekker, 1994), 61.

5. Luisa Dillner, "Doctor at Large: Inject Some Fun to Beat Fatigue," *The Guardian*, May 19, 1995, 10.

6. Arthur Kleinman and Stephen Straus, "Introduction," *Chronic Fatigue Syndrome*, proceedings of CIBA conference, May 12–14, 1992 (London: Wiley, 1993), 3.

7. Karyn Feiden, *Hope and Help for Chronic Fatigue Syndrome* (New York: Simon and Schuster, 1990), 3.

8. Komaroff, "Clinical Presentation," 52.

9. Simon Wessely, in *Chronic Fatigue Syndrome* (London: Wiley, 1993), 338.

10. See also Hillary Johnson, "Journey Into Fear," *Rolling Stone*, July 16 and August 13, 1987.

11. "America's Next Epidemic," ad for *Osler's Web* in *New York Times Book Review*, March 31, 1996, 5.

12. Hillary Johnson, *Osler's Web* (New York: Crown, 1996), 6.

13. Feiden, *Hope and Help for Chronic Fatigue Syndrome*, 29.

14. Johnson, *Osler's Web*, 33.

15. Jon Kaplan, quoted in Johnson, *Osler's Web*, 51.

16. Simon Wessely, "New Wine in Old Bottles: Neurasthenia and 'ME,'" *Psychological Medicine*, 20 (1990): 35–53.

17. "Neurasthenia and Modern Life," *British Medical Journal*, 1909, cited in ibid., 44.

18. Wessely, "New Wine," 47.

19. Johnson, *Osler's Web*, 118.

20. Simon Wessely, "The History of Chronic Fatigue Syndrome," in Stephen E. Straus, ed., *Chronic Fatigue Syndrome* (New York: Marcel Dekker, 1994), 29.

21. Johnson, *Osler's Web*, 50, 65–66, 138.

22. Hillary Johnson, "Journey Into Fear," *Rolling Stone*, 16 July and 13 August 1987.

23. David S. Bell, *The Doctor's Guide to Chronic Fatigue Syndrome* (Boston: Addison-Wesley, 1995), 8–9.

24. Feiden, *Hope and Help*, 63–65.

25. *USA Today*, February 1993.

26. Neenyah Ostrom, *What Really Killed Gilda Radner? Frontline Reports on the Chronic Fatigue Syndrome* (New York: TNM, 1989).

27. Ryan Murphy, "Whatever Happened to Cher?" *McCall's*, May 1994, 108–111.

28. Betsy Kraus, *Library Journal*, June 15, 1992, 94.

29. Wessely, "History of Chronic Fatigue Syndrome," 24.

30. Wessely, "New Wine," 20.

31. Lawrence B. Altman, "Study Ties Chronic Fatigue Syndrome to Abnormality in the Control of Blood Pressure," *New York Times*, September 27, 1995, A16.

32. Bell, *The Doctor's Guide to Chronic Fatigue Syndrome*, 232.

33. Quoted in Johnson, *Osler's Web*, 146.

34. Deanne Pearson, "Unwillingly to School," *Times* (London), August 20, 1995, 23.

35. Johnson, *Osler's Web*, 612, 629.

36. Review of Timothy P. Kenny, *Living With Chronic Fatigue Syndrome: A Personal Story of the Struggle for Recovery*, *Publishers Weekly*, March 4, 1994, 69.

37. Gail MacLean and Simon Wessely, "Professional and Popular Views of Chronic Fatigue Syndrome," *British Medical Journal* 308 (March 19, 1994): 776–77.

38. Wessely, "The History of Chronic Fatigue Syndrome," 39.

39. See Komaroff, "Clinical Presentation."

40. Bell, *The Doctor's Guide*, 52–53.

41. Wessely, "New Wine," 39.

42. Edward Shorter, *From Paralysis to Fatigue* (New York: The Free Press, 1992), 317.

43. See Johnson, *Osler's Web*, 348, and ibid., 317, for examples.

44. Johnson, *Osler's Web*, 680.

45. Carol Midgley and Liz Jenkins, "BBC Defends Rantzen Over TV 'Shout-in' Claim," The *Times*, August 7, 1996, 5.

46. Victor Lewis-Smith, "A Paid-up Member of the ME Generation," *Evening Standard*, August 6, 1996, 27.

47. Lisa O'Carroll and Nick Pryer, "Trial by TV for the Doctor Who Dared to Disagree with Esther," *Evening Standard*, August 6, 1996, 3.

48. Cited in Johnson, *Osler's Web*, 260, 684–85.

49. Arthur Kleinman, in Straus, ed., *Chronic Fatigue Syndrome* (London: Wiley, 1993), 258, 329.

50. David Mechanic, in Straus, ed., *Chronic Fatigue Syndrome*, 327–28.

51. Wessely, "New Wine," 50.

52. Johnson, *Osler's Web*, 684.

53. Deanne Pearson, "Unwillingly to School," 23.

54. Johnson, *Osler's Web*, 680.

9. Gulf War Syndrome

1. David France, "The Families Who Are Dying for Our Country," *Redbook*, September 1994, 117.

2. Ibid., 116.

3. Melanie McFadyean, "Soldier On," *The Guardian Weekend*, May 27, 1995, 25 ff.

4. Gregory Jaynes, "Walking Wounded," *Esquire*, May 1994, 74.

5. France, "Families," 148.

6. Jaynes, "Walking Wounded," 71.

7. Edward Pilkington, "Gulf War Veterans Fear for their Families," *The Guardian*, June 12, 1995, 4.

8. Jaynes, "Walking Wounded," 71.

9. Jonathan Freedland, "Cover-up Alleged as US Denies Gulf War Syndrome Exists," *The Guardian*, August 3, 1995, 2.

10. France, "Families," 148.

11. Ibid., 116.

12. Quoted in Kenneth Miller, "The Tiny Victims of Desert Storm," *Life*, November 1995, 62.

13. Jaynes, "Walking Wounded," 73.

14. See Philip Shenon, "New Report Cited on Chemical Arms Used in Gulf War," *New York Times*, August 22, 1996, A1, B13.

15. France, "Families," 147.

16. Scott Allen, "Gulf Troops Received Experimental Drug," *Boston Sunday Globe*, July 3, 1994, 1, 16.

17. France, "Families," 116.

18. "Report Offers No One Cause for Gulf War Illness," *New York Times*, December 14, 1994.

19. Philip J. Hilts, "Study on Ailing Gulf War G.I.s Called a Failure," *New York Times*, January 5, 1995.

20. "Study of 19,000 Finds No 'Gulf War Syndrome,'" *New York Times*, April 4, 1996, B11.

21. David Fairhall, "Gulf War 'Fever' Rejected by MoD," *The Guardian*, June 8, 1995.

22. Michael Evans, "Gulf War Syndrome Inquiry Supported," *The Times*, July 28, 1995, 4.

23. Simon Wessely, "What Is This Mystery Illness Which We Call Gulf War Syndrome?" *The Times*, July 27, 1995.

24. Laura Flanders, "Bringing the War Home," *The Women's Review of Books*, 11 (July 1994): 10.

25. Laura Flanders, "A Lingering Sickness," *The Nation*, January 23, 1995, 96.

26. Ibid., 96.

27. Miller, "Tiny Victims," 46–62.

28. Jaynes, "Walking Wounded," 75.

29. France, "Families," 147–48.

30. Ibid., 147.

31. "Comprehensive Clinical Evaluation Program (CCEP) for Gulf War Veterans," Department of Defense, August 1995.

32. Wessely, "What Is This Mystery Illness?"

33. Scott Allen, "Gulf Troops," 1, 16.

34. Statement to Committee, September 29, 1992, *Illness of Persian Gulf Veterans*, serial no. 102–51, U.S. Government Printing Office, Washington, D.C., 1993, 84.

35. Flanders, "Bringing the War Home," 10.

36. Joseph P. Kennedy, Monday, September 21, 1992, in *Illness of Persian Gulf Veterans*, 30.

37. Paul Cotton, "Veterans Seeking Answers to Syndrome Suspect They Were Goats in Gulf War," *JAMA* 271 (1994), 1559, 1561.

38. Richard A. Kulka et al., *Trauma and the Vietnam War Generation* (New York: Brunner/Mazel, 1990), 232.

10. Recovered Memory

1. Judith Lewis Herman, *Trauma and Recovery* (New York: Basic Books, 1992), 28.

2. Bessel A. Van der Kolk and Onno Van der Hart, "The Intrusive Past: The Flexibility of Memory and the Engraving of Trauma," in *Trauma*, ed. Cathy Carruth (Baltimore: Johns Hopkins University Press, 1995), 176.

3. Herman, *Trauma and Recovery*, 122.

4. Ibid., 178, 188. The term *unstory* comes from Lawrence Langer, *Holocaust Testimonies: The Ruins of Memory* (New Haven: Yale University Press, 1991), 39.

5. Herman, *Trauma and Recovery*, 185–86.

6. Louise Armstrong, *Rocking the Cradle of Sexual Politics: What Happened When Women Said Incest* (London: The Woman's Press, 1996), 4, 210.

7. Katy Butler, "You Must Remember This," *The Guardian*, July 23, 1994.

8. Frederick Crews, *The Memory Wars: Freud's Legacy in Disrepute* (New York: New Yale Review Books, 1995), 159.

9. Richard Webster, *Why Freud Was Wrong* (New York: Basic Books, 1995), 511.

10. Armstrong, *Rocking the Cradle*, 207.

11. Claudette Wassil-Grimm, *Diagnosis for Disaster* (Woodstock, N.Y.: Overlook Press, 1995), 350.

12. See Elizabeth Loftus and Katherine Ketcham, *The Myth of Repressed Memory: False Memories and Allegations of Sexual Abuse* (New York: St. Martin's Press), 1994.

13. Michael Yapko, *Suggestions of Abuse: True and False Memories of Childhood Sexual Trauma* (New York: Simon & Schuster, 1994), 20.

14. Richard Ofshe and Ethan Watters, *Making Monsters: False Memories, Psychotherapy, and Sexual Hysteria* (New York: Scribner's, 1994), 305–12.

15. Ellen Bass and Laura Davis, *The Courage to Heal*, 2d ed. (New York: Harper Perennial, 1992), 107.

16. Ibid., 24.

17. Armstrong, *Rocking the Cradle*, 52n.; Diane Russell, *The Secret Trauma* (New York: Basic Books, 1986), 10.

18. Ofshe and Watters, *Making Monsters*, 48.

19. Lisa Watts, "The Career Price of Sexual Abuse," *Harvard Magazine* (October 1994): 18, 20.

20. Mike Lew, *Victims No Longer* (London: Cedar, 1993), 55, 57.

21. Ibid., 69, 152.

22. Bass and Davis, *The Courage to Heal*, 3d ed., 410.

23. Ibid., 532.

24. Rebecca Peppler Sinkler, "Picks, Pans, and Fragile Egos," *Civilization* (July/August 1995): 51.

25. Judith Herman, "Backtalk," *Mother Jones* (March/April 1993): 4.

26. Katy Butler, "Did Daddy Really Do It?" *Los Angeles Times Book Review*, February 5, 1995, 11.

27. Carol Tavris, "Beware the Incest-Survivor Machine," *New York Times Book Review*, January 3, 1993; see Ofshe and Watters, *Making Monsters*, 200.

11. Multiple Personality Syndrome

1. Ian Hacking, *Rewriting the Soul: Multiple Personality and the Sciences of Memory* (Princeton: Princeton University Press, 1995), 39.

2. Flora Rheta Schreiber, *Sybil* (New York: Warner, 1973), 5, and Mark Pendergrast, *Victims of Memory: Incest Accusations and Shattered Lives* (Hinesburg, Vt.: Upper Access, 1995), 155.

3. See Hacking, *Rewriting the Soul*, 51–52.

4. Richard Kluft, "Treatment of Multiple Personality Disorder: A Study of Thirty-Three Cases," *Psychiatric Clinics of North America*, 7 (1984): 69–88.

5. G. B. Greaves, "President's Letter," *Newsletter of the International Society for the Study of Multiple Personality & Dissociation*, 5 (1987): 1; quoted in Hacking, *Rewriting the Soul*, 52.

6. C. A. Ross, "Epidemiology of Multiple Personality Disorder and Dissociation," *Psychiatric Clinics of North America*, 14 (1991): 503–18

7. Colin Ross, quoted in Richard Ofshe and Ethan Watters, *Making Monsters: False Memories, Psychotherapy, and Sexual Hysteria*, 206.

8. Ray Aldridge-Morris, *Multiple Personality: An Exercise in Delusion* (London: Lawrence Erlbaum, 1989), and Harold Merskey, "The Manufacture of Personalities: The Production of Multiple Personality Disorder," *British Journal of Psychiatry*, 160 (1992): 337.

9. Paul McHugh, "Multiple Personality Disorder," *Harvard Medical School Newsletter* (Fall 1993), quoted in Ofshe and Watters, *Making Monsters*, 209.

10. *DSM-IV* (Washington, D.C.: American Psychiatric Association, 1994), 485.

11. Hacking, *Rewriting the Soul*, 33.

12. James M. Glass, *Shattered Selves: Multiple Personality in a Postmodern World* (Ithaca: Cornell University Press, 1993), xv.

13. See Rosaria Champagne, "True Crimes of Motherhood: Mother-Daughter Incest, Multiple Personality Disorder, and the True Crime Novel," in *Feminist Nightmares: Women at Odds*, ed. Susan Ostrow Weisser and Jennifer Fleischner (New York: New York University Press, 1994), 143–44.

14. Armstrong, *Rocking the Cradle*, 61.

15. Quoted in ibid., 64.

16. Ofshe and Watters, *Making Monsters*, 222—23.

17. Hacking, *Rewriting the Soul*, 73.

18. Ian Katz, "Marriage Most Foul," *The Guardian*, June 19, 1995, 5.

19. Hacking, *Rewriting the Soul*, 171.

20. Jim Schnabel, "Splits in the Search for Self," *The Guardian*, June 9, 1995, 5.

21. Sherrill Mulhern, "Embodied Alternative Identities: Bearing Witness to a World That Might Have Been," *Psychiatric Clinics of North America*, 14 (September 1991): 777, 778.

22. Hacking, *Rewriting the Soul*, 74.

23. Margo Rivera, "Am I A Boy or a Girl? Multiple Personality as a Window on Gender Differences," *Resources for Feminist Research* 17 (1987), 41–43.

24. Sylvia Fraser, *My Father's House* (London: Virago, 1984), 149, 228, 154.

25. Judith Lewis Herman, *Trauma and Recovery* (New York: Basic Books, 1992), 99.

26. Fraser, *My Father's House*, 211.

27. Roseanne Arnold, *My Lives* (New York: Ballantine, 1994), xiv, 342.

28. Hacking, *Rewriting the Soul*, 50.

29. Mark Pendergrast, *Victory of Memory*, 170–1.

30. Sherrill Mulhern, "Satanism, Ritual Abuse, and Multiple Personality Disorder," *Journal of Clinical and Experimental Hypnosis* 1002 (October 1994), 280.

31. Ibid., 277, 279.

32. Ofshe and Watters, *Making Monsters*, 321n., 223–4, 239; Hacking, *Rewriting the Soul*, 124–5.

33. Hacking, *Rewriting the Soul*, 50–51, 53, 54.

34. Aldridge-Morris, *Multiple Personality*, 107–8.

35. *DSM-IV*, 485.

36. *International Society for the Study of Dissociation News*, 13, no. 3 (June/July, 1995): 1–4.

37. Hacking, *Rewriting the Soul*, 236.

12. Satanic Ritual Abuse

1. David K. Sakheim and Susan E. Devine, *Out of Darkness: Exploring Satanism and Ritual Abuse* (New York: Lexington, 1992), xi.

2. Leslie Bennetts, "Nightmares on Main Street," *Vanity Fair* (June 1993): 45.

3. Ellen Bass and Laura Davis, *The Courage to Heal*, (New York: Harper Perennial, 1994), 421.

4. Michael Horsnell and Robi Dutta, "Inquiry Dismisses Satanic Abuse as Evangelical Myth," *The Times* (London), June 3, 1994, 4. See Jean La Fontaine, "The Extent and Nature of Organized Ritual Abuse: Research Findings," 1994, Her Majesty's Secretarial Office, P.O. Box 276, London SW8.

5. Jan Larson, quoted in Bennetts, "Nightmares on Main Street," 48.

6. George Ganaway, "Historical Truth versus Narrative Truth: Clarifying the Role of Exogenous Trauma in the Etiology of Multiple Personality Disorder," *Dissociation*, 2 (1989): 207.

7. John Briere, *Therapy for Adults Molested as Children* (New York: Stringer Verlag, 1989), 128, quoted in Richard Ofshe and Ethan Watters, *Making Monsters: False Memories, Psychotherapy, and Sexual Hysteria* (New York: Scribner's, 1994), 179.

8. Sherrill Mulhern, "Satanism, Ritual Abuse, and Multiple Personality Disorder," *International Journal of Clinical and Experimental Hypnosis*, 1002 (October 1994): 267.

9. James M. Glass, *Shattered Selves: Multiple Personality in a Postmodern World* (Ithaca: Cornell University Press, 1993), 105–106.

10. Claudette Wassil-Grimm, *Diagnosis for Disaster* (Woodstock, N.Y.: Overlook Press, 1995), 6–7.

11. "A Woman's Memories from Childhood Lead to Murder Charges," *New York Times*, November 25, 1994, A27; Ian Katz, "A Deadly Memory," *The Guardian Review*, December 28, 1995, 2.

12. Bennetts, "Nightmares on Main Street," 52.

13. See Alan Dundes, ed. *The Blood Libel Legend: A Case Book in Anti-Semitic Folklore* (Madison: University of Wisconsin Press, 1991).

14. Jeffrey S. Victor, *Satanic Panic: The Creation of a Contemporary Legend* (New York: Open Court, 1993), 286.

15. Bass and Davis, *The Courage to Heal*, 428.

16. Leslie Wilson, "Salem's Lot," *London Review of Books*, March 23, 1995, 16.

17. Bass and Davis, *The Courage to Heal*, 518, 519, 522.

18. See Wilson, "Salem's Lot," 18.

19. Bennetts, "Nightmares on Main Street," 48.

20. Debbie Nathan and Michael Snedeker, *Satan's Silence: Ritual Abuse and the Making of a Modern American Witch Hunt* (New York: Basic Books, 1995), 120–23. Nathan and Snedeker base their analysis on the study *Behind the Playground Walls*, funded by the federal government's National Center on Child Abuse and Neglect.

21. Nathan and Snedeker, *Satan's Silence*, 4.

22. Linda Alcoff and Laura Gray, "Survivor Discourse: Transgression or Recuperation?" *SIGNS*, 18 (Winter 1993): 297.

23. Nathan and Snedeker, *Satan's Silence*, 6–7.

24. Ibid., 247.

25. Sherrill Mulhern, "Investigating Allegations of Ritualistic Sexual Abuse" (October 22, 1989, Eighth National Conference on Child Abuse and Neglect, Salt Lake City, Utah), 3.

26. Patrick Casement, "The Wish Not to Know," *Treating Survivors of Satanist Abuse* (London: Routledge, 1994), 23.

27. Mulhern, "Investigating Allegations," 4.

28. George Greaves, quoted in Ofshe and Watters, *Making Monsters*, 185.

29. Mulhern, "Satanism," 279.

30. Mark Pendergrast, *Victims of Memory: Incest Accusations and Shattered Lives* (Hinesburg, Vt.: Upper Access, 1995), 172, 173.

31. Walter Goodman, "Who Programmed Mary? Could It Be Satan?" *New York Times*, October 24, 1995, C18.

32. Pendergrast, *Victims of Memory*, 177, 178; Judith Peterson, "When the Therapists Who Have Sat with Shattered Souls Are Themselves Shattered," *Treating Abuse Today*, 4 (March/April 1994): 26–27.

33. See Ofshe and Watters, *Making Monsters*, 188.

34. Quoted in ibid., 189.

35. Ibid., 190, 195.

36. Joan Coleman, "Satanic Cult Practices," in Valerie Sinason, ed., *Treating Survivors of Satanist Abuse* (London: Routledge, 1994), 242–43.

37. Rob Hale and Valerie Sinason, "Internal and External Reality," in Sinason, ed., *Treating Survivors*, 243, 281.

38. Coleman, "Satanic Cult Practices," 251.

39. Joan Coleman, letter to the editor, *London Review of Books*, April 20, 1995, 5.

40. Horsnell and Dutta, "Inquiry Dismisses Satanic Abuse," 4.

41. Wilson, "Salem's Lot," 18.

42. Valerie Sinason, "Introduction," to Lawrence Wright, *Remembering Satan* (London: Serpent's Tail, 1995), vii.

43. Sherrill Mulhern, "Satanism and Psychotherapy: A Rumor in Search of an Inquisition," in James T. Richardson, Joel Best, and David G. Bromley, eds., *The Satanism Scare* (New York: Aldine de Gruyter, 1991), 145–72.

44. Horsnell and Dutta, "Inquiry Dismisses Satanic Abuse," 4.

45. Ben Macintyre, "Beast That Runs Wild in US Imagination," *The Times* (London), June 4, 1994, 4.

46. Dorothy Rabinowitz, "Verdict in Wenatchee," *Wall Street Journal*, December 15, 1995, and Timothy Egan, "Pastor and Wife Are Acquitted of All Charges in Sex-Abuse Case," *New York Times*, December 12, 1995, A24.

47. See Hass, "Margaret Kelly Michaels," 38.

48. Nathan and Snedeker, *Satan's Silence*, 281.

49. Kenneth V. Lanning, "A Law-Enforcement Perspective on Allegations of Ritual Abuse," in Sakheim and Devine, *Out of Darkness*, 109–46.

13. Alien Abduction

1. Keith Thompson, *Angels and Aliens: UFOs and the Mythic Imagination* (New York: Random House, 1991), 144–45.

2. See ibid., 60, 66.

3. David M. Jacobs, *Alien Encounters: First Hand Experiences of UFO Abductions* (London: Virgin, 1994; New York: Simon & Schuster, 1992), 21.

4. Ibid., 50, 51.

5. Ibid., 95.

6. Ibid., 114.

7. Ibid., 122, 305, 316.

8. John E. Mack, *Abduction: Human Encounters with Aliens* (New York: Simon & Schuster, 1994), 3–4.

9. Ibid., 421–22.

10. James Wolcott, "I Lost It in the Saucer," *New Yorker* (July 31, 1995): 77.

11. John Mack, "Foreword" to David Jacobs, *Alien Encounters*, 9, 10, 12.

12. C. D. B. Bryan, *Close Encounters of the Fourth Kind: Alien Abduction, UFOs, and the Conference at MIT* (New York: Knopf, 1995), 229.

13. Mack, *Abduction*, 3.

14. Jacobs, *Alien Encounters*, 51.

15. Ibid., 106.

16. Bryan, *Close Encounters* , 225.

17. Jacobs, *Alien Encounters*, 203.

18. Mack, *Abduction*, 191.

19. Bryan, *Close Encounters*, 50–51, 232n.

20. See Douglas E. Winter, *Faces of Fear* (New York: Berkeley Books, 1985), 192–206.

21. Whitley Strieber, *Communion* (London: Arrow, 1988), 121.

22. Ibid., 138, 142.

23. Ibid., 214.

24. Ibid., 34.

25. Winter, *Faces of Fear*, 202.

26. See Thompson, *Angels and Aliens*, 206–7.

27. Bryan, *Close Encounters*, 4.

28. Tom Hodgkinson, "Why It's Easier to Believe in UFOs Than God," *The Guardian*, July 11, 1995, 15.

29. Ian Katz, "Aliens Land on Main Street," *The Guardian*, July 25, 1995, 3.

30. See William H. Honan, "Harvard Investigates Tenured Professor Who Wrote of Aliens," *New York Times*, May 4, 1995, A18; Christopher B. Daly, "Psychiatrist for Alien 'Victims' Cleared by Harvard," *International Herald Tribune*, August 5–6, 1995, 1.

31. Jacques Vallee, interviewed in Thompson, *Angels and Aliens*, 194.

32. Mack, *Abduction*, 12; John Carpenter at MIT conference, quoted in Bryan, *Close Encounters*, 30.

33. Mack, *Abduction*, 12.

34. Anne Enright, "Diary," *London Review of Books*, September 21, 1995, 25.

35. Mack, *Abduction*, 13.

14. *The Crucible*

1. Ian Hacking, *Rewriting the Soul: Multiple Personality and the Sciences of Memory* (Princeton: Princeton University Press, 1995), 75.

2. Mark Pendergrast, *Victims of Memory: Incest Accusations and Shattered Lives* (Hinesburg, Vt.: Upper Access, 1995), 461, 477.

3. Richard Webster, *Why Freud Was Wrong: Sin, Science, and Psychoanalysis* (New York: Basic Books, 1995), 520.

4. Quoted in Wright, *Remembering Satan*, 78–79.

5. Judith Lewis Herman, *Trauma and Recovery* (New York: Basic Books, 1992), 181.

6. James William Gibson, *Warrior Dreams: Paramilitary Culture in Post-Vietnam America* (New York: Hill and Wang, 1994).

7. Charles Mackay, *Extraordinary Popular Delusions and the Madness of Crowds* (Ware: Wordsworth, 1995), 554.

8. Garth L. Nicolson, "Gulf War Illness Linked to Fatigue Syndrome," *New York Times*, April 10, 1996.

9. Dorothy Rabinowitz, "The Forces of Dimness," *Wall Street Journal*, April 1, 1996. Thanks to Dr. Jacqueline Mislow for this reference.

10. Wayne R. Anderson, "The X-File Factor," *New York Times*, August 29, 1996, A25.

11. Miller, "The Crucible," (New York: Viking, 1971) Act One, 7.

Index